MEMORIES
OF MEXICO

A History of the Last Ten Months of the Empire

by

Dr. S. Basch

Personal Physician
to His Late Majesty the
Emperor Maximilian, Officer
of the Imperial Mexican Eagle and
Guadalupe Order, Knight of the Imperial
Austrian Order of the Iron Crown.

*Translated
by
Hugh McAden Oechler*

TRINITY UNIVERSITY PRESS  SAN ANTONIO

iii

Originally published in German by Verlag von Duncker & Humblot, Leipzig, Germany (1868)

iv

To
J. C. S.

Dr. Samuel Basch

The Author

Samuel Siegfried Karl Ritter von Basch was born in Prague on September 9, 1837. After studying in his native city and in Vienna, he became a protégé of Ernst Brücke, a pioneer in the field of comparative physiology. As a result of his research, Dr. Basch was asked to Mexico to become Professor of Pathological Anatomy. Upon arrival he was assigned to the military hospital in Puebla, and he later became personal physician to the Emperor Maximilian. After the latter's execution in Querétaro, Dr. Basch returned to Europe, where he published *Memories of Mexico: A History of the Last Ten Months of the Empire* (Leipzig, 1868). The rest of his life was devoted to the study and practice of medicine. He did special research on intestinal histology and blood pressure. Credited with the invention of a new sphygmomanometer and cardiagraph, Dr. Basch was the author of numerous medical articles. He died in 1905 at the age of sixty-seven. (Dawson Wilhems, ed., *The British Medical Journal*, I [January to June, 1905], p. 1304.)

Contents

Preface

With this translation of *Memories of Mexico,* the English-speaking reader has available for the first time a principal primary source for one of the most controversial and romanticized periods in Latin American history. Depicting the last ten months of the Second Mexican Empire, the book describes events from the viewpoint of a European who was a trusted friend of the Emperor Maximilian and a witness to his downfall.

Without question Dr. Basch presents a minority opinion. Many of his factual statements flatly contradict other authors. Yet, his work has not been ignored by writers on the period. They refer to him; they cite him in their bibliographies; they sometimes quote from him. But points of disagreement remain unreconciled. Such inconsistencies emphasize the need for thorough and dispassionate scholarly investigation of the history of the Mexican Empire.

Much of the book's value lies in the insight it offers into the prejudices and misconceptions of Europeans who thought themselves called upon to govern a people of whom they were almost totally ignorant. They looked upon themselves as the bearers of enlightened rule and saw Mexican nationalist resistance as benighted ingratitude.

In my translation from the German I have tried to capture this spirit. I have attempted to convey as well the excitement and frustration of Dr. Basch's career with Maximilian. If I have sometimes taken the liberty of pruning back the verbosity of nineteenth-century German diction, I hope, in so doing, I have remained faithful to the original while adding to clarity and smoothness. Spanish passages in the work I took verbatim from the author, making no attempt to edit out or correct mistakes. I have, however, tried to be accurate about spelling and accents in the English portion. Finally, in an effort to present a fluent narrative, I have imposed uniformity of tense in passages where Dr. Basch was inconsistent. One final word to the reader: the author's notes in the volume are indicated by asterisks; those of the translator, by daggers.

Among those to whom I am grateful for assistance and encouragement in preparing this translation are my colleagues at the Fourth United States Army Language Training Facility. On the pretext that I was correcting French papers, they allowed me to slip away from military duties so that I could wrestle this book out of German. I must also thank the Trinity University Press, especially its managing editor, Joe Nicholson, for commissioning me to undertake the project, thereby providing a mental escape from the tedium of army life. The press also later furnished comfortable surroundings in which to complete my work. Mrs. Nora Herrera greatly contributed to the book by twice typing the manuscript and showing unflagging patience with my running commentary. I am grateful to my editor, Laura Barber, without whose painstaking supervision this translation would be far bulkier and much less readable. Her fertile imagination has enabled me to see and avoid nuances incompatible with the high seriousness of my intentions. To Professor Dick Woods of the Trinity foreign language department goes thanks for his careful insertion of accents. Finally, this project would never have been undertaken without the constant support of Margaret King Stanley and her family, who contributed so much to my stay in Texas.

H. McA. O.

Foreword

By publishing the following presentation of what I have personally seen and experienced in the most memorable months of my life, I make a new contribution to the history of the Mexican Empire which at least can claim to be authentic. At the same time, I fulfill a sacred duty to the memory of the noble and unfortunate prince who singled me out with his trust and at whose side I remained almost without interruption during the time of his greatest distress and danger, until the fateful catastrophe of June 19.

Right at the beginning of the siege of Querétaro, with the liveliness of spirit peculiar to him and in the midst of pressing cares, Emperor Maximilian thought to make timely provision for future historical description of military events which, whatever way the dice might fall, would decide his fate and that of his throne.

The Emperor initially commissioned me to prepare him a part of the materials by combining the reports of two officers with my own observations in the form of a diary. These officers were Lieutenant Colonel Pitner and Major Becker. Comparing reports of individual observers with different points of view would facilitate his gaining a general picture of events which as Supreme Commander he knew most rightly how to evaluate. It would guarantee the most complete and accurate description of detail. The press of business hindered his continuing the diary, whose first sheets he had dictated to one of his assistants—actually an Austrian officer of the *Guardia Municipal* named Kaehlig, assigned to me as secretary.

Since I was the only person of his entourage with a mastery of German whose professional duties left him any spare time and since I had previously been occasionally employed to compose political reports in German, the Emperor requested that I now continue the diary in the manner in which it was begun. He put at my disposal his own manuscripts and the reports which I had drawn up myself—all the material from the war cabinet including battle orders, orders of the day, and all the papers and records of the war council.

Along with everything I owned this valuable material was lost on the day of the betrayal. I succeeded in recovering only a part in the Cruz Convent, our former command post and our first prison. Among the pages scattered about the floor of my previous quarters were the remains of these diaries as well as my own notes. Probably because they were written in German they had escaped the notice of the Mexican soldiers. All Spanish manuscripts were lost.

But I still remembered many details from my compilation; moreover, I also succeeded in saving a notebook containing numerous notes Maximilian had dictated to me. Almost everyone in his entourage carried such a notebook because he insisted that his orders and instructions be immediately written down. For the history of the period before Querétaro, I have many of His Majesty's letters, official papers, and memoranda. Much of this material had remained behind with my effects in Mexico City, and it came to Europe on the Austrian warship *Elizabeth*.

Later in prison Maximilian repeatedly requested, once in the presence of Prince Salm-Salm, that after my return to Europe I publish an impartial narration of events. On one such occasion he told me: "You are really the only one who can be sure of returning to Europe. You must intercede for us and take care that we are done justice. What will you call the book?" he asked, in a sudden burst of the humor which never left him in the gloomiest days of captivity. "I would suggest: *A Hundred Days of the Mexican Empire.*"

I remarked that a complete and clear insight into the course of events would be possible only if I went back to the days in Orizaba.

"Good," he said, smiling, "then simply call it *Memories of Mexico*."

May these pages find a friendly reception. The kind reader must decide for himself whether, as I myself believe, I have really preserved the necessary impartiality and objectivity, despite my personal participation in events portrayed, despite my many bitter experiences. But I can fully vouch for the truth of the factual information. I have reported nothing I did not see with my own eyes or obtain from sources of whose reliability I was personally in a position to convince myself. I have not the slightest motive to conceal anything at all which might contribute to a clear insight into an historical episode which by its nature is certain to be a subject of deep, tragic interest for future generations.

CHAPTER I

The Court at Chapultepec—Journey to Cuernavaca—The Tlalpan Plot—Return—Meeting of the Junta.

On September 18, 1866, I began my duties as Imperial Mexican Court Physician.

This was two days after the last festivities during the Mexican Empire celebrating the memory of the Mexican Declaration of Independence by Father Hidalgo. On this occasion Emperor Maximilian, in a speech which has since become famous, had expressed his firm resolve to persevere despite the bleak outlook.

I had served as military physician in Mexico from February 10, 1866 until that date, and I owed my promotion to this new post to the recommendation of the imperial physician-in-ordinary, Dr. Semeleder. In this connection I must remark that, a few days after I began work, Dr. Semeleder discontinued his medical visits to the Emperor. From this time on I was, and remained in fact, the monarch's sole physician, although it was not until two months later, in November, that Dr. Semeleder requested and received his formal dismissal.

At that time the court was in residence in Chapultepec, former palace of the Viceroys of Mexico, one hour distant from the capital. This the Emperor had ordered put into liveable condition at considerable expense.

I was entering an entirely new field of activity. Because I was so averse to involvement in the political machinations of the various parties, I strongly felt the need to become oriented to the situation at court as quickly as possible. Expecting to meet with mistrust and reserve, I found these predictions confirmed in fullest measure, particularly at first. With my position not yet established, it did not seem to be worth the trouble to include me in any political combination, and virtually all the people I came in contact with gave the impression of cardplayers who did not want to show their hands.

The Emperor, whom I then saw for the first time, received me with his usual amiability. As Chapultepec etiquette required, I was

1

immediately welcomed to the imperial dinner table. Here it was not necessary to have a special invitation, as was the case at the Palace in Mexico City. It was the custom of the court at Chapultepec, as at Cuernavaca, for Maximilian to dine personally with his assembled entourage.

Among the people at the table, some of them high officials and ordnance officers, were two men who played particularly prominent roles in the Empire: Father Fischer and State Councillor Herzfeld.

On this occasion I came to know Father Fischer, a man who from his coarse and weighty appearance could be more easily taken for an able swordsman than for a cleric. His figure as well as his smooth, well-fed face certainly did not betoken an ascetic way of life. This contrasted strangely enough with a certain sweet and unctuous tone he usually gave his speech and the manner in which he raised his glance to the ceiling and then lowered it again to the floor when any potentially risky theme came up for discussion.

State Councillor Herzfeld impressed me as an adroit courtier who took pains to give the conversation a pleasant tone and to chase away the cares which occasionally furrowed the brow of his imperial master. Not exactly fastidious in his topics of conversation, he mixed in many a calculated allusion to the spiritual condition of the Emperor's table partners.

Nothing of special importance occurred during my first days at court; my position became clearer only as we moved to Cuernavaca towards the beginning of October.

Cuernavaca lies eighteen leagues to the south of Mexico City in a deep circular valley. The tropical scenery and temperate climate made it for His Majesty, who loved both, his favorite vacation residence. He had long rented a house there, the Casa de Borda, and he also acquired a small property nearby belonging to the village of Acapatzingo. This he named "Olindo."

I had been instructed to go with the court to Cuernavaca and set out two days before the Emperor. With me were Father Fischer, Professor Bilimek, Director of the Natural History Museum in Mexico City, and Luis Arroyo. Maximilian followed, accompanied by Herzfeld, under the escort of Count Khevenhüller and his hussar squadron.

Chapter One

With this trip to Cuernavaca and the sojourn there began my close relationship with the sovereign. There he had his first detailed conversations with me. These were initially concerned with his state of health, but from the way he talked to me from then on, I was soon assured that he would share with me his fullest confidence.

Maximilian remained in Cuernavaca six days. Mornings were regularly taken up with government business, and during the afternoons we took excursions on horseback through the surrounding countryside. On the last day he invited the Alcalde of Acapatzingo and his scribe to dine with him. The latter appeared in shirt-sleeves. "Do not be upset," remarked the Emperor, noticing my amazement. "In my trips to the interior I have more than once received Indians whose dress was even simpler."

For the seventh day was planned an excursion to the Hacienda de Temisco about five leagues away. Preparations for this trip were suddenly cancelled, and we left very early the next morning for Mexico City.

On the last afternoon before our departure, I concluded from the disconcerted and distrustful expressions of Herzfeld, Fischer, and Arroyo that this sudden decision—His Majesty had originally intended to stay in Cuernavaca twelve days—must have a peculiar reason. My suspicion was correct. In fact, news had reached Cuernavaca of a plot in Tlalpan to assassinate Maximilian on his return trip to Mexico City and proclaim a republic. This information came from General O'Horan, Prefect of Tlalpan, who also surprised the ruler with the news that he had discovered the conspirators and had hanged twelve of the ringleaders.

To this day it has not been completely explained whether O'Horan was fully in the right about this plot, or whether he made it up. During his entire political and military career he had played a problematical role, changing colors repeatedly, fighting with notorious cruelty, now for the conservatives, now for the liberals. To mask his own ignoble intentions toward the Emperor, he might have dissembled. At any rate this information was the reason for our sudden return trip, which took place without incident. The assassination attempt, for whose prevention extensive military precautions were taken, did not occur.

Coincidental with Maximilian's arrival in Chapultepec, news arrived from Europe that the Empress was on a French warship, beginning the return trip from her mission, and would shortly arrive in Veracruz. I learned this directly from the Emperor, who immediately ordered me to prepare for travel. I was to accompany him to Orizaba, where he hoped to await the Empress. He told me, "You should not say anything about this project to Dr. Semeleder because you do not yet know how things go on at court, and I do not want to hurt Dr. Semeleder's feelings unnecessarily."*

A few days after the Emperor's return to Mexico City, he called together a junta at Chapultepec, composed of members of the ministry, the state council, and some of the biggest financiers in Mexico.

On the road from Cuernavaca to Mexico City His Majesty and Herzfeld had worked out a project to propose to them. According to their plan a national congress would be entrusted with deciding the future form of government. Strange to say, the convocation of the junta, whose arrangements Father Fischer had taken over, and its deliberations were most carefully concealed from Herzfeld. Its results marked an important turning point in the internal politics of the Empire, and I find it appropriate here to give a short résumé of the political situation at that time.

---

*This agrees with two letters cited by Kératry from the Emperor to Marshal Bazaine and addressed accordingly. They said that since he expected the arrival of the Empress between October 20 and the end of the same month, the Emperor requested the marshal to take over appropriate arrangements for procuring an escort.

CHAPTER II

Political Parties—Behavior of France and the United States—The Conservative Ministry—The Emperor's Speech at the Independence Celebrations.

In September, 1866 the Emperor ruled with the Lares conservative ministry. Members of this cabinet, all archconservatives, were: Lares, Minister President and Justice Minister; Arroyo, Minister to the Imperial Household; Marín, Minister of the Interior; Aguirre, Minister of Public Worship and Education; Mier y Teran, Minister of Public Works (*Fomento*); Tavera, Minister of War; State Undersecretary Pereda, Minister of Foreign Affairs; State Undersecretary Campos, Minister of Finance.

In the previous fusion ministry War and Finance had been occupied by Frenchmen: Generals Osmont and Friant. But France had now given up its game in Mexico and considered it dangerous to show the Empire open sympathy. Paris forbade participation in and cooperation with the government. On Napoleon's orders Osmont and Friant resigned their portfolios. Previous ministries, composed of liberal party leaders, were required to withdraw from the scene because of the poor results of their administration; the Empire, viable when they had taken over, had withered and faded under their control.

The government was now driven to the last resort of forming a ministry composed of clerical conservatives. This was the party which had wanted the Empire and had called Maximilian to the throne. They were now to show by deeds whether they were capable of maintaining their creation, even without French intervention.

I have briefly mentioned here facts whose significance I can better illustrate and explain by first examining somewhat more closely the chief factors of Mexican political life: the political parties, French intervention, and the influence of the United States.

Mexican party life is not at all understandable in European terms. Party programs, if one can even speak of such, contain fewer principles than clear questions of personal interest. The struggle for material possessions leaves the factions here continually out of breath

5

and undermines the calm political development of the land. Roughly speaking, parties are *puros* (reds), who in manifold gradations make up the liberal faction; *conservadores* (clerical conservatives), and *moderados* (the middle party), conservative-liberals or compromise people, who in no respect are worth much.

In addition to the three main parties a fourth was formed when the Emperor ascended to the throne. The Maximilianists, His Majesty's personal supporters, revered him with unfeigned sympathy and put themselves at the disposal of his cause. This last group was composed of liberals who were originally republicans. Recognizing the preeminent need to create a consolidated government, they attached themselves to Maximilian, whose personal attributes guaranteed he would carry out a program centered around pacification, integrity of Mexican territory, and national independence. Other adherents to the Empire were remnants of the previous regular national army and the Indians.

Nevertheless, only the clerical conservatives and the liberals had actual importance as parties. They formed closed bodies with settled goals: The former wanted to recover properties lost under the liberal presidents; the latter wanted to continue owning property taken away from the clergy. The church had once owned the most land in the country, and even today hints of its previously extensive property are evident in the great number of monasteries and red houses. (The clergy have houses belonging to them painted red.)

The Juárez Ministry of Lerdo de Tejada had seized the church possessions through the *Leyes de Reforma*. The Reform Laws, with their carefully thought-out stipulations, were from the first applied in such a way that, within a few years, it became almost impossible to reestablish the *status quo ante;* but the clergy had not given up hope of winning back their property. Their main ground of conflict with the liberals lay in their efforts to this end.

Closely allied with the clergy were the large property holders, for whom it was above all a question of preserving their wealth. They had the same worries about their property as the clergy. For years the republicans had confiscated their goods under the pretext that the property of traitors reverts to the state. Nearly everything left was destroyed as war contributions to revolutionary leaders looking for

6

means to survive.

As for the liberals, their liberalism had very little meaning. It was essentially formal, and the trappings of republicanism completely satisfied its demands. Liberal efforts were merely nationalistic though the supporters called themselves republican liberals. They had only anticlericalism in common with real liberals. Unlike Europeans of the same party, they did not work for religious enlightenment and free development; their motives were purely socialistic and rooted in hostility to clerical property.

A Mexican, liberal or conservative, is a strict absolutist and intolerant to the highest degree; intolerant about religion, intolerant about his political opinion, and, above all, intolerant about everything foreign to him. Intolerance is thus not a party characteristic but a character trait of the Mexican nation left over from the time of the Spanish Inquisition and priestly rule.

Common to almost all parties is the complete lack of men loyal to their convictions. In Mexico one joins a party primarily for opportunistic reasons.

Perhaps nowhere else is political activity so closely paired with the vilest egoism. It naturally follows that in no other country in the world are there so many sudden political deserters. According to Mexican philosophy it is not at all dishonorable to change sides. Mexicans are very far from calling deserters by their real name. "Se ha pronunciado contra el gobierno" (he has pronounced himself against the government), they say. That certainly sounds innocent enough and satisfactorily characterizes the popular conception of such behavior.

Individual *pronunciamentos* only infrequently have the character of open political reaction or revolution; this becomes clear upon investigation of how most of them arise. A military leader in charge of troops finds, after smart calculation, that things are no longer going so well with his party and that more advantages are to be hoped for on the other side. Therefore, he revolts. That is, when, with his troops, he is the sole master of a city or a district, he deposes the existent authorities; then to give his new faction some evidence of real loyalty, he has a few people shot. If the leader with the men sworn to him is subordinate to another big body of troops still true to its cause, he runs away like a thief in the night and rebels in the next town.

In the large republican army which later besieged Querétaro, there was an immense number of such deserters. As long as the Empire had money and as long as there was something to profit from it, they had been strict imperials.

Pure liberals, who even here were to be found in only very small numbers, are in the first and last instance nationalists. They defend national independence and hold out for the form of government established by the first fighters for freedom: the republic.

When the Emperor accepted the crown in Miramar, the government in Mexico was in the hands of conservatives. The regency installed by Forey was composed of members of the clerical conservative party, the party which called Maximilian to Mexico. When he arrived in the country people generally expected that in due course the Empire would somehow become a continuation of this regency and that the Emperor would now rule with the French and the clerical conservatives.

But Maximilian saw it was impossible to satisfy their demands. The *Leyes de Reforma* could no longer be revoked without totally revolutionizing present property ownership and interfering in the smallest private relations. The logic of facts compelled the Emperor to adopt these laws. Thus, to their very great disappointment, the clerical conservatives were shunted aside. They had no alternative but to restrain themselves patiently and await the day when they would be needed again.

Why the Emperor did not attach himself to his natural allies, the French, becomes evident from the following defense notes in his own hand, which are appended to this book:

"Llegado al pais, vista la trahicion de los franceses todo mi trabajo protejer la independencia y integridad; negocio de la Sonora. En consecuencia enemistad con los franceses.—Los franceses roban todo el dinero, de los dos prestamos no entran que 19 mill. en las arcas del tesoro y la guerra que ellos hacen cuesta mas que 60 mill. Sobre todo esto quejus fuertes a Paris, documentos."

(Arrival in the country, in view of the betrayal of the French, my work to protect territorial integrity, dealings about Sonora. As a result, enmity of the French—the French steal all the money, only 19 million came into the state coffers from both loans, and the war they wage costs more than 60 million. About all this, strong complaints to Paris, documents.)

Firmly believing he would be guaranteed fullest sovereignty, Maximilian had taken up the crown which Napoleon offered through the notables. He would never have agreed to be used as the naked tool of French intervention. As Emperor of Mexico he had to be Mexican and oppose any foreign intervention threatening the independence and territorial integrity of his country. And that the French intended such encroachment showed in their efforts to acquire Sonora, a large and very rich province in the north of the country.

The Emperor confided in me that he wished immediately after taking office to summon a national congress elected according to the most liberal methods so as to rid himself of these confining chains. At the same time, he came to view the *suffrage universel* introduced by the French as not entirely genuine. In this congress, because of the way it was to be chosen, all parties would doubtless have been represented. They would decide the future of the country and its form of government. Maximilian repeatedly said in my presence that the idea was never carried out mostly because of the machinations of the French. Unwilling to give up their position as conquerors, they thwarted the establishment of a national army and generally did everything to prevent the Empire from standing on its feet.

If the congress had ever come about, its results would have been valuable for two reasons. Internally, since the republican party was then completely disorganized and incapable of offering active opposition, this act would have evoked the sympathies of the whole country. The prospect of liberation from foreign troops would even have insured the liberals' vote to the Emperor's cause and freed him from clerical influence. Thus it would have been possible to bring about a national Empire and, ultimately, peace.

Externally, such a solution of the Mexican question would have offered the United States (I can say so with conviction) the desired excuse to extricate itself from the matter.

Europeans had much greater notions of the pressure the United

States exerted on the Empire than was really the case or was estimated in America itself. As for the situation in Mexico, the United States could by no means look upon the founding of an Empire with complacent eyes. But internal conditions of the Union (the struggle with the South)—it was generally thought in Mexico as well as in the United States—would prevent active, aggressive intervention. I even know from reliable sources about private statements by American government officials, who maintained that the Union was only interested in seeing peace established in Mexico. Empire or republic made no difference, as long as all future European interference was precluded. Union diplomatic recognition of the republican government was in no way to be viewed as intervention. If internal conditions had been allowed to consolidate, the Union would have endangered the Mexican Empire in the weakest manner.

The Empire needed only fulfill the tasks of bringing the machine of state to an ordered path, of creating general national interests in place of the previous decisively party interests, of unchaining latent national strength, and it would have been assured permanence.

There is nothing daring about this contention to one who observed on the spot what deep roots the Empire already had fastened in its first two years, despite unfavorable circumstances, despite restraints by the French, despite mismanagement by Mexican authorities.

If he now wanted to realize his idea of building the Empire on liberal-national foundations, Maximilian would first of all have ruthlessly to clear the main hindrances out of his way; that is, break completely with the clerical conservatives and treat the French as national enemies. He did neither.

Conservatives were merely shoved aside, and a paper war was waged with the French. Only a part of the liberal-national program was really carried out: the first ministry was composed of leaders of the liberal party. Their efforts were doomed from the outset because of basic deficiencies and the liberal ministers' lack of conviction; they cannot be credited with real honesty.

One should not be misled if at the beginning the attempt looked like a success. That initial triumph was due to the full deployment of

10

French forces. As long as the French defended the Empire with both their influence and their strength, any opposition against the still unconsolidated regime could be successfully suppressed. It made absolutely no difference whether the Emperor ruled with conservatives or liberals, precisely because by calling on their forces the French protected any government and lent necessary force to its actions.

Had Marshal Bazaine been what he should have been, a commander of auxiliary troops under the Emperor, and had Napoleon, instead of unsettling the Empire with his demands, only honestly observed the Miramar agreements to the extent of putting the auxiliary corps at Maximilian's disposal for the six years agreed upon, the Empire would have had sufficient time to survive the crises of its birth. It would certainly have succeeded in consolidating itself. But with a completely independent command, Bazaine acted as master of the country. In fact he stood next to, not under, the Emperor. He pursued only his master's objectives and lent his strong arm to the imperial government just as long as its dispositions did not clash with his very flexible conception of French interests. However, from the moment instructions from Paris suggested Napoleon's total abandonment of the Empire and troop withdrawal seemed more than a possibility, the sensitive marshal worked single-mindedly for the downfall of Maximilian and his throne.

From then on the French army lay like a monster in repose looking on indifferently as the dissidents, emboldened by Bazaine's passivity, took one position after another. Weapons in hand, the French stood and watched. His Majesty's last military support, the Austro-Belgian volunteer corps, was systematically destroyed as the marshal exposed it to the enemy in small detachments.

Circumstances inducing Napoleon to withdraw his army from Mexico are well known. The Union, victorious in the war with the secessionists, now wanted to settle accounts with the Emperor of the French for support he had given the South. Categorical notes from the Washington cabinet proved successful. The Caesar did not feel strong enough to pick a quarrel with the American colossus and hastened out of the way of conflict.

That by agreeing to Union demands he broke solemn agreements with the Empire and that Emperor Maximilian, whose throne was basically his creation, must fall touched no scruples in the man of the second of December.

Once his decision to liquidate the Mexican venture was settled, he had to use all means to extricate himself with at least the appearance of honor. He addressed Maximilian a humble letter, begging him to renounce the throne on his own initiative. Such an abdication would have afforded Napoleon the opportunity to withdraw his troops from Mexico without breaking an agreement.

The Emperor repeatedly spoke to me about this letter. He described how Napoleon implored him to give up the throne, which he (Napoleon) no longer was in a position to support. "Remember I have a son," Napoleon wrote. Maximilian informed me he had replied that solicitude for the Bonaparte dynasty should by no means prevent the French ruler from carrying out the Miramar agreements.

The Emperor made one last attempt. It is well known how the Empress went to Paris. Even if it was no longer possible to break off Napoleon's dealings with the United States, at least perhaps she could delay their execution. Her efforts were in vain: Napoleon had already negotiated with the Union about the future Mexican Republic.

In the meantime the cabinet in Washington followed proceedings with increased interest. As long as the Empire was on its feet and offered the prospect of an assured existence, the North Americans remained passive.

In accordance with what I have remarked above, they would certainly have continued this policy had the French departure not caused the Empire to totter. A golden opportunity presented itself for speedy exploitation of the situation through an expenditure of money and arms insignificant for a power like the Union. It began openly to support the rebels, who therefore favored the United States more than did the Empire, whose continued existence by now was in doubt.

As things stood, people did not have great hopes for Mexico. The Emperor's abdication would not have caused surprise; in fact, an announcement of that kind was expected daily. Instead, there appeared in the *Diario del Imperio* the list of members of a newly formed ministry, and its program. This was at the beginning of September, 1866.

The conservatives, earlier completely without connection to the Emperor, now had in the person of Father Fischer a powerful ally in immediate proximity to the monarch. His intervention made it possible for them to approach Maximilian with their promises and offers. Now these proposals found a willing ear. The thought of carrying on the government of Mexico without the French, and despite them, made conservative cooperation in this effort appealing to the Emperor, although he had previously rejected it.

The conservatives were only doing what was necessary to secure the last anchor to safety, the only remaining chance for their cause. The ministers assumed office with great plans; their announced program impressed one as if they alone knew how to meet the challenge. They promised the country prompt pacification, although the proposed method for achieving it was a secret, of course. But people believed them and impatiently looked forward to September 16, the date of the independence celebrations, when the Emperor usually addressed a state reception.

The great Iturbide Hall in the imperial palace had never seen such a crowd as on that day. Those entitled to be there because of their position did not miss the occasion. After a *Te Deum* the hall quickly filled to capacity. Breathless stillness prevailed as the sovereign appeared on the balustrade and read the following speech in a strong voice:

Mexicans!

Sharing your enthusiasm, already for the third time as head of the Nation, I celebrate our great and glorious festival of brotherhood.

On this day of patriotic remembrance my heart urges me to direct free and loyal words to my fellow citizens and to take part with them in the general joy.

Fifty-six years have flowed past since the first call to rebirth. For half a century already Mexico has been fighting for its independence and its peace. This period doubtlessly seems very long to justifiably impatient patriots. But in the history of a developing people, this is only the hard time of learning, which each nation must pass through before becoming great and powerful. Without struggle, without blood, there is no

13

national triumph, no political development, no lasting progress.

The first period of our history teaches us self-sacrifice, unity, and unshakeable belief in the future.

Let all loyal friends of the Fatherland, each in his own sphere, energetically support the great enterprise of regeneration. Then my work will not be in vain, and I shall continue hopefully on the difficult path I follow. Have trust and goodwill so that one day we shall enjoy the fruits of peace and happiness we long for.

I still stand firmly in the place to which the will of the Nation called me: Unmindful of all difficulties, without faltering in my duties, for a true Hapsburg never leaves his post in the moment of danger.

The majority of the Nation has chosen me to defend her hallowed right against the enemies of order, property, and true independence. The Almighty must protect us, for it is a holy truth that the voice of the peoples is the voice of God. That was wonderfully shown in the days of the first national uprising, and it will also be shown by our rebirth.

The spirits of our heroes gaze down upon us. Let us follow their undying example without faltering, without trepidation, and we shall obtain the enviable goal of seeing secured and enthroned the cause of independence, which they consecrated with their blood.

Mexicans! Long live independence and the beautiful memory of its immortal martyrs.

The speech was received with enthusiasm, and on September 16, 1866, Mexico had one of the few beautiful days pervaded by happy confidence in the future.

CHAPTER III

Junta—The New State Council—Lacunza—Castelnau's Arrival—The Concordat Question—Two Letters from the Emperor to His Ministers —The Emperor's Address to the Bishops.

According to the Emperor's defense notes, the junta's primary task was to deliberate about the plan for a congress and the financial situation. "Deseo mio de un congreso. Junta en Chapultepec."

His Majesty avoided the meetings, not wanting to influence decisions by his presence. Since he would not see Herzfeld, I kept him company in his office and in the adjoining library.

I still remember the exact words with which he explained to me, among others, the basis for his nonparticipation in the sessions: "Previously, I have always done the work; this must change. Others must do the drudgery now and, if they are serious, above all come up with some money."

Deliberations were unsuccessful; the Emperor's congressional proposal was rejected, and, true to Mexican custom, money was only promised.

The conservatives had assumed mastery of the situation through the Lares ministry. They consequently showed at the first opportunity that they were primarily concerned with consolidating their party— not with fulfilling Maximilian's intentions. A fully representative congress might endanger these goals, so they vetoed his plans and clung to their well-worn philosophies.

The ministry's first task was to change the complexion of the state council. This body, composed mostly of liberals and moderates under the previous liberal ministry, was now to include conservative elements. Father Fischer had greatly influenced the choice of ministers. The same thing happened with the new members of the state council. I watched the Emperor give his consent to a string of Father Fischer's proposals about men supposedly qualified for these jobs.

The state council now took on a mixed character with a preponderantly conservative element. The president at that time was Lacunza, an official whom the monarch himself described as a great statesman and an honorable man. His later behavior, especially after Maximilian went to Querétaro and was captured, showed that he was neither one nor the other.

A former minister of finance, Lacunza in due course had mastered the art of always having money on hand in the state coffers. However, his methods were very singular, clashing with our conception of a financier's conduct. Lacunza well understood how to collect money, but seldom was he prevailed upon to make an accounting. That was the whole secret of Mexico's financial prosperity during the Lacunza ministry.

The Emperor's unhealthy condition, which, by his own statement, dated as far back as July, showed itself in Chapultepec to be malaria. I considered it my medical duty to advise him to move his residence from Chapultepec to Mexico City. Chapultepec Hill rises out of an extensive swampy plateau, and I had reason to suspect the topography, if not as the source of the illness itself, at least as the source of its obstinate persistence. In the first days of October, the sovereign moved from Chapultepec to the Residencia.

October 10, the day the French postal steamer arrived in Veracruz, word came that General Castelnau, Emperor Napoleon's personal adjutant, of whose arrival we had been forewarned, was a passenger. He would reach the capital around October 14 if, as we expected, he used the rapid coach line.

The situation in Mexico urgently required solution, and Maximilian eagerly awaited Castelnau's arrival. Examination of papers the Frenchman undoubtedly would bring would completely explain the nature of his mission. But for reasons unknown to us, the general took his time.

The Emperor saw mainly Bazaine's influence in this delay. He said to me: "For several reasons Castelnau's procrastination must suit Bazaine very well. If the mission is unfavorable to him, Bazaine will use the time to win over the envoy. If Castelnau has instructions to act in agreement with Bazaine, it is in the marshal's interest to manipulate Castelnau beforehand."

Castelnau's absence distressed him still further because, as he expressed it himself, he was infuriated over the general's inexcusable indiscretion in leaving him to wait unnecessarily. The French pleni-potentiary's conduct gave him little hope or encouragement. It could only create suspicion that delay meant the envoy was not bringing good news.

These days, ill health, even if only minor, chaotic political con-ditions, money problems, Castelnau's delay, and discontent with the conservative ministry's indifference to his wishes produced in the Emperor a deep mental upset and exhaustion which increased in later, much more unfavorable moments. At this time the Emperor was brought a *memento mori* as a souvenir of his last trip to Cuernavaca: the flintlock which, according to O'Horan, was taken from the man planning to murder the prince on the road to the capital.

Despite his ill humor, Maximilian was unflaggingly active during this period. He especially concerned himself with the increasingly crucial question of concluding a concordat. Father Fischer returned from his trip to Rome about this issue, reporting that preliminary negotiations with the Mexican princes of the church had resulted in an agreement. They would come to the capital for deliberation of the matter in synod assembly.

By concluding a concordat the Emperor intended first of all to reach final settlement with the clergy on the question of church property. This also meant legally establishing for the Empire the dis-amortization (release of goods in mortmain) introduced by the *Leyes de Reforma* of the earlier republican government, thus binding rela-tions with Rome very much weakened over this issue. Given the com-pletely Catholic character of the country, this settlement had become a state necessity; it would win new support for the Empire. However, Maximilian never intended to deliver the state over to the discretion of the church.

The following handwritten letters to his ministers best clarify the Emperor's ideas about the relationship between church and state. I quote from the unpublished collection *Alocuciones, cartas oficiales é instrucciones del Emperador Maximiliano durante los anos de 1864, 1865 y 1866,* printed on highest orders as a manuscript in the court printing press.

Mexico City—December 27, 1864

My Dear Minister Escudero:

In order to reach a compromise on difficulties arising from the so-called Reform Laws, We have resolved to make excellent use of a means which will simultaneously satisfy the Nation's just demands and restore the peace of mind and quiet the consciences of all inhabitants of the Empire. We made provisions for this purpose when We were in Rome and entered into negotiations with the Holy Father, as the Supreme Head of the Catholic Church.

The papal nuncio is now in Mexico City, but to Our great astonishment he has explained that he has no instructions and is only awaiting them from Rome.

The pressing situation We have faced for more than seven months with all Our efforts will allow no more postponement. It demands a quick solution and We call on you to propose as soon as possible measures by which impartial justice will be served and legitimate interests, created by those laws, remain insured. Excesses and injustices to which they have given rise must be eliminated. Provisions must be made to maintain public worship, to guarantee all sanctified objects under religious protection, to administer the sacraments, and to practice the other spiritual functions throughout the whole Empire without burdening the people.

Therefore, you will want to give Us, first of all, proposals about revising the disamortization and nationalization (confiscation as national property) of church goods previously carried out. They will sanction legitimate operations provided they are implemented honestly and in strict observance of the laws which decreed the proceedings against church property mentioned above.

Finally, act in accordance with the principles of the broadest and freest tolerance and continually hold before your eyes the fact that the state religion is Apostolic Roman Catholicism.

Maximilian

Mexico City—June 11, 1865

My Dear Minister Siliceo:

Public instruction in the Empire requires a fundamental reorganization in the most pressing way. When I entrusted you with leadership over educational affairs, I was completely convinced of your competence and your zeal, but, before you undertake this work, I want to point out the main features I hope to see in your proposals.

It is my will that public instruction in the Mexican Empire, since it makes use of the experiences of the most advanced peoples, be brought to a level which places us alongside those Nations.

As a guiding principle for your projects, you will want to keep in mind that education must be accessible to all, public, free of charge, and compulsory, at least as regards elementary studies.

Further, education should be organized so that it provides the middle classes with an adequate general education and yet can become the necessary basis for higher and specialized studies. The teaching of ancient and modern languages and the natural sciences must be considered essential. The study of ancient languages as a basis for a common humanistic education is a highly valuable mental exercise. In these days knowledge of modern languages is absolutely indispensable to a people taking part in world events and, with special reference to its exceptional geographical position, wanting to maintain an active commerce with other peoples. Attention to the natural sciences is characteristic of the times because they teach us to see things as they really are and to make natural forces subservient to human will.

I also wish that, in conjunction with intellectual development, physical education be given appropriate attention.

As for higher and professional studies, I think that to foster them successfully, special schools are needed. What in the middle-ages was called a "university" has become a word without meaning today. In establishing these specialized schools you must take care that in the different fields, all branches of the theoretical and practical sciences and the arts are represented.

I wish to direct your attention to a science hitherto only little known in our Fatherland. I mean philosophy; for this steels the spirit, teaches the person to know himself and, as a consequence of this self-knowledge, to perceive the moral order of society.

I also want to disclose to you my ideas about religious education. Religion is a matter of individual conscience; the less the state gets involved in religious questions, the truer it remains to its mission. We have liberated the church and sciences. To the first, I want to guarantee the full enjoyment of her legitimate rights as well as the greatest freedom in educating and training her priests according to her own rules without state intervention. But she has other important duties. Among these is, first of all, religious instruction, in which, regrettably, the clergy of the land until now has not taken any interest. As a result, in your offers and proposals you will give recognition to the principle that religious instruction in the lower and middle schools is to be given through the respective parishes according to books sanctioned by the government.

At all educational establishments examinations must be organized according to a new plan—openly held and administered with real strictness.

Since we require a basic education for our youth, we must provide for good teachers and means of instruction.

Therefore, you must first of all keep in mind the need to establish normal schools for excellent teachers. You will appoint to those posts the best personnel for this country and abroad. Likewise, I commend your special attention to the procurement of good teaching books.

Maximilian

The Emperor had drafted a speech in German for the opening of the synod. Since he wanted to give it in the language of the church, he commissioned me to translate it into Latin. My resistance, based on a more than eleven-year lapse in study of the Roman classics, was to no avail. I had to do it because Maximilian wanted to keep the contents of this speech secret for the present and did not trust the translation to any of the clergymen more skilled in Latin than I.

Since the German original drafted by His Majesty is not at my disposal, I give here the Latin text and the retranslation into German. May the admonitions of Cicero and the Piarists of Prager Neustadt forgive my offenses against classical style.

Reverendissimi et fidelissimi Archepiscopi et

Episcopi Imperii Mei!

Voluntas mea est, ut pax perennis inter Imperium ejusque Ecclesiam regnet. Hoc animo motus desiderio sanctissimi Patris libentissime occurri atque concessi, ut veniretis in urbem Meam et conferretis consilia de variis quaestionibus adhuc non judicatis cum Delegatis Gubernii mei. Hae quaestiones non judicatae nascuntur ex legibus sancitis per Gubernia Imperio Meo antecedentia, quas mihi legitimo eorum successori tueri necesse erat, usque dum tractatus cum sede Pontificia novum fundamentum posuissent.

A primo initio Imperii Mei omnia haec perspexi, atque necessitatem conciliationis pacificae agnoscens, Ipse in urbem sacram profectus sum et a Patre Sanctissimo petivi, ut cito mitteret Nuntium cum plena potestate agendi et tractandi.

Haud ignoti sunt Vobis, o Reverendissimi Principes Ecclesiae, eventus, qui subsecuti sunt. Nuntius Pontificius ex insperato profectus est; atque Ego semper aspirans ad conciliationem pacificam ac beneficam, ad alias rationes compulsus eram.

Ad comprobandam voluntatem Meam bonam ac sinceram, legationem diplomaticam cum primo Ministro Meo ad Patrem sanctissimum misi. Hi viri dignissimi optima voluntate et amore patriae praediti difficultates praecipuas ita sustulerunt, ut Gubernium Meum nunc cum dignissimis Archepiscopis et Episcopis Imperii Mexicani tractare possit.

Gubernium Meum ad has tractationes, quae rem decernere debent et ad perficiendam perennem conciliationem inter Imperium ejusque Ecclesiam optimam et sincerissimam voluntatem affert, nec non paratum est omnibus rationibus uti, quae ad tollenda impedimenta utiles esse videantur.

Iis rationibus vero nunquam accedet, quae felicitati atque commodis populi adversae sunt, aut quae jus Nationis Mexicanae a Majoribus traditum violare possint.

Persuasum Mihi est de amore patriae et de voluntati quam habent conciliandi Archepiscopi et Episcopi Imperii Mei: et hac ex causa spes optima Me tenet fore, ut clare verum statum perspicientes ingenio Vestro complectamini difficultates et obligationes conscientiae quibus nunc Gubernium Nostrum occupatur, et consecretis omnes vires ac diligentiam huic operi pacis.

De Mea igitur ergo Vos benevolentia certiores facti suscipite alacri animo munus Vobis commissum et patriam nostram, Imperatricem et Me Ipsum Deo in orationibus Vestris commendate.

Very Reverend and Very faithful Archbishops

and Bishops of My Empire!

It is My imperial will that perpetual peace reign between our state and the church. Inspired by this thought, I have eagerly cooperated with the Holy Father's wishes and have agreed for you to come to My capital to consult with representatives of My Government about various questions not yet discussed. These unsettled questions have their basis in laws sanctioned by the previous government which I had to protect as its legitimate successor, until an agreement with the Holy See laid new foundations.

I recognized this clearly at the beginning of My reign, and, understanding the need for peaceful reconciliation, I traveled to Rome to request that the Holy Father send us an envoy plenipotentiary as soon as possible.

What followed is scarcely unknown to you, Very Reverend Princes of the Church. Contrary to all expectations the papal nuncio departed, and, still striving for a peaceful and beneficial agreement, I am forced to other expedients.

To demonstrate My sincere goodwill, I have sent a diplomatic mission to the Holy Father with My prime minister at its head. Our estimable men, inspired by sincerity and patriotism, have succeeded in removing the main difficulties so that My government can now enter into negotiations with the Very Reverend Archbishops and Bishops of the Mexican Empire.

Desirous of effecting a lasting reconciliation between the state and the church, My government brings to these negotiations the best and most sincere goodwill. It also stands ready to employ all means which appear to be conducive to removing difficulties.

However, My government will never agree to means which prejudice the happiness, the freedom, and the welfare of the people or might violate the rights of the Mexican Nation inherited from our forefathers. I am convinced of the patriotism and the conciliatory spirit of the Archbishops and Bishops of My Empire; therefore, I hope that in just condemnation of the present situation, completely understanding the difficulties and responsibilities of conscience which occupy our government, you will dedicate your whole strength and activity to this work of peace.

Accept now, Very Reverend Archbishops and Bishops of My Empire, the assurance of my benevolence and go with fresh courage to the work entrusted to you.

I commend the Fatherland, the Empress, and My person to your devout prayers.

CHAPTER IV

Report on The Empress's Illness—The Emperor's Decision to go to Europe — Countermoves by the Conservatives — Resignation of the Ministry and its Reconstitution — The Emperor's Departure for Orizaba.

At this period Maximilian lived completely secluded at the Palace. No one but Herzfeld, Father Fischer, and I were invited to eat with him. Only on October 16 did he again begin to increase his table company by inviting guests. A great dinner was planned for the afternoon of October 18, preceded by a meeting of the ministry presided over by the Emperor. After that, I entered his office, as usual, and, while I was there, two cable dispatches arrived from Europe. The Emperor was visibly alarmed when they were handed to him; his gloomy suspicions had indeed not deceived him. One of the telegrams was from Count Bombelles, addressed from Miramar; the other cable, from foreign minister Castillo, came from Rome.

Herzfeld, who had immediately undertaken the deciphering, did not want to inform Maximilian of their sad news about the Empress's illness. He therefore feigned inability to interpret them correctly. Herzfeld maintained that he was only able to learn from the dispatches that someone in Miramar was sick, and the Emperor consoled himself with the thought that this probably referred to the Empress's Mexican lady-in-waiting, Madame Bario.

However, Herzfeld could not long keep the real meaning secret. Realizing that he held back the truth out of consideration for him, Maximilian himself demanded accurate interpretation of the dispatches.

He said, "I know that it must be something frightful. Please inform me; I expect the worst." While Herzfeld pretended to finish deciphering the dispatches, I went to my room. However, a few minutes later the Emperor called me back. "Do you know Dr. Riedel in Vienna?" he asked me, tears welling from his eyes.

I knew this name, and everything was clear to me. Herzfeld had already told him the truth. Even if I wanted to spare His Majesty, I couldn't lie. "He is the director of the insane asylum," I was forced to reply.

This sad news gave direct impetus to developing the crisis at hand and hastening catastrophe. In recent days Maximilian had faced so many difficult trials. Now his last hope had disappeared; he saw himself abandoned by fate and overcome with pain. Indifferent to everything, he could only find solace in the thought of leaving this land of misfortune and hurrying to his wife. Had he, since accepting this fatal crown, experienced suffering and only suffering? Had the whole period of his rule been a perpetual physical and moral struggle for his sovereignty and his idealistic intentions? Had he now to see them founder both on the opposition of the nationalists and on the intrigues of the French? The last stroke of fate darkened these gloomy clouds of care and disappointment. Everywhere he looked—no hope, no light.

The Empress had fallen victim to Mexico. Scant prospect remained that he could maintain his regime without French bayonets. Under the circumstances he need not fear the one factor which might have kept him there: European public reproach at a withdrawal. Even a sovereign may comply with human obligations.

All this heavy misfortune persuaded Maximilian to think earnestly and independently about the problem of Mexico and his throne. I say independently and lay particular emphasis on the word because I can give the best explanation of the sovereign's intentions, perhaps even the only one. At this time I already enjoyed his closest confidence and was the first whom he let in on his thoughts. The evening of the same day the news of the Empress's illness arrived, on his usual walk on the *azotea* (the flat roof) of the palace, he informed me of his tentative plans by asking whether or not he should leave the country.

My clear conviction, created by the unpromising state of affairs, drew me to his way of thinking, and since I considered it a holy duty to make no secret of my opinion, I answered him candidly. "I do not think Your Majesty will be able to remain in the country."

The Emperor asked, "Will anybody really believe that I am going to Europe because of the Empress's illness?"

I answered, "Your Majesty has reasons enough, and Europe will admit that you are no longer obligated to stay in Mexico since France prematurely cancelled its agreements." He then exclaimed "What do you think will be Herzfeld and Fischer's opinion about this?"

"I believe," I openly explained, "that Herzfeld will share my view. As for Father Fischer, as a matter of fact, he does not inspire much confidence in me. He is a cleric, and in all honesty, which I assume he has, his party's gain will come before Your Majesty's special interests."

In the further course of conversation, the prince then asked me my opinion as to whether he should put his decision into effect immediately or for the time being state it to be his definite plan. Upon conscientious reflection of everything this suggested, I felt I also had to answer that at the present time there was no reason to hurry, that the calm execution of such an important decision required preparations lasting weeks, perhaps months.

After this conversation, around six o'clock in the evening, His Majesty summoned State Councillor Herzfeld and Museum Director Bilimek, who both lived in the palace, to hear their opinions. As I had presumed, their judgment agreed with mine. That evening the Emperor Maximilian decided to leave Mexico.

After this transpired, he could no longer tolerate the Residencia. He retired to Chapultepec in strictest solitude and there succeeded in implementing his travel plans more quickly than I would have thought possible. At this time, State Councillor Herzfeld played the role of a man who, as a loyal personal aide and an Austrian, felt he was serving the Archduke of Austria rather than the Emperor of Mexico. Herzfeld had only one thing on his mind: to see the departure proceed as quickly as possible. I know, convinced though he was that Maximilian could not leave the country without first abdicating and winding up pending business in an orderly fashion, this one thought obsessed him. In his worried haste he was not at all frightened by the suggestion that his sovereign was flatly leaving everything in the lurch. He thought, "When I once have him at sea, then the many scruples will automatically disappear, and the Emperor and imperial family will thank me for having saved him."

Sheer human nature motivated the Councillor's calculation. Still under the fresh impression of the day at Tlalpan, he already saw imminent danger to Maximilian's life and advised the greatest haste. After three o'clock on the morning of October 21, he succeeded in effecting our departure from Chapultepec.

The events of October 19 and 20, which immediately preceded this, convince me to report these days at greater length. Scarcely had the Emperor moved back to Chapultepec, and scarcely had his decision to leave the country become public, when the combined conservative party protested violently against it. The conservatives knew only too well that they could present Maximilian very few arguments for remaining in the country. They were even convinced that he had reason enough to abdicate. But now fully awakened to the new political life and having worked with brisk passion to serve their own interests, they could see all their hopes, all their plans—clerical reshaping of the Empire, restoration of their property—destroyed by this one stroke. They had to exert all their powers to stop this, and they forcefully opposed the monarch's intentions.

The political effectiveness of the conservatives indeed began to make itself felt. Prelates had already arrived in Mexico City from all parts of the Empire; the synod was to meet in the next few days; the national army was to be organized; the struggle against the republicans would begin in all earnest. In the midst of all their beautiful plans, the decision to leave the country came as an overwhelming shock. As the conservatives said, it would expose their interests and leave them in the lurch. Selfishly, they supported the imperial form of government as a cloak for secret purposes and particularisms. If the regime collapsed, they would be without protection, and they would lose the ground under their feet.

The Emperor understood the conservatives' agitation, and, to dodge their indiscreet pressures, he barricaded himself in his cliff castle. As his physician, I had the highly unpleasant task of standing guard on the threshold of his room and refusing admittance with the words, "The Emperor is sick, and I can let no one in to see him." Among others also appeared the Princess Iturbide, maiden aunt of young Prince Iturbide whom Maximilian had adopted and appointed his successor in case of his death without an heir. I had a hard fight with this hot-tempered lady, who was very proud that the sovereign called her *querida prima* (beloved cousin). She would not believe my words and wanted to speak with Maximilian at all costs. When I explained to her harshly that this was impossible, she lustily abused all those who, she said, were misleading His Majesty into going away.

No one wanted to credit the news of the Empress's illness as the cause of the upcoming departure. People thought it invented, intentionally made up, to supply a plausible reason for abdication. It follows from this that the Mexicans were prepared for such a result and, for sentimental reasons, did not reproach the Emperor. If it were to judge fairly, public opinion could not refuse to see previous events as the basis for his decision. Moreover, the Empress was too beloved for them not to have inwardly wanted to disbelieve the seriousness of her condition.

The ministers' behavior towards Maximilian was highly peculiar. Through me the Emperor had given Father Fischer instructions to Minister President Lares to deliver in his name: Partly for health reasons, since the doctors had recommended a change of climate for the persistent malaria, partly because of the understandable wish to be closer to news from Europe, he was about to travel to Orizaba. However, his departure was not to change the government situation at all. The ministry would continue its work as before and send all important questions to Orizaba. In general, matters would take the same course as during the stay in Cuernavaca. The official journal, the *Diario del Imperio,* would inform the public of this news.

The morning of October 20, Maximilian sent State Councillor Herzfeld with a letter to Marshal Bazaine. He informed the marshal that he was traveling to Orizaba and cited the above reasons. In addition he instructed Herzfeld to discuss with Bazaine possible measures for maintaining the *status quo* during his absence from the capital. Marshal Bazaine's answer was more than reassuring. After the mysterious occurrences of the last days he could see the trip to Orizaba as a first step in complying with Napoleon's request.

I know the marshal informed us through Herzfeld that during the Emperor's absence he would suppress all opposition and provide adequate protection for the government.

Dispositions for the trip were settled. Of the imperial household only Father Fischer, the Emperor's aide-de-camp Feliciano Rodríguez, the ordnance officer Pradillo, Professor Bilimek, and I were to accompany the sovereign.

Around three o'clock in the afternoon, Minister President Lares appeared at the Palace of Chapultepec and demanded admittance to the Emperor. With an excited, trembling voice he told me he had to speak to Maximilian immediately; he had a document whose delivery would brook no delay.

I went in and announced that Lares had arrived and insisted on personally delivering an official document. But the monarch would not see even him. After I explained that until now no one, not even the Princess Iturbide, had been received, Lares handed me the paper. It contained nothing less than the resignation of the ministers en bloc in case of the Emperor's departure. Fear that without the ruler the government would collapse had driven the ministers to this decision. They had so little faith in their own strength and energy that, in the feeble balance which they believed characterized the situation, they trembled at every sudden change in the atmosphere. The ghost of revolution before their eyes, they clung helplessly to Maximilian. The ministry did not want, so to speak, to be surprised by the republicans *in flagranti*. They completely forgot that a short while before, they themselves had suggested taking up the fight with the rebels without French support. It was their precipitous retreat that most clearly displayed the impotence of their party.

The ministry's action which, by the way, came as a complete surprise, did not unsettle His Majesty. He had decided once and for all to depart and wanted to carry through despite all hindrances. First, through Herzfeld he informed the marshal of the ministry's intention to resign, giving no instructions for the present. He had made up his mind to let matters reach a crisis. While the ministers panicked, he carefully considered the situation and set up two contingency plans in case they did not revoke their decison:

1) To install a mixed regency.

The members of the regency would be Lares, minister president; Lacunza, president of the state council; Bazaine, chief of the army. The regency would call a congress and present it with the Emperor's decision to abdicate. Maximilian dictated to me a decree by which the regency would be transferred to Bazaine, Lares, and Lacunza during his absence. The regency decree was to be sealed in two copies; one for Lares, one for Bazaine. They would be delivered with orders to open only on later special instructions.

2) To transfer the seat of government to Orizaba.

Minister to the Imperial Household Arroyo, dependable under all circumstances, would be the only minister to go to Orizaba, while Bazaine in Mexico City took over security for the capital.

Father Fischer, whom the monarch also refused to see at this time, had to watch these events in involuntary passivity. Regretfully he learned of the impending departure; seeing his impotence in the matter, he acquiesced against his will. The only available means of averting catastrophe was to persuade the ministers to reconsider.

I know the following because Father Fischer personally told it to me. The afternoon after Lares delivered the resignation to Chapultepec, Fischer sought the officials out in the city and made energetic remonstrances. He succeeded in his task of persuasion by proving to them that resignation would provoke exactly what they wanted to hinder—Maximilian's abdication. By opposing the trip to Orizaba, they could only increase the Emperor's mistrust and move him to make Europe, not Orizaba, the goal of his trip. The only means, if not of preventing the abdication, at least of postponing it, was to remain in office and let the trip to Orizaba proceed calmly.

This argument was totally correct. Had the resignations not been withdrawn, Maximilian would undoubtedly have gone immediately to Europe. But the ministers withdrew their request. Marshal Bazaine contributed greatly to the result by bluntly reprimanding them for their disloyal behavior and at the same time promising his protection.

At ten o'clock at night the decision was made, and Arroyo conveyed the ministers' explanation. Acknowledging the reasons for the trip to Orizaba, they promised to attend to government business as prearranged, during the ruler's absence.

Before learning the decision, Maximilian received a letter from Bazaine, stating that there would be no hindrance to the move to

Orizaba. It also contained very comforting assurances that the marshal would take care of all eventualities. In case the officials really did resign, he advised the Emperor (thus agreeing with his plan) to take Arroyo to Orizaba as sole minister.*

Around eleven o'clock in the evening the travel arrangements were changed by adding Arroyo, the minister to the imperial household, and secretariat official Ybarrondo to the entourage previously decided on.

His Majesty left Herzfeld behind in the capital temporarily with instructions to use his influence in settling doubts about the Empress's illness. Also he was to calm the Austrians and Belgians, who with the departure of their sovereign towards Europe surely saw themselves abandoned. He was to assure them that whatever else the Emperor intended, he would never lose sight of their interests. Moreover, Herzfeld was to welcome Castelnau in Maximilian's name, explain the move to Orizaba, and ask him to send his papers there for a direct answer.

In addition to these instructions, which Herzfeld received directly from the prince's mouth, Maximilian dictated the following to me on the afternoon of October 20:

> Herzfeld is to prepare a secret letter concerning the Austro-Belgian Volunteer Corps. Bazaine must provide for this unit to be embarked and sent away. In due time, Colonel Kodolitch, Lieutenant Colonel Hotze, and Colonel Van der Smissen are to be informed of the contents of the letter. Furthermore, Herzfeld is to prepare, according to drafts already at hand, letters of farewell to the aunt and mother of Prince Iturbide. In the letter to the princesses, Herzfeld is to mention that the Emperor is thinking of their welfare and that they will be commended to the future government. Moreover, Herzfeld will draft an order handing over all inventory in Mexico City, Chapultepec, and Cuernavaca to the chief of the imperial secretariat, Captain Pierron, and to Colonel Schaffer. They

---

*Kératry puts the following words in the sovereign's mouth after he had received this letter: "Je ne puis plus en douter, ma femme est folle, ces gens la me tuent à petit feu. Je suis épuisé—Je m'en vais—Remerciez bien le maréchal de cette nouvelle preuve de dévouement. Je pars cette nuit et s'il désire m'écrire, voici mon itinéraire." To whom would Maximilian make such a remark? That day he only saw State Councillor Herzfeld and me. Certainly no one from general headquarters was admitted to him on that day.

will be jointly responsible for safekeeping and maintenance.

Finally, he is to draft a secret arrangement granting the imperial estate "Olindo" at Cuernavaca to the Emperor's aide-de-camp, Colonel Rodríguez, and giving all the imperial stables to the Emperor's ordance officers, Colonel Ormachaea, Lieutenant Colonel Uraga, and Major Pradillo.

All these instructions were later substantially modified and, in large part, cancelled; I have mentioned them here to confirm the intentions with which the Emperor left Chapultepec. At four o'clock in the morning, he set out from Chapultepec accompanied by a hussar escort, three hundred and four men strong, commanded by Colonel Kodolitch.

CHAPTER V

Journey to Orizaba—The Emperor's Meeting with General Castelnau in Ayutla—Annulment of the Decree of 3 October, 1865 in Socyapán —Naming of a Special Commission to Settle the Emperor's Private Affairs—Arrival in Orizaba.

We first stopped in a small village called Mexicalzingo. The Emperor drew my attention to the nearby sacrifice mountain, on which in Aztec times the great fires of joy blazed every fifty years. According to Aztec cosmogony, the world had fifty years' existence. When the fiftieth year approached, the Aztec people prepared themselves in gloomy resignation for the violent earthquake which was supposed to smash the universe to nothingness. On the sacrifice mountain near Mexicalzingo, the chief priests prayerfully awaited arrival of this most horrible catastrophe, from time to time bringing pious victims to appease the gods. When, after anxious hours, the world remained intact, the chief priest put a gigantic woodpile into the fire, thereby giving the signal for the fires of joy which, from all the high places of the Valle de Anahuac, now brought the happy news to the Aztec people. They could look forward to a new fifty-year period of the sweet habit of existence.

In Ayutla, thirteen leagues from Mexico City, we stopped for a noon rest and met Castelnau, traveling to the capital by slow day march.

Because of his recent behavior, the Emperor shunned seeing Castelnau, so the Chief of the Imperial Secretariat, Captain Pierron, went to meet him, and they entered Ayutla together. However, as close as his relationship was to Pierron, whose capability and effectiveness in the cabinet he constantly praised, Maximilian did not want to receive even him. I had to go to Pierron and make official excuses on grounds of ill health. Also, the frame of mind in which news from Europe had put the sovereign prevented his seeing Castelnau. He felt too weak, in his present indisposition, to discuss a matter of such significance. Indignation over Castelnau's behavior was also a reason why he avoided any such encounter, and this was supposed to convey his displeasure.

In Ayutla we also met Colonel Schaffer, just returned from the United States, where he had gone on a mission for the monarch. The reunion was moving. With tears in his eyes, Maximilian informed him of the Empress's illness.

Around five o'clock in the afternoon we reached the first night's resting place, the Hacienda Socyapán.

His Majesty was very silent and sunk in deep reflection. Without speaking to any of us, he walked back and forth in front of the hacienda with Professor Bilimek and me. Finally, he broke the secretive silence and informed us of what moved him so. "I want no more blood to be shed in the country on my account. What should I do?" he asked, in painfully agitated tones.

In his naive and straightforward way of looking at things, Professor Bilimek simply advised in favor of immediate abdication. I could by no means agree with his opinion and spoke out against it. Sudden abdication would have accomplished the opposite of what was intended. For from that moment civil war would rage even more violently, and bloodshed would only have just begun. Once he had abdicated, the Emperor himself would not be reproached directly. However, he would see it as a matter of conscience and ought not burden himself, even indirectly.

My opinion was to stick with the decision made in Mexico City. Revoking the martial law of October 3, 1865 would be enough to check the bloodshed. The much-discussed law, which the Emperor repeatedly described to me as the only injustice committed under his rule, was originally issued at the initiative of the French. Maximilian's own notes best reveal how the law originated:

En Setiembre, 1865 llega la noticia, que Juarez abandonó et territorio nacional. Impulso de los franceses para medidas fuertes, para como dicen terminar pronto y completamente. Se elabora la ley del 3. de Octubre. Bazaine dicta personalmente pormenores delante testigos. Los ministros responsables y muy liberales como Escudero, Cortez Esparza etc. etc. discuten la ley con todo el consejo de Estado. Todos los puntos principales de la ley existieron ya antes bajo Juarez; asi lo dijeron los ministros. La ley fué bien ejecutada de los Mexicanos, por lo, que hicieron los franceses no podémos tomar la responsabilidad.

> In September, 1865 word arrives that Juárez has abandoned
> the national territory. French impulse to strong measures in
> order, as they say, to finish quickly and completely. The law
> of October 3 is drawn up. Bazaine personally dictated details
> in the presence of witnesses. The responsible and very liberal
> ministers like Escudero, Cortez Esparza, etc., discuss the law
> with the whole state council. According to the ministers all
> the principal points of the law already existed under Juárez.
> The law was mildly enforced by the Mexicans. We cannot
> take responsibility for what the French did.

By lifting this law the Emperor could assuage his conscience, but
in his current mood he felt this step was still not enough. He wanted
to shift all responsibility from himself once and for all. He insisted on
laying down his crown here in Socyapán and continuing his trip as a
private citizen. The commander of the escort, Colonel Kodolitch, had
already received instructions to inform the officers of his abdication.

My complaint that since leaving the capital there was nothing
new to justify abdication on the highway was in vain. The prince did
not listen to reasons and only answered abruptly, "no more blood must
flow on my account."

I now pointed out to him that besides revoking the law of October 3, he could also order a temporary halt to hostilities. This would
relieve him of all responsibility.

Presented with the same questions of conscience, Father Fischer
agreed with me, and we succeeded in persuading the sovereign temporarily to be satisfied with these two measures.

During the long discussions with me, Professor Bilimek, Colonel
Kodolitch, and Father Fischer, His Majesty's agitation finally gave
way to calm reflection. He himself now realized that Socyapán was
not a proper place to undertake the important political act of abdicating. Instead he immediately conferred on Father Fischer the duty
of drafting two documents to Lares and Bazaine with orders revoking
the law of October 3, suspending all convictions, and immediately
ceasing all hostilities until further notice.

"Ida de Mejico a Orizaba, Anulacion imediata del decreto del 3.
de Octobre." (Journey from Mexico City to Orizaba, Immediate
revocation of the law of 3 October.) These are the Emperor's words
in his defense notes mentioning the day at Socyapán.

35

Count Lamotte, officer of the Austrian hussars, went as a courier to Mexico City with both documents.*

The story of this significant day has repeatedly suffered distortion. Romantics of both hemispheres, people writing for all kinds of purposes, have seized upon this "thankful impulse" and thereby given free rein to fantasy. I believe that if I offer here a strictly true report, only scoundrels, who, when opportunity and advantage so offer, play their frivolous game with what is noblest and best, will succumb to criticizing and deriding such sentimental battles of a noble heart. In the souls of all of us who spent those agonizing hours near the Emperor, the memories of that day are dug deep as among the most difficult and saddest we lived through in Mexico.

On the morning of the twenty-second we set out from Socyapán. His Majesty had found peace of mind again and talked with me during the trip about the settlement of his private financial matters.

At noon we stopped at Río Frío. From there the Emperor sent the following telegram to Captain Pierron.

The Emperor to Captain Pierron:

You, Piño, Trouchot, and Mangino are named as a commission under your leadership. As quickly as possible and with the help of an honest official of the finance ministry you are to audit the accounts of the civil list—mine as well as those of the Empress—so that it will be clear whether we owe the state or the state owes us. In this matter I demand from the commission a detailed presentation, with documents attached. In this account you must include the sum which the Empress took with her for her trip to Europe, what my secretariat received on the account of the civil list, the sum which Minister Arroyo received, and the work done in the palace and in Chapultepec after the reduction of the civil list.

I must further mention in this context the special arrangements which the Emperor made with the idea of leaving the country.

---

*In Kératry's book (page 207 of the French edition) is printed the Emperor's letter to Marshal Bazaine. The passage: "ces documents devront rester réservés jusqu'au jour, que je vous indiquerai par le télégraphe" has to do with the regency decree, which Maximilian had dictated to me in Chapultepec and which was naturally cancelled because of the later decision. The three points mentioned in the letter, on whose immediate execution the monarch put especial stress, are those which I have noted above.

Even monies from the civil list spent in Europe were to be taken into account. Herzfeld was therefore given the task of issuing in His Majesty's name relevant written directions to the prefect and treasurer of Miramar.

I was instructed to write Herzfeld that: "The Emperor wishes the greatest openness about all these steps and makes you responsible on your integrity and friendship. He wants to keep his honor and his name completely out of this shipwreck even if he suffers personal loss."

In the same scrupulous way Maximilian was concerned lest any amount of state property be touched, and he repeatedly sent Mexico City and Veracruz the strictest orders to forward to Europe at all costs only what was determined to be his private property.

On the twenty-second we stopped for the night at the Hacienda Molino de Guadalupe, a farm equipped with all European comforts, and the most beautiful estate on the Mexico City-Orizaba route to hospitably open its doors to the traveler.

We spent the night of the twenty-third at the Hacienda Molino del Puente, a half hour from Puebla. Upon arrival there Maximilian was welcomed by civil authorities and the officer corps of the Austrian garrison in Puebla.

I slept in the room with His Majesty, who was still bothered by malaria and insomnia. That night he got little rest. In addition to his illness he was disturbed by constant noise from horses, calves, and sheep narrowly penned in a nearby stall. The restless night and physical weakness induced him to halt for a day's rest.

On October 24, we left Puebla to move to nearby Hacienda del Molino, which offered more comfortable and agreeable quarters.

Our next night stops were Acatzingo and Cañada where we stayed in rectories.

Count Kératry reproaches the Emperor that "pendant tout le trajet Maximilien ne s'arrêta que chez le clergé mexicain." This is a definite lie, and, even if the Emperor twice spent the night with clergymen, Count Kératry was familiar enough with Mexican conditions to know that the saying "One sleeps well under the crozier" applies at least to Acatzingo and Cañada.

Along the whole way the inhabitants had greeted Maximilian

with the greatest sympathy.

In Mexico City itself only a day after his departure, a large procession was held, attended by all the representatives of the foreign powers, to entreat the Empress's speedy recovery.

Everywhere we stopped to rest deputations came to express their concern; people strew flowers on the road and tossed bouquets into the imperial coach. Often I saw the Emperor with tears in his eyes, deeply moved by the demonstrations.

Around four o'clock on the afternoon of October 27, we arrived in Orizaba. The French officer, Colonel Poitier, had ridden several hours to meet us.

In Orizaba itself reception by the citizens and the French garrison was cordial. Amidst salvoes of cannon, Maximilian made his entrance and took up residence in the house which the regency had prepared as a palace at the time of his arrival from Europe.*

*I must here correct Kératry's allegation that His Majesty stayed in Jalapilla, half an hour from Orizaba. During his entire stay in Orizaba he lived in the Bringas House as mentioned above.

CHAPTER VI

Orizaba—The Emperor's Mood—Preparations for a Journey—Father Fischer's Behavior—Campbell-Scarlett, Sanchez Navarro—The Fischer Clique—A Semiofficial Correspondence.

Herzfeld awaited Maximilian in Orizaba despite prior instructions to remain in Mexico City a few days longer. He had hurried on ahead by stagecoach, as he did not want to leave half done the enterprise he had started. He intended to have us continue to Veracruz and embark immediately for Europe, although his haste was less justified now than ever. The Emperor was only a day's journey from the coast; communication with Veracruz was neither broken nor endangered; there were no grounds for anxiety about his personal security. In Orizaba, besides the loyal imperial hussars—*sombreros chiquitos,* as they were called—there was a strong French garrison, and the dissidents properly respected both. If we returned to Europe under those circumstances, it would look like open flight.

Although the prince held fast to the plan to leave Orizaba soon, he did not intend to do so immediately. He saw that the ground was burning under Herzfeld's feet, so he sent the state councillor to Europe to prepare for the Emperor's arrival directly and through the press. His Majesty could now consider calmly how he should leave the land: whether as sovereign, in which case he would install a regency before embarking in Veracruz and leave further determinations to the congress it summoned; or whether he should lay down his crown completely in Orizaba or Veracruz.

Both solutions had things for and against them. As always the ruler failed to make a decision. First of all there was the question of the affairs of the foreigners who had come to the country with him, especially the problem of protecting the interests of the Austro-Belgian volunteer corps. Maximilian could not postpone arranging this if he wanted to leave the country with a clear conscience.

It is psychologically understandable that his mood in these days grew even gloomier. The hard moment had arrived in which by making his decision public, he would abandon the undertaking. He had never failed to recognize its difficulties, but with youthful enthusiasm, with readiness to sacrifice, and at great personal risk, he had dedicated his life to its success. He must abandon his grand idea of regenerating a degenerate people. After everything he had lived through in Mexico, he would have to turn away from his venture with a bitter feeling that only betrayal by those who called themselves his friends had brought the enterprise's downfall. He realized that this land would not be helped for a long time to come.

Inwardly, he had already given up Mexico. Determined not to remain the vassal of France, he intended Orizaba to be only a rest stop. Abdication as such cost him no further struggle. But his self-esteem bristled at having to admit to the whole country by this act that he could no longer maintain himself without French support and that he had let himself be deceived by Louis Napoleon. His sense of honor would not let him leave the country as sovereign and maintain in Europe his full rightful title and legal claim. It would relieve his troubled soul to free himself from the oppressive burden of this rank without power—this obtrusive label without truth—and travel to Europe to the sick Empress whose fate gnawed at his heart so deeply. Only because of these reasons and not because of indecisiveness, only because of this ambivalence of feeling, did the Emperor vacillate and refuse to speak his final word. In his diary of Querétaro he himself tried to depict his state of mind at that time. Later on, during the description of the march from Mexico City to Querétaro, I shall give the complete text of the only page of his diary which remained intact and which also contains this passage.

No one desired this indecision more than Father Fischer. He now followed the tactic of nervously dodging every specific comment, every expression of firm opinion, as he endeavored to keep His Majesty wavering. It was also his incessant endeavor and his sole aim to have Maximilian remain in Mexico and as soon as possible be delivered over to his party. He made sure that his own viewpoint was noticed and for the present restricted himself to averting all haste about the abdication, every irrevocable *fait accompli* on the Emperor's part. To this extent, he worked harmoniously with me, with the essential difference that for me the abdication was merely a question of time. For him it was the whole question.

At that time my position was such that the monarch's trust in me permitted my influencing his decision. I had to behave according to true convictions, using my position for the sake of the Austrians and Belgians, to delay departure until the fate of the auxiliary corps was decided. It was some months before the French departure, and there was time enough to wind up all business without haste so that His Majesty would have absolutely no doubt as to its complete settlement.

Father Fischer could only support my endeavors. Any postponement, any delay, benefited him; every day the Emperor remained in Orizaba was a victory. By all kinds of little maneuvers, he painstakingly dodged every open yes or no. Forgetting and delaying instructions for the departure, he operated adroitly behind the back of the man whose plans and intentions he was conspiring against. Fischer never had the courage to say the truth in front of Maximilian himself. If he were asked "should I abdicate," it was predictable that Father Fischer would sigh in agreement. If the question followed, "should I depart without abdicating," the cleric again agreed, with a gloomy shrug of his shoulders.

Maximilian meanwhile made all preparations for his departure. By virtue of a general grant of authority, Colonel Kodolitch was ordered to go to Marshal Bazaine in Mexico City and negotiate about the Austro-Belgians.*

During this same period the whole Mexican court household and retainers were discharged and sent away. Only two European servants remained with the Emperor, and of the Mexicans only the colonels, Lamadrid and Ormachaea, imperial adjutant, were to escort him to Veracruz.

From the special commission reports which arrived in the interim, it was ascertained that His Majesty owed nothing to the state. On the contrary the civil list still had outstanding claims of 180,000 pesos. He was completely reassured that he was leaving behind no kind of

---

*Kodolitch's letter of authorization is found on page 216 in Kératry's French edition. In his second letter of November 12, likewise to the marshal (page 238), are set out the Emperor's last wishes before his departure. They refer to settlement of the affairs of the volunteer corps, to payment of certain sums to the Princess and Prince Iturbide, and to settlement of the civil list.

responsibility and thus could quietly carry out his intention to return to Europe.

Farewell letters were written to all the ministers and diplomats, and Maximilian dictated to me the following plan for the sea voyage: "The Emperor goes immediately with the *Dandolo* to St. Thomas; there, after it has taken on all baggage, is to be sent the sailing ship ordered by Résseguier. From St. Thomas to Gibraltar. From there telegraph, and, if possible, order the Empress to Corfu. If the Empress cannot come, someone will call from Miramar to Corfu. The sailing ship brings to St. Thomas all dispatches which have arrived before departure."

In mentioning this travel plan, I am compelled to refute Kératry's shameless insinuation based on a letter from Éloin (page 220 of the French edition). Kératry gives a self-serving coarse report from Éloin about the internal situation in Austria after Königgrätz, alluding to the Emperor's supposed intention of exploiting Austria's critical state to his personal advantage. Such a report and such reasoning best characterize Éloin and Kératry. Instead of discrediting the sovereign's memory, I vindicate him against such accusations. Herr Kératry will admit that I knew at least as much about Maximilian's intent as he, and, as far as I know, he had resolved then never again to step into public life. He wanted to make a longer voyage and see Austria only after one or two years.

These travel plans, described here as organized, proceeded under various interruptions. By presenting them clearly I intend only to demonstrate how firmly settled Maximilian was on his return to Europe and how he already had decided everything down to the most specific arrangement. If his wishes remained ultimately unfulfilled, the cause must simply be sought in the efforts of Father Fischer and his confederates.

At the beginning of our stay in Orizaba, Father Fischer was certainly isolated and without prospect of achieving his goals. He pretended to be the blindly attentive servant of his Emperor, with no opinion of his own, and when he eventually came forward with a definite proposal, he was surprisingly naive.

I still remember exactly a conversation Maximilian had with us one evening. He thought he had found the best solution in abdicating and specifying the Empress's illness as the sole cause for his decision. In his usual manner, the cleric answered with doubts. However, one could infer that he was expressing his opinion against it. I too disapproved this plan. I candidly answered, basing my disagreement on the doubt that people would cease to look for and find still other motives.

The sovereign, who shared my scruples, dropped this idea. As the conversation continued, I heard Father Fischer give the curious advice "of abdicating in favor of Napoleon." "This idea is Machiavellian," answered Maximilian. "It would be better if I went away without abdicating," he said, ending the discussion.

From then on Father Fischer followed the travel plans with apparent indifference. He behaved completely passively, expecting the imminent arrival of support from Mexico City.

From the chief of the secretariat, Captain Pierron, a letter had already arrived, definitely and directly reproaching the monarch for wanting to leave the country.

Early in November, Campbell-Scarlett, the English *Ministre Plenipotentiaire* for Mexico, arrived in Orizaba. He had just begun a vacation trip to Europe and stopped in Orizaba for more than two weeks. The Emperor's immediate departure was particularly inconvenient for the Englishman. His major concern was getting imperial approval of the commercial treaty already concluded with the ministry. This was the reason the practical emissary made an appearance in the interest of his country. Maximilian told me directly that Campbell-Scarlett had advocated his remaining. Whether he did so out of personal conviction, I cannot definitely say. I only know that lengthy conversations took place between him and Father Fischer and that the result of these conferences was a long letter to His Majesty, in which Campbell-Scarlett energetically counseled against abdication. Soon afterwards, the Englishman departed for Europe. Contrary to his own expectation, Father Fischer had won an ally whose power was enhanced by the fact that, as a foreigner, his position was apparently neutral.

After this visit, Sánchez Navarro arrived in Orizaba. An administrative officer and subsequently a minister to the imperial household, Navarro was a fanatical conservative. He had been Fischer's very intimate friend since the time the latter was a clergyman in Parras (in the state of Durango). Earlier assessed to be the greatest landowner in Mexico, Sánchez Navarro had had properties in Durango and bordering states of such great extent that estimates placed them equal to the kingdom of Spain. Most of his property had been confiscated under the liberal presidents, and he, with so many others, hoped for imperial aid in their restoration. Thus, his eagerness in crowding in on the Emperor was understandable.

Several former representatives (imperial commissioners), whose names escape me, as well as a number of influential conservatives also arrived in Orizaba shortly after Sánchez Navarro.

Father Fischer's cabinet included Campbell-Scarlett, Sánchez Navarro, Minister to the Imperial Household Arroyo, the imperial commissioners, as well as the Mexicans belonging to the court household. These men were the hearth where the dying glory of the Empire would burst into new flame. By calling on all available means, the Fischer clique soon spun a whole net of threads, reaching to the capital and the individual states.

The secret agitation was principally applied in two distinct directions: first to stir up an apparent *vox populi;* then to convince Maximilian that his Empire could rise again more glittering than ever if he remained on the throne and granted unrestricted rule to the conservative ministers. As Fischer never tired of pointing out, they had the best will and were in a position to recover buried treasures.

All at once the cleric displayed previously unknown energy. Certain of his Mexicans, he turned to the Austrians, winning several of the latter to his cause. He knew I had influence, so he had no choice but to try his powers of persuasion on me. Aware of my scepticism, he took unbelievable trouble to show me my error in so little valuing the resources of his party. He painted for me golden mountains in the future; I placed naked reality before his eyes.

At that time Fischer and I managed the ruler's private funds. In reply to his bombastic tirades about unearthed millions, I recommended the imperial cash reserves, about which he knew as much as

I, for immediate improvement. He quickly escaped this dilemma. He could not help now, but he swore on his life that as soon as Maximilian decided to return to Mexico City, 50,000 pesos would be in the cash box ready for any eventuality.

In anticipation, I must mention that when the Emperor set out for Querétaro, the ministry was capable of raising a total of only 50,000 pesos for his war and private purse. Once again I was correct in coldly doubting Father Fischer's sanguine promises and attempts at persuasion. His efforts and those of his confederates still found no fertile ground with their ruler.

After only a day, Sánchez Navarro was sent back to Mexico City, on the specific pretext that as an official of the imperial household he would be in his rightful place only in the capital, where there was enough pressing business for him. Maximilian then bade ceremonious farewell to him forever. Seizing the opportunity, Sánchez Navarro made one last try to change His Majesty's mind. "Ingrato pais" (ungrateful country), he ended his speech, vainly trying to touch the sovereign with his usual pathetic display.

Of Father Fischer's other fellow conspirators, no one but Campbell-Scarlett obtained admittance to the Emperor. Consequently, little hope beckoned for the conservatives unless they succeeded in enlisting new, stronger allies. Preparations had been made for us to leave Orizaba at any moment. In this event, all their efforts would have been in vain.

On November 8, 1866, at the Emperor's order I wrote the following correspondence to the imperial authorities in Vienna. This letter, intended for publication to prepare for his arrival in Europe, informed them of the situation as His Majesty perceived it. It represented his most personal views.

Mexico City, November 8

The French army of occupation continues the policy of *laisser aller* it has been unabashedly pursuing with disastrous results for nearly two years. The more dangerous posts are manned by foreign and national troops. They keep such a respectful distance from the rebels that it looks as if the dissidents shy away from them. No one today doubts the ability of the French soldiers, and we here are completely convinced that the French army acts this way only because of inspiration from Paris and Washington. In any case it is peculiar that the timidity with which they give way to the dissidents is so extreme. Not once has the great line of retreat from Mexico City to Veracruz, all important points of which are garrisoned by them, been safe against temporary dissident incursions. Only a short while ago, on his trip through, the English envoy Campbell-Scarlett had to be escorted by the Austrian Volunteer Corps hussars on special order of the Emperor. The dissidents had broken into Palmar, on the route mentioned. The Empire is on the verge of a decisive crisis. Its cause is the illness of the Empress, on whose arrival we had based the most sanguine hopes. The first news of this illness came by cable dispatch from New Orleans to Mexico City. It provoked the greatest sensation and the most vivid sympathy among the inhabitants.

Shortly after receiving this news Maximilian traveled to Orizaba at the suggestion of the doctors, who advised a change of air because of persistent malaria. At the same time he wanted to be nearer to the couriers bringing detailed reports from Europe. It is generally believed here that the Emperor will not return to the capital and will soon leave the country. This rumor does not seem so unfounded. It is very possible that he will decide to leave. He is completely disillusioned by latest reports from Europe and aware that United States pressure and their ever-increasing support of republican dissidents insure either the Empire's collapse or continued bloodshed. Conceivably, he will decide to leave the country to avoid personally hindering peaceful political union. In addition, the fact that the Emperor's marriage is childless and his family interest is presently firmly rooted in Europe must be taken into consideration.

At that time no mortal could promise success to the efforts of Father Fischer and his friends. For the conservatives there was a critical imminent danger, and they would have certainly not obtained the slightest results if at the last moment two more men, Márquez and Miramón, had not stepped onto the stage. They already had repeatedly played a fateful role in Mexican history. In contrast to those who dealt in hollow phrases, "the old wigs and mandarins," as the Emperor called them, these two men threw their tested swords into the balance.

CHAPTER VII

Márquez and Miramón—Deputations from Mexico and Puebla— Father Fischer and the Conservatives—Convocation of the Ministry and State Council to Orizaba—The Emperor's Opening Handwritten Document—Votes of the Ministry and State Council—Their Motivation—Demonstrations by the Conservatives—The Emperor's Way of Life in Orizaba.

Márquez and Miramón, two old comrades-in-arms, landed together in Veracruz. Both came from Europe, to which they had been banished by the Emperor. At the beginning of his reign he had tried to exclude conservatives even from diplomatic missions. Back on Mexican soil, the two men had to be considered pillars of the conservative party. Although there was little prospect of Maximilian's receiving either general, especially Miramón, who had come back without his permission, their timing could not have been better for the conservatives.

Miramón once again was playing *va banque*. He returned to Mexico perhaps to serve His Majesty and if not—to work for himself. For this reason he had disagreed with State Councillor Herzfeld, who informed him at a meeting in Havana of the monarch's intention to leave Mexico.

Bureau, imperial commissioner in Veracruz, considered it his duty to report Miramón's arrival by telegraph, asking whether to let him pass. The Emperor answered "yes." On the other hand, nothing hindered Márquez's progress since he had returned with Maximilian's knowledge and consent. The defense notes read: "Marquez era llamado desde 6 meses como otros diplomaticos por razones de economia; Miramon no fué llamado." (Márquez was recalled for reasons of economy six months ago like the other diplomats; Miramón was not recalled.)

During this interim, the longer temporary conditions dragged on, the more His Majesty's apathy gave way to industrious participation in government affairs. At the beginning of the stay in Orizaba, only the travel preparations retained any interest for him. The return of good health rekindled his desire for work, and, after regaining peace of mind, he also shunned the solitude he had previously sought. By the time Márquez and Miramón arrived in Orizaba, his spirits had already improved substantially. He received both generals; a few days before he would have certainly sent them away.

The audience granted the generals in no way suggested that Maximilian had changed his mind about returning to Europe. He clung to his idea, until now unshaken. However, his behavior had changed to the extent that he could weigh the situation more calmly, and he wanted to avoid rashness. The first of his conversations with Miramón and Márquez was unproductive. He remained firm with them too, and they could not give Father Fischer an encouraging report. Deputations which arrived from Mexico City and Puebla at Fischer's instigation also received an unfavorable answer. There were three such missions: two, from the *ayuntamiento* (municipal representative body) and the most prominent townspeople; the third, from Puebla, delivering an address affixed with a thousand signatures. One of its spokesmen remarked to the Emperor that unlike the rebels, he had at his disposal the most capable and experienced generals. "No war can be fought with generals alone," Maximilian replied, "even if they are the best. Troops and money are also necessary." Without obtaining a definite answer, the deputations were dismissed.

On November 12, the sovereign once against wrote to Bazaine. This document most distinctly indicates his changed mood. However, he still held fast to the same basic thought: departure for Europe.

In his letter of October 31, he limited himself to generalities and left disposition of the volunteers to Colonel Kodolitch. In this second letter, he specified and sharpened his demands and requested the clearest guarantees.

On November 16 arrived an explanatory answer to both letters, signed by Marshal Bazaine, the French envoy Dano, and General Castelnau. Essentially it agreed with Maximilian's requests. At the same time, in cheerful anticipation that the Emperor would voluntarily quit the field, Napoleon's plenipotentiaries improvidently told tales out of school. At the close of the official document they spoke of negotiations with a "nouveau gouvernement du Mexique."

Open declaration of the hitherto secretly conducted French intercourse with the United States powerfully impressed His Majesty. He felt the offence keenly, and his pride bristled at such dispensation while he was still alive, at such a disregard of the first rules of diplomatic decorum. It was clear that Napoleon wanted to cover up his breach of agreement. Forced to show the world his impotence since he could not redeem his pledge, he now planned to throw sand in people's eyes and go from there. Maximilian's abdication would be nothing more than the recall of an administration with which Napoleon was no longer content. He would magnanimously respond to Mexico's cry of pain. Europe would be amazed by Napoleon's versatility: For once, he was blessing society with a republic.

The Emperor's travel plans remained unchanged. He had gradually become too accustomed to the idea of abdication to throw it overboard immediately. Now all he had to do before leaving the country was deny yielding to the French. Rather, of his own free decision he was returning the power entrusted to him by the Mexican nation.

For this reason, on November 24, Maximilian convoked the ministry and state council. In a confidential message he also invited the marshal to a discussion in Orizaba. The following letter inspired by him, which went to Vienna for publication, best explains the Emperor's inner transformation during these events.

Mexico City, November 19

Events now cluster around two locations: around Orizaba, where the Emperor has been nearly four weeks; around the capital—headquarters of the conservative ministry, conservative and liberal party leaders, and Marshal Bazaine. In Mexico City reigns the most agitated uncertainty over whether the Emperor will return or leave the country. We are particularly embittered against the French; both because of the rumor of an agreement between France and the United States, and because we are beginning to perceive the main cause of the present crisis to be the behavior of the French Government vis-à-vis the Empire. This embitterment has come clearly to the fore despite the strong French garrison in Mexico City. It erupted recently during a theatrical performance in repeated stormy cries, "fuera los franceses." People here fully grasp the possible results of overt action by the United States. They realize that America is in no way interested in preserving Mexico's nationality and independence. People are disturbed by fear of the North American colossus, and everywhere, with all their strength, people cling to the hope of the Empire's preservation and particularly the Emperor's remaining. Without the second for the present, the first is unthinkable. Frightened by the specter of impending anarchy and North American business interests, the people demonstrate unsuspected sympathy for the Empire. It suddenly comes to light, as if by magic.

In the midst of this restless agitation, Maximilian lives modestly in Orizaba like a man in private life. Only dealing with a few trusted members of the entourage, he is without an imperial household. Of the diplomatic corps, only the envoy from the English court, whom the Emperor frequently sees, is here. Generals Márquez and Miramón, well-known heads of the conservative party, have returned from their posts in Europe and offered their swords in the struggle with the dissidents to establish peace and order. In the same way General Uraga, reputed by the French to be the most capable strategist in Mexico, with a forceful statement from Europe has pledged his strength to the imperial cause.

Today the Emperor received three deputations: two from Mexico City and one from Puebla, conveying professions of loyalty and the good wishes of the people.

In Orizaba itself the conservatives proceeded unflaggingly with their work under Fischer's leadership. Márquez and Miramón conferred repeatedly with the sovereign, but their efforts always failed. Fischer had to exploit every resource to keep their patience. "What do you want to do?" he once asked both generals, when they complained loudly. "The Emperor is not going to Mexico City in his current mood. Do you want to carry him to the palace? It is like demanding that a sick person get up and work. In His Majesty's present condition, you can only profit by forbearance. You see how patient I am."

Father Fischer in fact had to exert superhuman self-control not to lose heart. The promises of the conservatives, for whom he was still spokesman, found no credence with Maximilian. Although he now at least listened, the ruler made no commitment to Father Fischer. During these weeks the conservatives and their leader played a peculiar game among themselves. Fischer's final goal was the concordat. For the moment that was a matter of secondary importance to the conservatives; for them the issue was the restitution of property. Both could realize their plans only within the Empire. It was therefore natural that his fellow conspirators sought to exploit the cleric's access to the Emperor until they could stand on their own feet. In fairness, I must grant Fischer honorable intentions towards the conservatives. He always represented their interests warmly, even though they repaid him with little thanks. Later I will tell how the ministers, whom he took care of and pampered like children, neglected him and shoved him aside after Maximilian left Mexico City.

Under the circumstances, Fischer naturally could do nothing for the concordat in Orizaba. "The Emperor is returning to Mexico City," he said one evening, beaming with joy, when it appeared that this was the case. "Now I shall get to my real work, the concordat."

In prison at Querétaro I learned how Father Fischer had promoted the concordat, for whose sake he had been sent to Rome. The sovereign's words provide the most thorough judgment of the cleric's achievement.

On November 21, a semiofficial article appeared in *Patria,* the Mexican *Fatherland,* as a kind of ministerial program. Before obeying Maximilian's summons to Orizaba printed in the *Diario del Imperio,* they issued this statement. Because of the revelance to the situation I quote it fully here.

Mexico City, November 21

Although two ministers and the chef de cabinet have traveled with the state council to Orizaba, this does not disturb the cabinet's activities. Work proceeds under the remaining ministers and state secretaries. The provisional minister president is His Excellency, señor Manuel García Aguirre. Our readers can be certain that the current undermining of the Empire little deters the present cabinet.

Fortunately people of strong character, energy, strength, and civic spirit have united. Free of the nervous activity which some confuse with energy, they possess that strength of belief, of conscience, and patriotism, which never yields to flattery and threats. Victory in politics and in the field will never be achieved by fear, by vacillation, or by doubting the cause one supports. Victory is always on the side of those who endure, and neither the sad babble of the despondent nor the outcry of the demagogue will divert the cabinet from its path. It will only yield to insuperable force. It entered the Palace with full knowledge of the legacy it had accepted, and the life of struggle and sacrifice demanded. With these in mind it works tirelessly. With these in mind, it makes progress. People will later learn of this work. Only then will those blinded by alarmist rumors realize that the cabinet has unassumingly fulfilled its difficult mission. Neither the present nor the absent ministers lose spirit. They are firm and determined to go down with the throne or to earn fame for having saved it.

Considering the situation at that time, one must admit that the program was more than daring. Apart from the total financial confusion, the Empire was already restricted to Mexico City, Puebla, Orizaba, and little more than their immediate environs. The so-called interior and the whole North were completely under liberal domination, and, according to the latest report arriving in Orizaba, Oaxaca and Jalapa had also fallen into liberal hands.

In Oaxaca, after the city had been taken by Porfirio Díaz, the small Austrian garrison under Captain Beskoschka held the fort there for several weeks. In the end they too were forced to yield. The Austrian garrison under Major Hammerstein in Jalapa shared the same fate. Unable to wait longer for relief troops promised by the French, they were compelled to lay down weapons after street combat with the enemy, who had already forced entry into the city.

At the Emperor's invitation, some of the ministers and almost the entire state council followed him to Orizaba. Prudently avoiding a personal meeting, Bazaine excused himself by letter, saying that the security of the capital required his presence there. At about the same time a letter arrived from Pierron. In peculiar contrast to the reproachful stance he took in his first letter, he now eloquently counseled abdication. It was not difficult to fathom who had inspired the drafting of these notes. If I mention them at all, I do so not for their contents but rather for the position which their author (the French chief of the secretariat) takes in them. Besides, they failed completely. The first one Maximilian scarcely noticed, in his depression, and the second came at a time when the advice of a Frenchman defeated its own purpose.

Around ten o'clock on the morning of November 24, Lares and

Chapter Seven

Lacunza paid their respects to the Emperor. They had arrived the previous night with the other ministers, the state council, and several dignitaries. It was no longer the stooped Lares of Chapultepec, whose knees had trembled as he presented me his resignation request. Rejuvenated and with a light step, the old premier rushed towards Maximilian, who had no chance to refuse the impetuous *abrazo* (embrace), according to Mexican custom the intimate form of greeting. Somewhat more cautiously and with a solemn mien, the corpulent Lacunza stepped forward.

After the formal visit Lacunza remained alone with the Emperor a long time. Now for the first time since departure from the capital, a councillor of the crown directly expounded the wishes and viewpoints of the government. Lacunza's presentation was particularly effective because he had not been a strict conservative. He had repeatedly occupied different posts under the former liberal ministry, and the sovereign himself had a high opinion of him.

Lacunza, a man endowed with a dignified appearance and that winning eloquence almost universally characteristic of Mexicans, understood how to play the right notes. Touching upon the question of honor, he struck the most sensitive chord. He told His Majesty that the whole country expected him to remember his words of September 16—"a true Hapsburg never leaves his post in the moment of danger" —exactly as the country remembered them. He ought not yield to the hidden enemy; rather he should stand up to all his foes and vanquish or fall. Still vivid in my memory is the impression made by these propositions on Maximilian. He informed me of their contents immediately after Lacunza had retired, and I saw that he was greatly affected by them. He said to me, "Lacunza has done his task in an upright manner." He sincerely believed what he said.

I felt less edified by Lacunza's success. Appeal to the ruler's chivalry seemed to me the most horrible weapon in the Mexican's arsenal of craftiness. I fully understood Maximilian's feeling that with his honor at stake, he would have to renounce abdication even against his own conviction. I was inwardly enraged over the cold calculation with which Lacunza cut off his retreat at the decisive moment.

Nevertheless, I still cannot prove that His Majesty would have left the country if the conservatives had not used their last strategem. In the last days his resolve to abdicate and return to Europe had lost much of its original intensity in the face of insidious French activity and the vigorous approach Márquez and Miramón were taking in the military question. However, when the Emperor called both corporate bodies, it was firmly established that he would lay before them his abdication and its causes and would by no means engage in further negotiations. "Deseo de salir, llamado de los consjeos." (I want to leave, convocation of the councils.) These are the words in the defense notes.

It would have been the only way to satisfactorily solve the crisis. However, Maximilian had already taken a step backwards in a hand-written letter informing the combined ministry and state council of his decision to return his mandate to the nation; in the same breath he implied that he was prepared to make further sacrifices for the Fatherland.

The letter, which Lares read aloud in the opening session, went as follows:

> The seriousness of the Fatherland's present situation has moved us to convoke the councillors of Our government so that, strongly supported by their wise judgment, We may legally resolve the current crisis.

> A heavy duty now weighs on Us. We are deeply convinced that the well-being of the Fatherland requires its fulfillment. After free deliberation unclouded by partiality and passion, and after long and painstaking examination, We have determined that it is Our duty to return to the Mexican Nation the mandate bestowed on Us.

> The following are the grounds for our firm opinion:

> 1) We regret that civil war continues and, with the blood of thousands of Our fellow citizens, unfortunately widens its tracks.

> 2) The hostility of the United States is now more evident than ever.

> 3) Our allies have explained that for political reasons they are no longer able to offer Us further support.

> It has even come to Our attention recently through

French representatives that negotiations now proceed between the French government and the United States toward settling the civil war which so long has rooted up the marrow of Our country. We have learned that, in the considered opinion of a great majority of the American people, this goal might only be reached with installation of a republican government through the mediation of both states.

We are justly apprehensive of jeopardizing this achievement.

Even if Our spirits and Our strength are humbled in the process, We do not hesitate an instant to make any sacrifice on the altar of the Fatherland.

We have therefore assembled here Our ministers and state councillors, who have already given so much proof of their devotion and loyalty, so that united with Us they might solve this difficult matter.

Maximilian

Twenty-three people attended this session, and the voting results were as follows: Two liberal state councillors, Siliceo and Cortez Esparza, both former ministers, voted unconditionally for abdication. As the basic reason, they cited the viewpoints expressed in the Emperor's message.

Members, on the motion of Minister President Lares, spoke out unconditionally opposing Maximilian's departure. The welfare of the country required him to stay, they argued, and there was a good chance to restrengthen the Empire for the well-being of the nation.

A third faction of eleven votes concurred in principle with leaving the country, but they objected to immediate departure. Without being explicit they basically agreed with the two republicans, but they petitioned His Majesty to remain at his post at least until the interests of those compromised by the Empire could be successfully insured.

Before giving the sovereign's reply, I must discuss motives. First, the liberal vote favoring abdication expressed the opinion of two republican imperials, who by conviction and behavior still hoped to compromise with the liberals, or better, with the republican government certain to follow the Empire.

Ten votes belonged to strict conservatives, who had no choice but to preserve the Empire at all costs. In view of the hatred between their party and the republicans, they had no alternative. Only in the imperial state could the conservatives maintain their ground; only through its survival could they protect their interests from further compromise. An alliance with the republicans was impossible. In the long struggle and under the pressure of numerous severe reprisals, conservatives and liberals had changed from political opponents into embittered enemies. There could be no thought of a reconciliation, particularly if the republicans regained power. These two opinions were based on at least a trace of political sense; in contrast, the plurality of eleven seemed completely without conviction. They urged the Emperor to remain conditionally or, in effect, to abdicate conditionally.

Lacunza proposed and formulated how these eleven voted. This was the same Lacunza who the day before had so warmly spoken to His Majesty about duty, honor, and sacrifice. The man's behavior best characterized his whole party, for which I can find no right name. They called themselves *moderados*. Yesterday, exuberant and full of the purest intentions; today, shamelessly flaunting their naked egoism, they were always suspicious and inconsiderate of friend and foe.

Both liberals said a Mexican Empire was impossible; the strict conservatives believed Empire to be the only possibility; the *moderados* were concerned only with themselves. They emphasized the Emperor's remaining, even though in their view he could not do so permanently. The *status quo* must endure only long enough to insure all their interests. In a way, this party was the most honest because it openly admitted the necessity for Maximilian's personal sacrifice. And in fact he did so; the sacrifice was made when he answered the combined majority's resolution: He intended to make another attempt at ruling.

His reply to Lares read as follows:

My Dear Minister!

We are deeply moved by the loyalty and sympathy shown in the official communiqués of the last session of the ministry and state council held here, which have just been presented to Us by their presidents. We have not hesitated a moment to walk the path prescribed by duty and our openly confessed patriotism.

Ready for any sacrifice for the national welfare We nevertheless believe that caution commands alertness lest Our sacrifice be in vain. If we grant the request of Our ministry and state council and make a firm decision on that basis, We require a practical solution of the present situation. It must be based on measures deemed necessary and indispensable if the sacrifice on behalf of Mexico's development is to be fruitful and completely successful.

1) Calling a national congress completely representative of all classes of the Mexican people. This congress should asemble not only to decide the form of the future regime but also to organize it according to constitutional principles. Our state council should determine a meeting place, establish convention procedure, and declare appropriate means for securing the most complete popular participation.

2) Financial means to cover government expenses must be suggested. Proposals and estimates already formulated by Our finance ministry offer insight on this point.

3) Recruiting laws for definitive organization of a national army must be proposed.

4) Laws for colonization of the country must be suggested.

5) Appropriate proposals must settle the question between Mexico and France.

6) Means must be found to cement good relations with the United States.

If Our ministry and state council make successful and practical proposals, then We shall continue our efforts and loyally and gladly resume the burden of Mexico's regeneration.

"Llamado de los consejos dictamen y apelacion al deber y al honor" (calling of the councils; declaration and appeal to duty and honor) reads the fateful passage in the Emperor's handwriting.

It was predictable that the state councillors and ministers gathered in Orizaba would concur with Maximilian's stipulations. When he declared his willingness to renew the attempt to rule Mexico, they had achieved complete success. Against his will and without his knowledge, they had made him an ally of their party.

They scarcely considered the possibility of fulfilling even one of his stipulations, not once cautioning him about the difficulties which even in favorable circumstances a partial execution of his program would involve. Without hesitation they acquiesced to his demands, acting as if it would be child's play to fulfill them. In this the conservatives and, indirectly, Father Fischer were guilty of supreme dishonesty. Had they and their current allies, the moderates, been at all truthful, they would have had to refuse His Majesty's terms because there was no prospect of fulfilling them.

As I have already indicated, most of the country was in republican hands. On the heels of the retreating Frenchmen concentrating in the Valley of Mexico, the rebels occupied the abandoned positions. Thus, it was impossible to convene a really general congress—the first and most essential of Maximilian's demands.

As for financial help, I am convinced that even if the ministers had good intentions, as they did not, they were not in the slightest position to alleviate the hardship. The possibility of establishing a national army and colonizing the country was also complicated by the real hopelessness of financial improvement.

The last point in the imperial program, apart from the French question—opening the way for good relations with the United States— naturally could have relevance only after complete consolidation of the Empire.

Maximilian had no illusions about the actual state of affairs. He himself wrote: "If Our ministry and state council make successful and practical proposals, then We shall continue Our efforts and loyally and gladly resume the burden of Mexico's regeneration." Even if he were also convinced of the hopelessness of solidifying his throne, he could by no means leave the country without exposing himself to conservative reproaches. They would accuse him of not even having made an attempt to maintain his rule, although unforeseen circumstances and happy coincidences might have favored its survival. These were the factors which the conservatives usually took into account.

In explaining my hard judgment of the conservative ministry, I want to cite one other fact mentioned by Kératry. I reported above that on October 21 in Socyapán, when the Emperor repealed the martial law of October 3, 1865, Bazaine conferred with the ministers in Mexico City about the imperial decree. Lares and Marín responded negatively to the just and noble-minded decision, and the decree in question was merely set aside.

Consequently, one can be certain in assuming that the ministers thought and reacted to the idea of a congress and the other points in exactly the same way. Having agreed in Orizaba to everything requested of them, they then did as they pleased.

As was later revealed, they concentrated particularly on directly thwarting the congress. They had already proved to be its sworn enemies at the junta of Chapultepec. Never even considering a peaceful solution, they only wanted war. The history of Mexico shows that good luck had often come to their rescue on the field of battle.

The Emperor's decision to return to the capital was understandably received with enormous jubilation by the conservatives. The joyful message was telegraphed to Mexico City, Puebla, and to small villages everywhere. On the evening of November 30, His Majesty learned that an elaborate celebration with torchlight procession, music, and fireworks would be held in Orizaba. This distressed him. "I find this very tactless of the ministers," he said. "They should show honest endeavor, work, raise troops and money. These empty demonstrations are even less appropriate because they have done nothing yet but talk." Minister to the Imperial Household Arroyo transmitted the order cancelling the demonstrations. But the conservatives did not let themselves be dissuaded. Their main goal was to display Maximilian's person and to parade his popularity, the first accentuating the second. Also they wanted to show the sovereign how overjoyed the people were at his decision to remain. Nevertheless, despite all their reports, he did not agree to this comedy, as he called it.

The public appeared in front of the palace, rejoicing and cheering. I now had to resume my role as guardian of the gate. To Lares, mincing about frenetically in his obsession to have the Emperor appear before the rejoicing multitude, I reported that His Majesty was ill in bed and I must forbid any excitement. Moreover, I had to entreat Lares to thank the populace in Maximilian's name from the balcony of the Palace.

The demonstrations continued peacefully, according to the prearranged program, even if the conservative coup to make the monarch a collaborator had completely miscarried.

Before I turn to the sovereign's departure from Orizaba, I still want to sketch briefly his life-style at that time.

In the first days after arrival in Orizaba, he remained in the Palace, dejected and suffering physically. Cloistered from the world, he saw only Father Fischer, Professor Bilimek, and me. With the return of good health and the awakening desire to work, his way of life also changed. Every morning at ten o'clock after breakfast and afternoons at four o'clock, the Emperor went for a drive with Professor Bilimek and me. Half a league from the city he usually had the carriage stopped, and then we exercised for several hours. The inviting countryside, with its charming variety of yucca, castorbush, acacia, and coffee trees and its sap-green meadows luxuriant with flowers displayed the most captivating scenery.

On these lonely excursions into the precarious surroundings of Orizaba, we must have appeared to every stranger as three harmless naturalists under the leadership of Professor Bilimek. A zealous collector, he did not let political events interfere with his activities. Armed with gigantic flycatchers and butterfly nets we looked for insects, under Bilimek's direction tracking them down even in putrefying tree trunks. The Emperor collected with great zeal. Anyone who did not know him well would have believed that he took these excursions only to support Bilimek in his raids on "innocent animals," as the Indians gazing at us in comical wonder called them.

Initially, Maximilian continued the excursions even after the arrival of Márquez and Miramón, and during council sessions he went along only for amusement. Later however, he combined pleasure with a repeatedly mentioned purpose. There was a French air about Orizaba; the garrison there was French, and His Majesty did not trust the honor guard Colonel Poitier had given him. In order to evade espionage and to keep his thoughts private, he withdrew into the forests under the guise of a naturalist.

Given the ruler's well-known enthusiasm for nature and his outspoken inclination toward natural-scientific pursuits, the most suspicious could find nothing shocking or calculated in these excursions. In this way the Emperor also held meetings with Miramón that he wanted to conceal from the argus eyes of the French. Moreover, Maxmilian had another intention behind such a harmless pursuit. It contrasted with the serious situation, as did his whole ostensibly simple way of life throughout the stay in Orizaba.

He did not dare let the Mexicans believe, as was all too possible in their one-sided approach to things, that he had not been entirely serious in his determination to leave the country. He would not have them speculate that he could not tear himself from the pomp and luster of the imperial crown. Mexicans, like all half-cultivated people, appreciate only superficialities. An Emperor without his court, without a display of magnificence, is to such people nothing more than a butterfly grown plain because the colored dust has rubbed off its wings. Maximilian could no more clearly show how little stock he put in his crown than by renouncing all pomp, living without an imperial household, and going on excursions in a coach rented from an Orizaba *haciendero,* señor Vallejo. (Only recently had he even made the concession of using a carriage with six horses.)

The Emperor could not expect the Mexicans to understand the hard struggles he had endured in the last weeks. He was fully aware that the self-conquest cost him by the resumption of government remained absolutely incomprehensible to them. Still he wanted to throw into bold relief the fact that only their interests, not personal considerations, prevented his departure.

Of late even Father Fischer took part in these excursions. He disliked walking, and I kept him company while His Majesty and Professor Bilimek devoted themselves to zoology. On one such occasion Father Fischer opened his heart to me. He was elated that he now enjoyed Maximilian's confidence. This happy feeling, the father felt, was only clouded by one thought. "I am convinced," he said, "that the Emperor believes in my honesty and candor, but I am afraid he considers me immoral." To a doctor unaccustomed to giving much credit to so-called clerical morality, Fischer's comment appeared so comical that I felt obligated to comfort him. I assured him that I at least had no knowledge of any suspicion on Maximilian's part. His anxiety, I knew, was based on diverse rumors circulated about his private life, rumors which might have found their way to the Emperor.

CHAPTER VIII

Agitation in Mexico City—The Emperor's Manifesto to the Nation—Circular of State Undersecretary Pereda to the Embassies and Foreign Courts—The Emperor's Handwritten Message to the Imperial Commissioners Sherman and Campbell-Scarlett—Military Division of the Country—Dissolution of the Austro-Belgian Volunteer Corps—The Emperor's Manifesto to the Austro-Belgians—Protest of the French Officers Against Bazaine.

Echoing the demonstrations in Orizaba were the congratulations and addresses of allegiance which arrived from everywhere the conservatives could operate freely. Even from the capital, where the joyous atmosphere likewise openly prevailed, came congratulations, some from liberals. The latter expressions were significant; they were more than addresses from magistrates and municipal representatives ordered by high-ranking conservatives. They expressed the hopes of that liberal faction called Maximilianists.

Immediately after the Emperor's departure for Orizaba, a sudden change of opinion in his favor occurred in the capital. Honestly exploited, it would have had lasting effect. The possibility of abdication vividly brought *quid nunc* before the eyes of the few patriots, who in the midst of all these party squabbles had maintained a real patriotism. They were aware that laying down the crown would in no way end the civil war. A peaceful union of the parties under a liberal monarch, immune to partisan interests as Maximilian had always proved to be, should be accomplished at the earliest date. Moreover, fear of undermining national independence attracted recognition for these efforts. The fate of Texas stood as a threatening example before their eyes. Similar annexation could be imminent for Mexico itself.

It was the last chance, but the conservatives thwarted every peaceful statement. While an imposing faction, hoping for a final solution, stood ready to cooperate, the conservatives did nothing to indicate an interest in compromise. Such a solution of the conflict would be inopportune for these people who wanted at any price to hold open the hind gate of reaction. They needed the war to gain victory for themselves. Their answer was "Márquez and Miramón."

These names alone were sufficient to make any rapprochement with the liberals impossible. None of the parties could deal with Miramón, much less with Márquez, who was stained with the blood of the victims of Tacubaya. Yet Father Fischer and the ministers described both of these men as the saviors of the Fatherland. They were represented as the only ones who through bravery, experience, and old soldiers' luck could bring victory against the rebels.

With the Emperor's letter to Lares, after the interregnum of October 21 to November 30, began the new operations of the government. On December 1, 1866, His Majesty issued the following manifesto.

Mexicans!

Circumstances of great importance intimately connected with the prosperity of Our Fatherland and increased by domestic misfortune, had convinced Us that we should restore to you the power which you had entrusted in Us.

The meeting of the ministry and state council We summoned has expressed the opinion that Mexico's welfare requires Our keeping this power. We deemed it Our duty to yield to this request. While doing so, We at the same time expressed a desire to convene a national congress in which all factions should participate on the widest and freest basis. This congress should vote whether the Empire is to endure and, if so, should help create viable laws for consolidating public institutions.

Our councillors are presently occupied in taking the appropriate steps to secure total party agreement.

Until then, Mexicans, We count on all of you, including those of opposing political opinions. With courage and persistance We will strive to carry on the task of regeneration which you have entrusted to your fellow citizen.

Maximilian

This manifesto was sent to all the courts of Europe, along with the following circular by State Undersecretary Pereda.

Chapter Eight

Ministry of Foreign Affairs and the Navy

Circular

Mexico, December 10,[†] 1866

Before assuming the crown of Mexico His Majesty the Emperor Maximilian desired the documented support of the people themselves, assurance of further assistance from allies who expressly were to share in pacifying the country, and finally, extraordinary resources to supplement regular ones, which could not then be procured in the usual way.

To this end we made treaties and agreements, solemnly concluding a tight and strong alliance to secure the peace.

In the meantime, the civil war dragged on longer than anyone had originally expected. Concessions the Emperor made to the dissidents went unnoticed. Government efforts to establish a national army were complicated by various obstacles. Funds authorized for this purpose were depleted, and the government was compelled to engage in oppressive credit operations, which heightened the strain on the already heavily burdened treasury.

At this point, His Majesty the Emperor Napoleon announced that for political reasons he could no longer support the Empire with money and troops and that the French army would withdraw before the agreed time period.

On the basis of this announcement, French troops began to concentrate. Those cities, towns, hamlets which the government momentarily could not defend in default of organized forces fell captive. Now most of the abandoned villages are occupied by the dissidents and, in many cases, by robber bands.

Withdrawal of the allied powers from the most important points, which only they had garrisoned, and news of their imminent departure from the country, which of course would no longer be supported by France, encouraged the bands of dissidents and equally discouraged the friends and defenders of the present government.

The revolutionaries gained new support. They by no means owed this to their own strength, but rather to the fact that whole districts were left completely defenseless. Enemies of the existing order were confident that they would no longer

†This date is apparently incorrect. It should be December 1.

have to fight French troops. The bloody struggle increased, and, in the wake of the civil war, theft and the burning and destruction of cities flourished.

In the midst of this deplorable crisis the activities of the United States underscored the country's objections to foreign political intervention in the Americas. His Majesty the Emperor learned that negotiations had begun between the French government and the United States to establish a Franco-American mediation to end the civil war destroying Mexico. The government created under the protection of this new alliance was to be—this was deemed unavoidable—a completely free republic.

The hopes of His Majesty's government, partially based on the sincerity and firm continuance of the French alliance until the restoration of a self-supporting order, proved fruitless. The country was not pacified, and the civil war raged on. Defenseless villages capitulated to the mercy or the displeasure of the dissidents; the blood of citizens was spilled in vain; war outlays exhausted all resources. Negotiations, which supposedly would lead to restoration of a Franco-American alliance, promised to be incompatible with continuation of the Empire and the integrity of the national territory.

After scrupulous and unprejudiced investigation, His Majesty the Emperor deemed it his duty in the extraordinary and difficult situation to return to the nation the power entrusted to him. The proposed agreement eliminating the monarchy promised to give Mexico peace, and he did not want to stand in the way of that outcome.

With still greater denial than that with which he took up the crown, he resolved to sacrifice his throne on the altar of the Fatherland.

He did not want to execute a plan of such great significance without first hearing the judgment of his ministers and state councillors. He summoned them to Orizaba, where he had been for some time because of ill health.

To these two bodies His Majesty the Emperor submitted all the problems analyzed earlier. Both felt that under the present circumstances, far from curing existing shortcomings, his abdication would contribute to the certain ruin of the country. It would cause the loss of national freedom and independence and total annihilation of the Mexican race.

In their deliberation they stated that the only vindication for all the bloodshed lay in sustaining the struggle in the face of constant opposition. It must be carried on for the maintenance of the interests of society and consequently for the endurance of the nation. To defend such valuable concerns, they argued, one must exploit all national resources to organize an independent Mexican army and make a supreme effort for the welfare of the Fatherland. One must also keep in sight considerations of foreign politics and the form of government, which only the nation can decide.

After this declaration from both advisory bodies, the sovereign solicited their opinion about a practical solution of various vital questions concerning politics and administration. He sought assurance that his sacrifice in continuing the government would be fruitful and strategic.

The most crucial issue was to convene a national congress on the widest and freest bases. Parties of the most divergent political complexions were to participate, immediately deciding whether the Empire should continue, and, if not, what form of government the nation should adopt for the future.

The congress would further propose appropriate measures for complete and definitive organization of the country. Finally, it would suggest methods toward funding the budget and legislate a productive system of colonization. Both advisory bodies recognized the importance of maturely considering all these points. The state council will examine them and propose suitable measures for dealing with each one.

As a result, acquiescing to the declaration of both advisory bodies, His Majesty decided to continue the government entrusted to him by the nation, and he is now striving with courage and perseverance to resume the work of regeneration.

In order to apprise the nation of his decision to convoke a national congress, His Majesty at this time published the enclosed manifesto in edition 583 of the *Diario del Imperio*. He also approved several of the most urgent laws to replenish the public treasury and gave necessary orders for organization of independent military units. In achieving the pacification of the country so ardently desired by all worthy Mexicans, they will be supported by the French as long as they remain.

At this time His Majesty the Emperor received from His Excellency Marshal Bazaine, who agreed with the sovereign's directives, the guarantee that as long as French troops remained on national territory, he would support government measures and collaborate in consolidating order with peace.

By order of our high sovereign I have the honor of communicating the above, in order to bring it to the attention of your Excellencies' governments, and I authorize you at the same time to submit this note to your Minister of Foreign Affairs and to leave a copy for him if requested.

The State Undersecretary of the Ministry of Foreign Affairs in Charge of Dispatches, Juan Nepomunceno de Pereda, His Excellency the Envoy Extraordinary and Minister Plenipotentiary of the Empire, etc.

Apropos this manifesto the Emperor himself addressed the following letter to the imperial commissioners Salazár, Jlarregui, Luis Robles, José Esteva, Domingo Bureau, and Iribarren:

My dear Commissioners:

You will have seen in official documents, especially My proclamation to the nation, how I intend to proceed politically. In this I seek solution to the difficult questions which increasingly assail Us. Dividing Our Fatherland into factions, they not only weaken it, but also make it certain and easy prey to Our mighty neighbor state.

When the different parties accept the idea of the congress, We will end the sad spilling of blood, a result which I have long ardently desired. With acceptance of this idea, all parties will create a free and loyal field for their political endeavors.

Power comes from the nation; only the united and legally represented nation can definitely decide about the form of government and the future of the country. I shall be the first to submit to this legal decision with pleasure, whatever the result.

In order to establish now a real national representation in which all parties can unite, I most warmly and urgently recommend two things especially to you who so worthily conduct the Empire's affairs: In the first place, we must convince the loyal as well as the dissident population by all possible means that the ideas in My program are thoroughly sincere and express My inner conviction. In this I have no reservations; nor do I respond to indirect influence by any party. I firmly resolve as a loyal Mexican to set an example as the first willingly to submit to the decision of legal national representatives.

To advertise this point of view, you can utilize all direct and indirect legal means: letters, the press, even clerical influence.

Secondly, where possible We must conciliate the more respectable segments of the dissident leadership so as to win them over to the idea of a congress based on neutral principles and free speech. Such a body should end the horrible civil war.

If there are skeptics among the leaders mentioned above, I am ready to see each of them personally so that from My mouth he may hear My word of honor that there are no ambiguities in the new government program.

If, with your well-known efficiency and loyalty, you pursue this end, which in my opinion can bring about the lasting salvation of Our beloved Fatherland, you will be able to believe more than ever in My thanks and friendship.

Yours with kindest regards,
Maximilian

On December 2, word came from Veracruz that the Americans, Campbell-Scarlett and Sherman,[†] had arrived there and immediately departed. Convinced that the Emperor was already on his way back to Europe, they had come to establish direct relations with Juárez. Greatly disappointed when they learned that His Majesty was not only still in the country but also intended to stay, they very promptly headed for home.

Maximilian's manifesto was followed by decrees from the ministers. Those issued by Under State Secretary of the Finance Ministry Campos sufficiently illustrate the real worth of the promises given in Orizaba.

The ministers spoke incessantly of the unsuspected rich sources of income at their disposal, and it now finally became apparent how they were obtained.

To establish a school fund they set up a national lottery with twelve drawings a year and prices of 10 and 5 pesos. In addition four new taxes were introduced: a tobacco tax, 16 per cent of value; an income tax, to raise two million pesos; 6 per cent levy on property, and a 2 per cent rent tax. To be introduced at the beginning and middle of January, 1867, the taxes yielded very acceptable results on paper.

Even so, the ministers could display no more striking evidence of

†The Englishman, Campbell-Scarlett and General William Tecumseh Sherman

poverty than to expect any kind of financial improvement through taxes. Only Mexico City, Puebla, Orizaba, and Veracruz were taxable. From them revenue flowed in only with news of an enemy defeat. As long as ready money could not be plentifully raised, even the best financial plans—those of the under state secretary scarcely deserved that name—were nothing but pipe dreams.

Organization of the army was handled in the same fashion. A European would have difficulty conceiving of such an enterprise without money and troops, but it is different with Mexicans. Anyone acquainted with circumstances in their country will understand to some extent their custom in this regard. Troops were impressed and confined to barracks; otherwise, they certainly would have run away. Officers were promised a salary, of which they received only half per month. As for providing uniforms, no one foresaw any difficulties on that account. The army was not trained for parade but set right on a war footing, and in the mild Mexican climate troops can go to the field without uniforms if necessary.

By making every possible effort, the ministers collected barely enough money to raise the first companies even though several weeks had elapsed in the meantime. Army organization was enthusiastically pursued.

Mexico was divided into three large pacification districts. Miramón, chief of the not yet organized First Army Corps, assumed command of the first district, comprising Baja California, Sonora, Sinaloa, Chihuahua, Nazas, Durango, Nayarit, Jalisco, and Colima.

The second district contained Guanajuato, Querétaro, Michoacan, Toluca, Tula, Valle de Méjico, Tulancingo, Tuxpan, Tlaxcala, Puebla, Guerrero, Acapulco, Veracruz, Oaxaca, and Tehuantepec. This gigantic territory, stretching to both seacoasts, was to be pacified by the Second Army Corps under General Márquez. For the present this corps was 6,000 men strong: 4,000, the Méndez Brigade, were in Michoacan; 2,000 made up the garrison of Puebla.

To the third district belonged Coahuila, Nuevo León, Matamoros, Tamaulipas, San Luis Potosí, Matehuala, Aguascalientes, Fresnillo and Zacatecas. This was assigned to General Mejía, with 4,000 men at his disposal.

Chapter Eight

Coinciding with these dispositions, the Emperor issued a decree disbanding the Austro-Belgian volunteer corps. The edict in question, dated December 13, read:

> Since the Army must be uniformly organized, ending any differences between units with different designations, We have deemed it necessary to disband both corps of the Austro-Belgian legion, after settling all accounts. Nevertheless, all individuals of these corps who want to belong to the Mexican Army, may enter the service of the Empire, retaining their respective rank. Those who want to return to their homeland will embark in conformity with their contracts. A commission, composed of the highest leaders of the relevant corps and two officers whom Our war minister will name, will concern itself with settling this affair.

> Maximilian

The Emperor addressed the following manifesto to the Austro-Belgian corps itself:

> We are gratefully mindful of the services you have performed with unshakeable faithfulness to Our government. We cannot forget the magnificent deeds by which you have honored the weapons of your country on Mexican soil, and We thankfully recognize your real military value and integrity, which have won the respect of all Mexicans, even Our enemies.

> While expressing Our thanks for your profitable and honorable achievements, We inform you of Our decision that the Austrian-Belgian volunteer corps be abolished as a foreign body of troops separate from the national army.

> Although every one of you has obligated himself to the service of Our government for six years, We do not want to force anyone now. We declare ourselves ready to release from their oath all those who in the present change of circumstances want to return to their Fatherland.

> In agreement with Our Ministers, We have made the following decisions about this matter:

> 1) All officers, noncommissioned officers, and volunteers of the Austrian-Belgian corps are to express freely whether they want to return to their homeland or enter the service of the Mexican national army.

> 2) Except for colonels, all those who enter the ranks of

the Mexican national army will advance one grade beyond their present rank. That is to say, lieutenant colonels are promoted to colonel; captains, to major; first lieutenants, to captain; second lieutenants, to first lieutenant. The same stipulation applies to enlisted men, with the limitation, however, that the necessary degree of education is not to be overlooked in their promotion. Only one spirit can and must inspire all soldiers of the Mexican national army. For that reason those who enter its ranks must declare themselves ready completely to change their attitude as members of a foreign corps and to familiarize themselves with the character and customs of the units to which they now belong.

3) As a result of these arrangements, after the expiration of six years all officers, noncommissioned officers, and volunteers of the Austrian-Belgian corps will obtain tracts of land to colonize, corresponding to the rank which they have held.

4) All officers, noncommissioned officers, and volunteers, who by their own choice wish to return to their homeland, will be taken to Europe at government expense and there dismissed accordingly.

5) Invalid officers, noncommissioned officers, and volunteers of the Austrian-Belgian corps will be cared for according to their rank. You will learn the more specific provisions from your commanders.

Orizaba, December 10, 1866

Maximilian

By dissolving this corps Maximilian intended first, since the French were leaving the country, henceforth to organize a completely national army and dismiss all foreign troops, inasmuch as they tactically comprised separate corps. His idea was to divest the Austrians and Belgians of their foreign military character and to blend them organically with the national army. They were to form part of the cadre for the new army and to assimilate into it completely. In the new Mexican era which the Emperor hoped to inaugurate, the peace he longed for would only be brought to the country through the efforts of national forces.

I know from His Majesty's repeated statements that he would very much have liked to see all the Austrians and Belgians enter the national army where possible. But only a remnant of the corps reenlisted, and few of the troop units were organized with preponderant Austrian elements.

There were two reasons why the majority of the Austrians did not comply with their sovereign's express wish. Above all, French influence made itself felt. Even high-ranking officers allowed themselves to be seduced and as a result used their authority to persuade the enlisted men to go home. However, the conduct of the Austrian and Belgian chargés d'affaires was primarily to blame. I reveal nothing at all new, nothing everyone in Mexico, at the same time as I, was not aware of. Both Baron Lago and M. Hoorricks exerted all their influence to remove the Austrians and Belgians from the country. By pointing out the hopelessness of our undertaking, they reached their goal almost completely.

Understandably, the same thing happened with the French in regard to their officers and soldiers who had already accepted service in the Mexican national army. In particular, several months previously some regiments of *cazadores* (scouts) had been established under French auspices. These troops were a permanent part of the national army, but most of the commanders and officers were Frenchmen. Even the enlisted ranks, though composed of mixed elements, were preponderantly French.

Here I must anticipate several weeks, in mentioning the order by which Marshal Bazaine curtly recalled all French officers and soldiers serving in the Mexican army. Once the withdrawal of the French was settled, he declared deserters those who ignored his summons to leave the country with the withdrawing French army. Clearly to delineate Bazaine's conduct regarding desertion, I want to show that blame for protecting the offense falls right back on him. The Frenchmen who had enlisted in the cazadores battalion had given up their original positions in the French army with the Marshal's express permission. Consequently, it was Marshal Bazaine who induced them to desert.

With this decree he declared outlaws all Frenchmen who remained true to the military oath they had sworn to the Emperor, and the dissidents later took over the infamous business of shooting "deserters." For this reason, after Miramón's defeat at San Jacinto at the beginning of February, Escobedo had 109 captured Frenchmen executed.

This atrocity evoked general horror, and ten French officers published in *Le Courrier* in Mexico City the following protest, which Herr Kératry did not incorporate in his books.*

Mister Editor:

We beg you in the name of our French, Austrian, and Belgian comrades of the imperial Mexican army, to accept in your paper our protest against Escobedo's infamous act after the Battle of San Jacinto.

Coldbloodedly sentencing to death soldiers captured in battle is an act which will remain an indelible stain in history, but to excuse it by insulting the loyally fighting opponent is infamous; it elicits our tears of rage.

In his report of the victory Escobedo calls us bandits because the French flag no longer flies in Mexico, and, in the service of the Empire, we continue faithfully to observe the obligation we have assumed. He calls us bandits because we are foreigners and no longer belong to any flag.

We have been brought to this pass thanks to Marshal Bazaine. This is the lot reserved for us because we did not want to break our word, which the Marshal himself authorized us to give and from which he had no right to absolve us.

We know exactly where the blow came from which struck our unlucky comrades-in-arms. We certainly know who will relegate us to such a death, if ever fate lets us fall into the hands of this enemy for whom "civilization" and "humanity" are just empty words.

How has his Excellency Marshal Bazaine answered the Emperor's appeal to the Mexican national army on behalf of the French soldiers enlisting in it?

He answered with an act we can find no words to describe. He evoked the law which deprives of his nationality any Frenchman serving abroad without his government's authorization.

Does this not mean degrading us to pariahs; we who dedicate ourselves to the service of a government founded and

*Since I have no copy of Montlong's *Enthüllungen* (disclosures) in front of me, I quote the translation of this protest whose original I sent to Europe from Querétaro on the Emperor's instructions.

supported for years by France?

But we had authorization for this: You yourself, Marshal, gave it to us; you yourself invited us to do it, and you are the one who now wants to break our oath.

That oath is holy, Marshal, and you cannot dispose of our consciences.

Escobedo has excused his insults and his butchery with the same invalid declaration, which, so to speak, puts us outside the law.

Will not the blood spilled fall on the head of him who first caused these scenes of murder?

That blood cries for revenge, and we will avenge it. Our only request is that the government form a legion composed of us Frenchmen, Austrians, and Belgians and designate us, under the command of General Miramón, as an advance guard. We will march, fight, even die until our poor comrades are avenged. One will then see whether we equal those fainthearted bandits who murder prisoners and plan new hecatombs for the wounded.

Finally, we appeal to the European soldiers who fight in the enemy ranks. They will understand that they cannot be comrades of those who cowardly murder their fellow countrymen.

During all these events Bringas House, the Emperor's residence, previously so silent, had taken on a quite different appearance. The Mexicans who once had crept in half furtively to see Father Fischer now entered without restraint, flaunting their expectations of victory. All day long lively activity reigned.

In the meantime all baggage had returned from Veracruz. Now it was time for new travel preparations, not towards the coast, but back to the capital, "*hermosa* Mexico."

CHAPTER IX

Departure from Orizaba—The Emperor's Meeting with Dano and Castelnau in Xonaca—The Customs Question—Junta in the Palace—Miramón's Victory at Zacatecas—His Defeat at San Jacinto—The Emperor's Order of the Day to the Army—The Emperor Takes Command of the Army.

On the morning of December 12, His Majesty left Orizaba. His escort, commanded by Colonel Kodolitch, was comprised of the hussars and the gendarmerie regiment, mostly made up of foreigners. The ministers still traveled with Maximilian and his retinue, although according to their instructions they should have gone earlier. But they preferred to travel with their prince because they wanted to put their precious selves under the protection of a strong escort.

Their sovereign's long-desired return to the capital supplied the ministers the occasion to give an intimate banquet on the last night in Orizaba. Naturally Fischer, who had proved himself to be such an excellent promoter of their goals, did not miss this gathering in his honor. The new era was greeted with fiery champagne. Father Fischer was well qualified as a drinker, but that night he must have really celebrated. On the next morning he complained to me of violent headaches. These became progressively worse during the trip, and in Acultzingo where we stopped at noon, the poor father suddenly became so sick that he protested he could travel no farther. His indisposition greatly worried the ministers, although it was probably less personal sympathy than fear. If at this critical moment he had to leave the Emperor, they would lose their most loyal and capable partisan and their strongest supporter.

They ran about deliberating as if it were a great matter of state and finally refused to leave the sick father behind. They requested that Maximilian stay until Fischer, whose condition probably would soon improve, could stand the hardships of travel.

The Emperor asked me if Fischer's indisposition was serious. I reassured him that it was only an aftermath of yesterday's banquet and there was nothing to fear. He decided calmly to continue his journey, bidding me ask Fischer to follow as soon as he recovered. I delivered this information to the ministers, who felt that I was responsible and were visibly displeased by my lack of concern. Only when I expressly explained to General Márquez that Maximilian wanted it this way did he give in.

Fischer remained overnight in Acultzingo and left on the following morning, overtaking us in Palmar, our second-night station.

On December 14, we reached Castle Xonaca, a quarter of an hour from Puebla, and formerly the property of the Bishop of Puebla.

To bypass noisy demonstrations Maximilian wanted above all to avoid stopping in Puebla itself. He could not evade notice entirely, however, for a great multitude of people from the city had come out to meet him in carriages, on horseback, and on foot, celebrating his arrival in Xonaca with typically Mexican gaiety.

In Xonaca the monarch finally met Castelnau after many postponements. He received the Frenchman on two occasions: the first time, accompanied by the French minister Dano; the second time, alone. I understandably was not present at either conference, but the Emperor discussed with me at length the subjects covered, immediately before and after each one.

He told me: "I gave Castelnau a dressing down, and it was a joy for me to see his great embarrassment. I positioned myself," and he showed me the place in the room, "so that I was standing in the shadows, and the light blinded him. Castelnau could not see me clearly, and I gloated at the impression which my remarks made."

I have no doubt about the tenor of His Majesty's answer. It ran, I must assume from all indications, just like his answer to a letter from the Emperor Napoleon. He persisted in standing by the treaties and certainly took the opportunity to denounce their breach.

"Los franceses exigen mi salida para arreglarse con Ortega y hacer pagar 'a Mejico, mi permanencia salva el pais de este peligro, tanto mas, que yo quebro el tratado de aduanas. Vuelta 'a Mejico, entrevista en Puebla con Dano y Castelnau."

(The French require my departure, to come to terms with Ortega and make the country pay. Because I stay the country is saved from this danger, all the more since I break the customs treaty. Return to

Mexico City. Interview in Puebla with Dano and Castelnau.)

Thus reads the passage in the Emperor's defense notes mentioning events in Orizaba.

Maximilian stopped about eight days in Xonaca. Excursions with Professor Bilimek and me resumed, but the bare, inhospitable surroundings and the meager catch of insects soon discouraged us. In the hours of relaxation he stayed busy, as he had in Orizaba, drafting plans for the park at Miramar and the abbey of Lacroma. After dinner there was target shooting with pistols, in the garden. The Father Confessor to the Emperor, Father Weber, field chaplain in the Austrian corps whom Maximilian once invited to dinner, enthusiastically participated in the shooting practice. Professor Bilimek's weak nerves could not stand the explosions, and he regularly bolted away. Even Father Fischer, now named acting cabinet secretary, was a permanent member of the shooting club.

From Xonaca the prince moved to Puebla, where he took up residence in the episcopal palace.

At this time the conduct of business in the cabinet became more organized.

The Emperor constantly dealt with Father Fischer and the ministers, and I had less opportunity to examine the proceedings. Moreover, matters discussed were essentially of a military and financial nature and therefore were far from my competence. Ever since the sovereign left Orizaba and started towards the capital, he generally had cooperated with his ministers and the conservatives. His behavior now seemed definitely in agreement with most of their wishes. He wholly followed their inspiration, and I remained completely passive as an observer and spectator. Henceforth, Father Fischer was Maximilian's sole advisor. To be sure the latter's dealings with me had lost none of their earlier friendliness, but I avoided expressing my opinion without being asked. The more gloom I saw in the future, the larger grew my obligation to forestall any reproach that I was shrinking from danger.

In Orizaba, after His Majesty had decided to return to Mexico City, he continued to ask my opinion. I straightforwardly stated that, if he stuck to his intention of leaving the country, I myself found the return trip to the capital for the purpose of abdication completely justified; I saw it as nothing but a formality. I overlooked no occasion to express my opinion in the same candid way, but it was fruitless. Full of confidence in the ministers and his duty, the Emperor went to meet his tragic fate.

The following typical incident will best bear witness to how worthy his advisers were of their prince's confidence and to how they justified it by performance.

In the last days of December, I once entered Maximilian's office just as Campos, the under state secretary of the finance ministry, was leaving. "That is quite a man," the Emperor said to me. "I have just been assured that the deficit will disappear with the beginning of the New Year."

Campos must certainly have known full well that he would not be in a position to remedy the existing financial crisis; nor could he expect any success at all from the taxes he had imposed. It was even less justifiable to give hope for financial improvement when the only resource of the Empire worth naming, the toll collection of customs at Veracruz, had stopped.

Seizure of the customs was one of the last acts of force committed by the French. According to stipulations in the agreement of July 30, 1866, from November 1, forward, half the daily toll collection of the port of Veracruz was to be consigned to the French. In the meantime, Napoleon arbitrarily suspended the agreements as a whole, so there was no reason for the Emperor Maximilian to enforce this particular provision and deprive himself of his last remaining expedient in favor of the French. Maximilian consequently could support his finance ministry with a quiet conscience. Despite a request from the French envoy Dano, they took no steps to deliver the French share of the customs collections. Violent measures were now threatened. By virtue of *force majeure* a separate French toll office was established next to the Mexican customs. Its chief, M. Maintenant, oblivious to the minister's protestations, calmly levied the toll.

After vain negotiations and after Marshal Bazaine had extricated himself from the affair by placing responsibility for his instructions directly on the French finance minister, the latter could do nothing but refuse to return the property of those who did not pay the toll at the Mexican office.

On January 2, the following announcement to the business community appeared in the *Diario del Imperio.*

"We are authorized to make an announcement to merchants coming from Veracruz who have wares stored in the customs of Mexico City which are not provided with documents prescribed by the Imperial Mexican laws. Monsieur Maintenant, who has made a declaration concerning such goods, does not have the authority to release your property. If you should obtain your goods without previous settlement with the official Mexican revenue bureau, further appropriate measures authorized by fiscal laws are to be expected."

This declaration from the finance ministry only increased M. Maintenant's daring. He answered with a direct infringement on the sovereignty of the Empire, by publishing in the *Ere Nouvelle,* the marshal's newspaper, an official proclamation to the merchants. He promised protection and ordered agents to the customs of Mexico City to help force the release of goods not covered by duty.

The protest that followed from Under State Secretary to the Foreign Office Pereda to Minister Dano was only a feeble self-defense against this brusque behavior. It changed little in the actual situation.

On January 7, the commercial community read a new warning in the *Diario.* Like the first one it disputed the qualifications of the French representatives "to order customs agents to the capital to deliver the above-mentioned goods, because even according to the most liberal interpretation of the convention of July 30, the authority of the French agents must remain limited only to the port and never extend to customs in the interior."

I know nothing about a proclamation from Dano and Maintenant concerning these new protests. In any case they did not change their conduct thereafter, for little or no money at all flowed in from the customs. Under such conditions how Campos could have had the impudence to promise the Emperor an early disappearance of the deficit is a matter, like so many others, which he and the ministers must settle with their consciences.

Maximilian left Puebla on January 3, after making an excursion

81

on the previous day to Cholula, three and one-half leagues away. With the Egyptologist Reinisch, Colonel Schaffer, Professor Bilimek; the commander of the *Elizabeth,* Captain Von Gröller; the commander of the *Dandolo,* Captain Nauta, and me, he saw the great pyramids made famous by Humboldt.

On January 5, we reached the Hacienda de Teja, a quarter of an hour's distance from the capital. The hacienda belonged to a Spaniard, and the prince had stayed there before.

His whole trip from Orizaba to Mexico City seemed to be made unwillingly. It was as if a friendly power restrained him and delayed his surrender to destiny. Slowly, stopping off for long rests, he neared the Palace.

Meanwhile in the capital opinions pro and con were more clearly expressed. Partisans of the Empire, because of their prescience and their concern for His Majesty, now openly opposed his remaining in Mexico. Among these were his former liberal ministers—Fernando Ramírez, Escudero, Robles y Pezuela. They considered it more advisable to leave their homeland and escape being dragged into the abyss along with their ruler.

In the Teja they took leave of the Emperor. The farewell of Ramírez whom, despite conservative disdain, Maximilian called his friend, touched the prince deeply. He told me: "Ramírez wept, and tears also came to my eyes; he took leave of me with the hope that his evil premonitions deceive him."

On the day that Imperial Commissioner Robles y Pezuela left the Teja, he too begging the monarch to go to Europe, the latter spoke to me, still under the influence of the departure scene. For the last time before the march to Querétaro, he voiced his resolve to remain only a few more months in Mexico. "I will remain," he said, "in no case longer than a few months only to put everything in order. Will the further stay in Mexico City harm my health?" he asked. "Will the fever return?" I thought I should take advantage of the moment and in my answer went as far as a physician can ever go in dealing with his lord. I answered, "I have no anxiety that the stay in Mexico City will harm Your Majesty's health, but I fear that it could endanger Your Majesty's life."

"That cannot determine what I do," he replied, ending the discussion. Never again did he mention this point with me.

The court household in the Teja was the same as in Chapultepec. The Emperor dined with his small private court, and nearly every day invited guests appeared.

The Archbishop of Mexico City and the Bishop of Puebla were also invited on different days. The first appeared in the full pomp of his high rank, seeking to renew the esteem of the Princes of the Church. After leaving the table, we went into a second salon, as was also the custom in Chapultepec, where cigars were passed around. Conversing further with his guests for half an hour, Maximilian then retired. The ostentation with which the Archbishop of Mexico took his leave contrasted singularly with the simple manner in which the Emperor treated his guests. In benevolent condescension the unctuous prelate stretched out his hand to everybody for a kiss. Only the Mexicans and Father Fischer complied with his friendly invitation. We Europeans were satisfied to pledge His Archepiscopal Grace our respect and devotion with a hearty handshake.

In the middle of January, the sovereign moved from the Hacienda de Teja to Mexico City.

Ever nearer approached the day fixed for departure of the French, and it was high time quickly to organize the necessary troops to replace them.

At this time were established Khevenhüller's hussar regiment, Hammerstein's infantry regiment, and the *Cazadores del Emperador* under the Mexican, Colonel Moso. These three units along with the gendarmerie, as already mentioned, comprised most of the elite troops assembled from foreign elements.

Creation of the cazadores regiment sparked a characteristic incident. The Emperor originally wanted to give command of these soldiers, who were certainly capable, to his adjutant, Colonel Ormachaea. Any other officer would have been highly honored to receive such a command with war so imminent, but Ormachaea did not want to exchange his comfortable and quiet position as adjutant to His Majesty for that of a genuine combatant. Lieutenant Colonel Moso, ordnance officer, was entrusted with the command in his place.

After the departure of the French, we expected an attack on the city by the republican army under Porfirio Díaz and began to ready the capital for war. For the first time since my appointment, I saw Maximilian wear a general's uniform and devote himself to military preparations—inspecting, holding reviews, etc.

On January 14, the Emperor once more summoned the ministry and state council to a junta in the Imperial Palace; Father Fischer and Marshal Bazaine were also present. A few days previously at a reception in the Hacienda de Teja, the marshal had been invited by the Emperor himself.

Very serious efforts to induce the dissident chiefs to cease hostilities and to have their party participate in a congress preceded this last ministerial council. Since these attempts, begun in Orizaba, met with no success, the junta had to reach a final decision on the path to be taken.

The crucial point among conditions for His Majesty's remaining was the convening of a congress. Its vote was to be the principal basis of his further activities. He also vowed, in case of abdication, to return only to a congress, as the single valid authority, the power which had transferred to him by popular decision. The conservatives again blocked the plans, and the junta had the same result as in Chapultepec and Orizaba: no congress, no attempt at pacification on a peaceful path.

To be sure, the few liberals in the junta had considered it their duty to point out the insufficiency of resources and the predictable failure of a military campaign. United as one man, the conservatives rose up against these cautious temporizers. Lares, Sánchez Navarro, and Father Fischer in long excited speeches demonstrated that all necessary means were at hand and victory certain. Sánchez Navarro, firebrand of the junta and bosom friend of Father Fischer, especially urged a war to the knives.

Even Marshal Bazaine, in an equally lengthy analysis, expressed his views. True to his role, still relying on his military, financial, and political experience for support, he recommended an end to the Empire. It was clear that the marshal's presentation was worth very little—especially regarding military points—when he deduced from experience as chief of the intervention that if the French yielded to the dissidents, the imperial army could not possibly stand before them.

He himself well knew that the French were not leaving Mexico because they had been beaten by the liberals, but because they voluntarily chose to abandon the country to the dissidents. Even in a financial and political connection, the marshal drew false conclusions from false premises. Under the circumstances, his description of the situation had no effect on the Emperor or the junta.

War was therefore the solution of the ministers and state council. Although still nourishing a slight hope for agreement with the republicans, Maximilian accommodated himself to the express will of the conservatives.

In a few words in his defense notes, the Emperor mentions this junta and the steps on his part which accompanied it:

"Otra junta de los consejos en Mejico, mismo dictamen. Trabajo assiduo para juntar el congreso, agentes 'a Juarez y Porfirio Diaz. Envio de Garcia con el hijo de Iglesias cerca de Juarez."

(Another junta of the council in Mexico City, the same decision —continuing efforts to come to an agreement on a congress—agents to Juárez and Porfirio Díaz. The dispatch of García with the son of Iglesias [justice minister] to Juárez.) This mission dated from the Querétaro period.

Military preparations were energetically pursued, and, considering the many hindrances, organization of the army made some progress after all.

On January 26, the Emperor addressed the following letter to Minister of Public Works Mier y Teran:

My Dear Minister:

The political complications which Mexico has suffered and presently suffers have brought the complete ruin of many foreign families, especially those of French nationality not in a position to make use of the French mission's invitation to return to their homeland with the expeditionary force.

I wish to improve the lot of these people as much as possible, so that we may procure for them the means to establish themselves in our country and provide them land to colonize.

I recommend that you make me the appropriate proposals to achieve this goal.

Be assured of my good will and kindest regards.

Maximilian

On the same day he issued the following Order of the Day to the army:

Generals, Leaders, Officers, and Noncommissioned Officers of our National Army:

There are among you a considerable number of worthy soldiers, who did not glimpse the light of day in Mexico but are Mexicans by adoption and sentiment. It is Our warmest desire that complete brotherhood reign between the native-born and those first named; united may they share the fatigues of campaign, the danger of battle, and the sweetness of peace.

We enjoin you to act accordingly, for We should be sorry to have to punish offences against unity, committed in words as much as in deeds, which could insult the sensitivity of those who are Our brothers. I demand the same behavior from them, and I do not doubt that We will all live on the best of terms.

The French Army is returning home, but a considerable portion of the sons of noble France remain among us. Some occupy posts in the national army; since they have already served in their fatherland, others dedicate themselves to commerce, industry, and the arts. It is Our duty to stay scrupulously alert lest, after unselfishly remaining in Mexico, these people find reason for disagreement with their brothers-in-arms. As for the latter, We must likewise take care that their persons and interests suffer no harm. We especially insist that these Our wishes be fulfilled.

Maximilian

National Palace—January 26, 1867

In the meantime action had begun. With several hastily collected bodies of troops, Miramón had advanced in forced march through Querétaro to Zacatecas, capturing this important position in the first attack. Juárez and his ministers escaped only because of the speed of their horses, which Miramón's wearied riders could not follow. News of this *coup de main* by Miramón filled the ministers with jubilation and conviction of victory. They envisioned the rebels crushed and field operations ended before they had started. But after only two days, on February 5, came a second dispatch, which completely destroyed the joyful mood.

Miramón had been repelled by Escobedo, and his troops completely annihilated at the Hacienda San Jacinto. Dispatches also brought to the capital the frightful news of the shooting of 109 French prisoners. Everyone was struck by confusion and terror. Profiting from this misfortune, many different people again attempted to induce the Emperor to join the retreating Frenchmen. The moment for such advice was in any case poorly chosen.

As long as he was in Orizaba, Maximilian could contemplate going to Europe, but to embark with the French, after the campaign had begun, was a proposition which as sovereign and soldier he had to refuse with indignation. He could not now leave headquarters at any price. He had troops enough, and he even had around him the best units, comprised of foreigners who had stayed behind. With this force he could hold Mexico City until a new attempt to convoke a congress was successful. Since all outside pressure ceased with the French withdrawal, this was a reasonable possibility. Should this attempt prove unsuccessful, His Majesty could in the worst of circumstances still make it with his escort to a point of his choice on the coast.

Miramón's defeat pressed the ministers to a decisive step. First of all they had to guarantee the sovereign's presence so as to eliminate any possibility of his leaving the country come what may. It was a question of intimately binding his fate with theirs and of his behaving as leader of their party.

Since Miramón's defeat had discouraged the troops, Lares and Márquez proposed to Maximilian the necessity of his putting himself at the head of the army and assuming command. Here I must particularly stress Father Fischer's total disagreement with these plans. He commented to me: "His Majesty must remain in the capital, not for the sake of his safety, for I think he is nowhere safer than in the midst of his army, but because of the principle that the Emperor belongs in the Palace."

The cleric completely agreed with an energetic war against the dissidents, but it is untrue that he prevailed upon Maximilian to go to Querétaro. I also vindicate the Prussian envoy Baron Magnus from the accusation that he had persuaded His Majesty to join the army. Even though the actions of both men were so described in a diplomatic report to the Austrian government, in fact this was not the case. Baron Magnus argued at length against a war which had only the aim of inducing negotiations. A comment to Father Fischer is amply descriptive of the opinion the baron had of the situation: "I have often heard of negotiating in order to go to war, but I have never heard of waging war in order to negotiate. The Emperor is playing a dangerous game when he wants to start peaceful deliberations with weapon in hand."

But all remonstrances were in vain. Maximilian had already promised Márquez to go to Querétaro.

CHAPTER X

The Last Days of French Intervention—Proclamation by Márquez— Khevenhüller and Hammerstein — The Emperor's Departure from Mexico City.

Although no longer in communication with His Majesty about events in the palace, Bazaine was well informed. He must have waited impatiently for the sovereign's decision. He still hoped that Maximilian would depart and return to Europe on a French ship accompanied by Frenchmen. If his wish had been fulfilled, as far as Marshal Bazaine was concerned, the French army of intervention could still have accomplished their final mission on the eve of their departure and given Mexico a republic. However, the marshal's expectations were not borne out. His Majesty stayed on and took up the fight with the republicans which Bazaine, who personally knew the situation, offered a reasonable chance for success.

Enraged that he had deluded himself, the marshal now dropped the mask which he had so long sought to wear. In his last days in Mexico City he unabashedly showed his bitterness. He did everything still within his power to undermine the Empire and to cripple the struggle for its survival.

I cannot attest to the charge leveled by many that Bazaine sold weapons to the dissidents, but before hundreds of witnesses he had whole loads of powder thrown into the water, gun carriages shattered, and cannons blown up. Grenades were buried in the earth to keep them hidden. In short everything was destroyed—nearly all the war materiel on hand which could be was destroyed. Once implicated in these contemptible activities, the Marshal of France did not hesitate to commit acts of crudest irresponsibility and dirtiest avarice. The Emperor had given him a palace in Mexico City as a wedding present, and the government had procured for it a great quantity of furniture. These were left at the marshal's temporary disposal. Ignoring property rights without hesitation, he sold the entire household furnishings; he did the same with the coach of former dictator Santa Anna, which belonged to the government and had been spared even by Juárez.

On February 5, the French left the capital. Even in leaving, Bazaine let his petty rancor show clearly. It had been agreed that the French would leave the city ramparts at six o'clock in the morning and withdraw. The agreement about time, as well as its observance, was understandably of military importance to the immediate reoccupation of the *garitas*. However, contrary to his own word, Bazaine departed at two o'clock, in the silence of the night. When the imperial troops arrived later, the ramparts had been empty and unoccupied for four hours.

Immediately after departure of the French, Márquez assumed command of Mexico City, informing the populace of this fact by proclamation. In this decree from which a quote—"ya me conoceis y no tengo que decir mas" (you know me, and I need say no more)— became proverbial in Mexico City, Márquez revealed himself completely to be the notorious soldier feared throughout Mexico. The full content read as follows:

> I have just assumed command of this beautiful city; you know me, and I need say no more. You have proof that I know how to sacrifice myself for a cause entrusted to me, and I would rather die than allow the slightest disorder. As a result I have taken precautions for your security. There is sufficient armed force at my disposal. You yourselves will see how the city will be guarded. I do not want any restless soul to come forward with the insane intention of disturbing the peace, compelling me to the sad duty of using the law as I am firmly resolved to do if it is broken.

On February 10, the Emperor informed me under the seal of deepest silence that I should prepare myself to begin a fourteen-day journey. The goal of our trip he told me would be Querétaro. There the situation, as Lares and Márquez had described it, required his presence to check the blind and thoughtless actions of Miramón and at the same time to restore the unity and confidence of the army.

With the best of spirits and with full confidence in success, Maximilian made preparations for this expedition. According to reports of the poor condition of Juárez's forces and the incompetence of their leaders, a protracted struggle was scarcely to be expected, and His Majesty's presence at headquarters could only inspire the young army to heroic deeds.

Chapter Ten

The ministers prophesied speedy success since a Mexican occultist had discovered the sovereign had five "M's" on his side: Maximilian, Márquez, Miramón, Mejía and Méndez. Victory was certain.*

Departure was set for February 12. Márquez, named by the Emperor to Chief of the General Staff, was to accompany us. He was to determine the strength of the column and to organize it. From among the ministers Maximilian had chosen Sánchez Navarro, Minister to the Imperial Household, to accompany him as countersigning minister. This was the very same Sánchez Navarro who in all juntas and ministerial sessions had pleaded the most rabidly for prosecution of the war and strong control of the dissidents. Now he refused to go into the field with his prince and declared that he wanted to remain in the capital. So His Majesty chose as his companion the stouthearted García Aguirre, then Minister of Public Worship, and the only honorable, loyal soul among the advisers. General Vidaurri, a former republican Maximilianist and embittered opponent of Juárez, was also to go along. Vidaurri had been governor of Nuevo León under the presidencies of Commonfort and Juárez and by good administration had created a significant following there and throughout the whole North. He was the person best suited to pacify this important district, and for him the Emperor intended just such a mission.

I alone of the Europeans at court—reduced to a small household indeed when the majority accompanied the Empress to Europe—was to go with Maximilian. Besides me two European servants were in attendance.

Despite our readiness to march, we could not leave on the twelfth because the ministers could not raise money. Their earlier tall tales of unsuspected, immense financial resources, which they now needed to tap, revealed their true value. The ministers stood helpless, without advice. But the sovereign, who refused to be further intimidated, brooked no delay, and departure was set for the following day. Finally after many exertions, by the evening of the twelfth, the ministers had assembled a total of only 50,000 pesos instead of the millions promised. This paltry sum was all they could put at the commander-in-chief's disposal for field operations.

*Just why the five "M's" were a good omen I have never been able to learn.

Departure was definitely fixed for the morning of February 13 at six o'clock. The hussars, whose barracks were located in the Palace itself, and the Hammerstein regiment had received the day before orders for a limited alert, and early on the morning of the thirteenth the Austrians learned with astonishment what until then had remained a secret. His Majesty himself was setting out on the march.

They were displeased that, according to the dispositions made by Márquez, they were not to go in the field with him. Their task was only to accompany the prince as honor escort, not attaching themselves to the column. This Márquez had assembled in such a manner that—with the exception of about seventy foreigners, mostly Austrians serving in the Municipal Guard of Mexico City—it consisted only of Mexicans. He left the Austrians behind in order to isolate the Emperor from foreign influence so he could decide matters himself. On the other hand, he found it satisfying to put the capital, which he valued only slightly more than he did Maximilian himself, under the protection of the reliable Austrians.

Khevenhüller and Hammerstein did their utmost to procure from the sovereign orders to accompany the march, entreating Father Fischer to use his influence in this direction. They protested to him that they would be powerless in Mexico City itself and that since they had remained only to vanquish or fall with the Emperor, their service would lose its sacred purpose in his absence. They declared themselves ready to march in an hour to follow the ruler to Querétaro.

All their efforts were in vain; Maximilian insisted that the Austrians stay. He told them that his reasons were purely political, that while taking the field in the name of Mexican nationalism, he wanted to be surrounded only by Mexicans. His Majesty, who had been awaiting departure since six o'clock in the Palace courtyard, then approached the officers of both corps, who were assembled in a group, and personally promised to let them come later.

In the meantime command of the capital was given to General Tavera, and the notorious General O'Horan was named prefect of the city.

At a quarter of eight, instead of six o'clock, we finally left the Palace. Through the streets of the city the Emperor rode alone with

Chapter Ten

Márquez, his adjutant Ormachaea, the ordnance officer, Major Pradillo, and several of Márquez's adjutants. Awaiting us in front of the garita was the 1600-men-strong column, commanded by the traitor López.

Thus Maximilian left the city, which he was to see for the last time. His departure was truly ominous. At his side, constantly high in his favor, and now engaged in friendly conversation with him, were Márquez and López, the authors of the catastrophe of June 19, 1867. With them, treason rode to Querétaro.

CHAPTER XI

Fragment from the Emperor's Diary—The March to Querétaro—Battle at the Hacienda de la Lechería—Battle at San Miguel Calpulálpan—The Emperor's Order to the Army—Arrival Before Querétaro.

[The following is a page from Maximilian's diary.]

comes, to force into a war—or robber's profession. Since recruiting efforts so far have consistently run aground on the silent opposition of the whole populace, the government was forced to grasp a horrible expedient from former times in order to set up the new army. The levy is precisely the same unjust procedure which England employed to impress its sailors.

Soon our route led us through the beautiful Hacienda de los Ahuehuetes, named after the gigantic trees of the same name which overshadow the streams of the hacienda with their gigantic branches. Most of these trees (*Taxodium Distichum*), which are also the pride of Chapultepec and several other picturesque spots in the Valley of Mexico, date from ancient Indian times. They always indicate the nearness of springs, places traditionally consecrated to the gods. The *Taxodium* is like the oak of the Teutons, like the linden of the Slavs, like the palms of Balbek and Palmyra. It is the true symbol of the old Indian empire. In the grove of the gods in Chapultepec, under the gigantic dome of the towering trees, grey with age, Montezuma celebrated his mystic sacrifices by the cool springs. On the shores of Lake Texcoco he had another favorite residence, likewise regularly planted with and shaded by these colossal titans of the plant world. One of the largest trees stands in what is now the site of the cemetery of Tacuba and is called by the people "el arbol de la noche triste." Under it sat the daring adventurer Cortéz after that famous night fight which momentarily forced him out of Mexico City. Here the man of iron wept bitter tears. It was the only time in a career so rich in risky adventures and dangers that his heroic soul was gripped by grief and weakness. This moment in the history of the great conqueror has always been extraordinarily interesting to me because it teaches us, as do so many historic examples, that men of the strongest and most domineering natures, usually as firm and tenacious as iron, have rare moments when they believe themselves abandoned by their stars and sink into the most complete prostration. If in such moments there is no recuperation, the man's luck has run out and his star has really sunk for good. Frederick the Great, in the first Silesian campaign, also had such a moment when his generals had to restrain him from cowardly flight. A passing cloud only darkened Cortéz's star for a moment. He rose from his affliction stronger than before and retook Mexico City, successfully concluding his daring undertaking.

Another group of these lordly trees, four in number, stands in the Valley of Mexico near the village of Atzapotzalco. Because of their gigantic size they form by themselves a stately grove in whose shadow two thousand men could encamp. The patriarch of these trees, perhaps the strongest tree on the globe, stands near Oaxaca and has a circumference of 36 vara (108 feet). The measurement cited was given me by General Gamboa shortly before my departure from Mexico City.

On these remarkable mystical trees appears that peculiar, gray, beardlike Spanish moss which people in the country call *heno* and whose great profusion gives the trees a stately silver shimmer. In the natural cathedral of Chapultepec they hang down from the dark tree vaults like stalactites in a grotto.

The hacienda was quieter than usual, and the people left there were worried. In vain the tempting hanging signs of the pulque vaults beckoned the wanderer with labels and illustrations to enjoy this national liquid.

The fermented juice of the maguey (*Agave Mexicana*) was spoiling, at great loss to the proprietors. Pulque does not keep like other fermented juices. The opal-colored liquid must be drunk right away; it is completely spoiled after two days. Since pulque is the principal product of the immense haciendas of Mexico, one can easily judge what an extraordinary loss this eternal political confusion entailed for the landowners.

I have already mentioned this page from Maximilian's diary in connection with the day at Socyapán. I retrieved it from the floor of my room in the Cruz at the time of his capture. Only the last paragraph—"the fermented juice of the maguey, etc."—was in the Emperor's handwriting. I have inserted it here because its description of places indisputably relates it to the early days of the march from Mexico City.

Our first rest station on the way to Querétaro was Tlalnepantla, which we reached at eleven o'clock in the forenoon. The march had been calm and undisturbed until then. In the house of the local parish priest, His Majesty had breakfast with General Márquez, Minister Aguirre, and me.

From the table conversation, I still remember the statement by Márquez, reassuring the worried clergyman with the words: "No tenga Vd cuidado yo verá Vd como iran las cosas." (Don't worry, you will soon see how things go.) Agreeing with the priest, Márquez inveighed against the liberals as destroyers of peace and order, declaring among other things that they were also enemies of progress because they cut telegraph communications.

Here in the priest's house we first heard shots. A small band, quartered shortly before in Tlalnepantla, had run into our rear guard. They withdrew, however, after exchanging a few salvoes with our men.

We stopped in Tlalnepantla for a full hour. Maximilian awaited General Vidaurri, who had been unable to break camp at the same time as we because the ministers could not procure horses for him and his escort. (He had forty trusted men accompanying him.) Unquestionably the incident implied malice on the part of the conservatives. To them the liberal Vidaurri was never *persona grata*. When the general did not come, we continued to march.

One half-hour after we left Tlalnepantla we had our first skirmish, on a mountain ridge between Cuautitlán, where we were to spend the night, and Tlalnepantla. In range of the Hacienda de la Lechería, the bandit chief Fragaso with several hundred horsemen ambushed our column.

The Emperor galloped forward from the center to head the column, which had taken up a position near the Hacienda de la Lechería. Approximately three steps in front of the sovereign, a sergeant of the municipal guard was wounded. On him, I performed my first operation under fire.

In the meantime Márquez ordered around ninety men of the mounted *Guardia Municipal* unit to advance. Under the leadership of the brave Colonel Joaquím Rodríguez they quickly succeeded in dislodging the enemy and freeing the road. Following guerrilla tactics, the enemy riders swarmed around us for a long time, firing multiple shots into our ranks without causing damage.

The weapons fire continued until nearly two o'clock in the afternoon. When the last rider vanished, we marched on unmolested to Cuautitlán where Fragaso had gone. He was soon driven out by a unit of our cavalry.

On the way from the Hacienda de la Lechería to Cuautitlán, one of the soldiers' women traveling with us discovered a member of Fragaso's band hidden in a ditch. According to Mexican custom, he would have been immediately shot on the spot if His Majesty had not intervened. Even so, our soldiers only grudgingly observed the order to let him live and bring him along as prisoner.

In Cuautitlán, Maximilian was greeted with enormous enthusiasm by the troops marching past. Unfortunately the joyful atmosphere was destroyed by a shocking sight. The dissidents had hanged a captured imperial soldier by the feet from a tree in the church yard. His skull was crushed.

Except for several shots fired in alarm, the night passed calmly and without further guerrilla attack.

Late in the evening Vidaurri marched in, accompanied by his trusted men and a squadron of Austrian hussars. With him also came Colonel Prince Salm-Salm, who, as a foreigner, was supposed to stay behind when the Emperor left. Wanting at all costs to take part in the field operations, he had attached himself to Vidaurri's staff.

On February 14, we headed out of Cuautitlán towards Tepejí del Río. The day passed quietly without our seeing Fragaso and his band or any other dissidents. This meant the rebel chieftain had barricaded himself in Zumpango, a small village on the lake of the same name, which we saw on the right side of the road. Naturally we did not concern ourselves with him and continued our march without stopping.

The next day, the fifteenth of February, also passed without incident, and we arrived at San Francisco unhindered.

During the march we rode past a troop of irregular soldiers, whose small detachments represented the different districts of the country. Maximilian called my attention to their peculiar attire. The only thing uniform about them was the white band twisted around their hats with the name of the districts where they were impressed.

Most wore jackets, but many lacked even these. There were quite a few whose military livery consisted of nothing more than a cartridge belt. Laughing at the sight of these figures, the prince remarked: "What would Europeans say about this procession? They have not even buttoned their coats."

February 16 was not to go by as quietly as the two previous days. On this day as usual we broke camp at six o'clock in the morning and halted after two hours of vigorous marching for a rest in the small village of San Miguel Calpulálpan. This place already had a name in the history of the Mexican Civil War. A few years earlier Gonzales Ortega and Miramón had fought a battle here. Success then had been on the side of Ortega, and Miramón had been throughly beaten.

San Miguel Calpulálpan lies immediately at the entrance to the narrow pass of the same name. In this defile the guerrillas of Cosío and Gelista—around 600 men strong—had taken a stand. If the enemy held the thickly forested high ground on both sides, we could not force our way through at all or only with the heaviest casualties. However, it soon appeared that the enemy only occupied the mountain on the left and that the heights on the right were free.

From Calpulálpan, where we rested an hour, we could see the enemy with the naked eye. In the isolated clearing on the left were small bodies of men, whom we would soon encounter.

By nine o'clock, the skirmishers were already out front, and our column advanced. According to the judgment of several staff officers, the battle orders which Márquez then gave were a complete blunder. If he had sent part of the column left around the mountain while at the same time forcing entrance to the pass, he would easily have cut off the guerrillas. But this way the enemy remained free on his flank and rear. While our skirmishers distracted him slightly from the mountain opposite, he was protected by trees and could concentrate his fire on the column in the pass. The enemy stood fifty paces off and fired one volley after another.

At this time the Emperor and his party were also forward with the advance guard. Suddenly we came to a standstill, at the very moment of heaviest firing. A stagecoach with twelve mules, which we had met on the outskirts of San Francisco, had been turned back because the passengers, who claimed to be traveling to Mexico City, appeared suspicious. The guerrillas thought Maximilian was in the stagecoach at the center of the column, and they launched an incessant barrage at it. The mules were skittish and overturned the coach, disrupting the column and detaining it for almost half an hour.

This whole time His Majesty stopped with his entourage in a clearing in the forest, and we were shot at like targets. Bullets flew thick over the prince's head into the trees. His cook, who rode with the train, sustained a face wound. (He was later present at Maximilian's death.) The sovereign could have secured some cover by taking advantage of a little dip in the terrain, but he would not move. Despite entreaties by General Vidaurri, his adjutants, and me he refused to protect himself. Warding me off he said, "I am of no use if I spare myself at the first opportunity."

Despite the intensive weapons fire which endured for nearly three hours, our losses were astonishingly light. Only one man was killed; two more were wounded.

We had already passed through the defile when we heard strong small-arms fire from our rear guard. Immediately the Emperor turned his horse around and hurried at full gallop towards the noise of battle. I had been by his side during the whole action thus far and now also followed him to the fighting at the rear. My impression of the soldiers' impetuous enthusiasm at watching Maximilian dash forward was truly overwhelming. In that moment I understood the exultation of battle.

By noon, around three hours later, the column had marched through the defile and reached the plains. We fired a few more grenades at the enemy and then continued to march. In the meantime, the guerrillas left the heights and swarmed about in range of our column, continually firing at it. Finally our troops lost patience. A whole platoon of cavalry requested permission to put an end to this teasing, and, obtaining it, they hurled themselves on the enemy with a loud cheer. The dissidents had not expected an attack at all and now fled instantly in wild haste. From this hunting expedition, for that was all it really was, our horsemen brought back two prisoners, a dead man, and two horses.

Only now could we continue our march unharassed, and at four-thirty in the afternoon we arrived at Arroyo Sarco, our stopping place for the night. From here to Querétaro the trip was free from attack.

On the morning of the seventeenth, we broke camp from Arroyo Sarco, at eleven o'clock reaching Soledad, a small neat, newly founded village. It was the site of an annual fair, but the populace reported they had not had the celebration in a long time because they were afraid of guerrilla bands. The marauders' conception of property rights was not very orthodox, and, especially since the withdrawal of the French, they continuously raided, robbed, and plundered. The people had heard of the Emperor's arrival, and in a singular way they demonstrated their trust in him—they held the fair. Here as in all other places on the way to Querétaro we met a friendly reception, and here, as everywhere, we heard expressed longings for an early peace.

On February 17, after a forced march of thirteen leagues, we came to San Juan del Río, where His Majesty issued the following order to the army.

To The Mexican Army

Today I put myself at your head and take over the supreme command of My army, which for scarcely two months I have striven to train and to assemble.

For a long time I have wished ardently for this day to come. Obstacles to My wishes restrained Me, but now free from all obligations I can exclusively follow My sentiments as a good and true patriot.

Our duty as loyal citizens commands us to fight for the two holiest principles of the country: for its independence, threatened by the blind egoism of men who dare to infringe upon the national territory; for its peace and order, which we daily see violated in the most shocking manner.

Free from any external influence and pressure we strive to hold high the honor of our glorious national banner.

I hope that the generals will give to their officers, and these to their brave soldiers, a worthy example of blind obedience and strictest discipline. This is necessary to an army which is to exalt national dignity.

I do not have to speak to Mexicans, of courage and lack of fear, for these attributes are national legacies.

101

I have named the brave General Márquez chief of my general staff and divided the army into three corps.

Command of the first I have entrusted to the daring General Miramón; that of the second, I leave to its previous leader; the third I commit to the dauntless General Mejía. Every day I expect the arrival of the belligerent General Méndez and his loyal, experienced troops, who will take their place in the Second Army Corps. Patriotic General Vidaurri also accompanies Me so that he can organize his troops as soon as possible and open operations in the North.

Let us trust in God, that now and in the future He will protect Mexico, and let us fight with courage and perseverance for Our holy cause.

Maximilian, m.p.

San Juan del Río, February 17, 1867

We camped for the night in Colorado, a small village approximately two miles from Querétaro, and at nine-thirty in the morning arrived at the Cuesta China, where the road toward Querétaro a halfmile away falls off steeply. We halted here in order to make a ceremonious entry into the city. Generals Miramón and Mejía, then in Querétaro, came with their staff and all the higher officers of the garrison up to the Cuesta China to meet the Emperor and join his suite.

In the meantime, the troops had adorned themselves with the few decorations at hand, and Maximilian tied on the large ribbon of the Order of the *Aguila* and placed himself at the head of the procession. Slowly the column climbed down the mountain road. It was ten-thirty when we reached the Garita de Mexico of Querétaro.

CHAPTER XII

Maximilian received a welcome of unfeigned cordiality from the populace of Querétaro. Dense masses of people were standing packed from the garita to the Spanish casino which had been prepared for him to live in. They greeted the Emperor with cheers and shouts of joy. Windows and balconies, decorated with flags and banners, were occupied mostly by women. From the *azoteas,* also teeming with people, thousands of copies of a hymn were thrown on the imperial procession. The parade stopped in front of the casino, and His Majesty entered the Great Hall, where he was received with ceremony by the prefect of the city, General Escobar, and the highest military and civilian authorities. Immediately afterwards the ruler, accompanied by all those present, went to the cathedral for a solemn *Te Deum.* Later there was a reception of the top military and civilian authorities, at which Generals Miramón and Escobar gave stirring speeches. The latter's address closed with the words, "Posterity will justly give Your Majesty the glorious title of Maximilian the Great."

The Emperor's reply, ending with the words "viva la independencia," excited lively enthusiasm. After the speeches Miramón's and Mejía's troops passed in review in front of the Palace.

In addition, the general had arranged for that day a banquet to which Maximilian was invited. However, he declined the invitation, excusing himself because of fatigue from the march. At this festivity Márquez gave a fulminating speech. With poorly disguised sarcasm he intimated to the youthful, foolhardy Miramón what a beneficial influence the monarch's presence would have on him. His speech was nothing but an expression of malicious glee over Miramón's recent defeat. At the same time, Márquez wanted to make former president Miramón feel the superiority of the position that he, a onetime subordinate, now occupied. Miramón went white with rage but controlled himself and replied curtly with a toast to the army.

On the next day, the twentieth, at two o'clock in the afternoon, the Emperor rode out to meet General Méndez, marching in from Michoacan with his brigade, nearly four thousand superb, highly trained troops. For hours he held an extensive review, personally awarding orders and medals to the officers and men. That evening all high officers and the imperial entourage—nearly fifty people— were invited to a large dinner, which Maximilian also attended. Immediately after this an adjutant of General Márquez brought before the prince a man in civilian clothes, who came from San Luis Potosí on a pass issued by Escobedo. The ensuing discussion revealed that he was First Lieutenant, later Lieutenant Colonel, Pitner of the Austrian corps, who on May 16, 1866 had been seriously wounded at Santa Gertrudis and captured by the Juaristas. Now he had returned after eight months' imprisonment. Pitner naturally protested his treatment in Querétaro and demanded to be brought before His Majesty. Trembling with shame and righteous indignation he told of insults suffered through the fault of Márquez. Maximilian calmed the young officer and prepared an outstanding reward for him. Several days later Pitner was assigned to General Márquez's staff as a major.

According to our information about the dissidents, Escobedo was located with the bulk of his army in San Miguel Allende; Corona was in Guadalajara. Some fifty leagues separated both enemy units, from each other as well as from us. For the time being the Emperor directed his main attention to reorganization of the troops assembled in Querétaro. Miramón was awarded command of the First Infantry Division; Castillo, the Second; Mejía, the cavalry division; Méndez, the reserve brigade.

While still on the march to Querétaro His Majesty had issued instructions that the Austrian troops in Mexico City—the hussars under Khevenhüller and Hammerstein's regiment, as well as the artillery located in Mexico City—should follow him to Querétaro. But the ministers were fearful for their personal safety. They refused to provide money, and they wanted to keep the foreign troops (the most reliable) in the city for their own security. Therefore, both units, whose commanders were unaware of the sovereign's order, remained in Mexico City.

Military activity did not deter Maximilian from also engaging in government business and private matters. He dictated to me, the only German in his entourage, several letters in German for my notebook. After I had transcribed them, he read over and signed them. It is questionable, in view of the uncertainty of communications at that time, whether all letters arrived at their destinations. I do know, from speaking to people to whom they were addressed, that some did in fact arrive.

Of these original dictations I include here three letters, given verbatim, with the omission of lines dealing with household matters or exceedingly delicate questions.

Even at the risk of being accused of indiscretion, I cannot avoid publishing these writings. I believe I would be untrue to my duty if I wanted to suppress such documents. Because of their origin and destination, historical research considers them valuable contributions to a correct judgment about people and events.

Querétaro, February 28

Dear Father Fischer,

I have read with interest your letter of February 23, which I received yesterday, and I heartily thank you for it. I await with suspense the brochure with the appropriate translations. A postscript confirming the last infamous actions of the French and the latest legal documents of our government will be very advisable. If letters from you go astray, quite possibly they are intercepted by our ministers.

I have long known that they want to destroy the secretariat. This proves the weakness of the men now in control. Only weak people have fear of command and criticize the skills of others.

You will tell Lares that the money for the secretariat must be paid; that this is my express wish.

Schaffer writes me that they do not give a sou for the loyal servants whom I have left behind in Mexico City. This is shocking. If they can no longer pay the last three or four servants their sovereign retains from his whole court, they should say so openly. To tell the truth in such cases is no disgrace, but to lie and avoid payment is a disgrace for the government, ultimately reflecting back on the sovereign himself.

You must continue to attend all ministerial councils and insist that at a favorable moment their minutes and the separate statements about the work of the different ministries be sent along.

Publication of my letter to Lares, addressed from Orizaba, has understandably displeased these men as party members. In Europe this publication has made an excellent impression. What personally amazed me was only that the letter did not appear verbatim. Perhaps this is the result of many translations.

I await with interest a concise summary of the European mail.

I am truly pleased that you have written all our diplomats in my name. You will be so good as to do so with each mail. . . . We are organizing and strengthening ourselves here and eagerly await *libranzas** from Mexico City. We are all very well. The climate of Querétaro has an excellent effect on me because of its beneficial warmth. All day long I am occupied with military matters. In the evening we play *boliches.***

Yours with kindest regards,

Maximilian

I believe I should add some explanation to this letter from the Emperor. The brochure he wanted Father Fischer to forward was an exposition of events preceding the withdrawal of the French, drafted by State Councillor Martínez. The letter to Lares is the one the ruler wrote him in Orizaba after accepting the resolutions of the junta, the relevant portion of which I have already quoted. Previously I hinted at the ministers' relationship to Father Fischer as it now developed, and Maximilian touched upon this in his letter. Since they had reached their goal and, with the help of the cleric, had arrived at the position they wanted to attain, the ministers sought to loosen the *entente cordiale* with their former confidant. As long as he worked with them and pursued the same goals as they did, he was agreeable to them. But

*Bills of exchange.
**ninepins.

now, as secretary to the monarch, in whose absence he was supposed to be independent and to some extent represent the sovereign's view to the ministers, he was only a stumbling block. This situation is what His Majesty designates in his letter as "fear of command." I need add no explanation about the ministers' conduct towards the secretariat, as well as toward the Emperor's household. Nothing adequately describes the baseness of such actions. Scarcely had Maximilian left Mexico City, scarcely did they know he was in a safe place, away from the port, when they brazenly revealed their dirty egoism, which had also expressed itself in the unheard-of detainment of the foreign regiments.

On the same date His Majesty wrote the following letter to Colonel Schaffer, to whom he expressed himself about the ministers in the same way as he did to Fischer.

Querétaro, February 28

Dear Captain Schaffer![†]

I have read with interest your letter of February 26, which I received yesterday evening and heartily thank you for. I am glad to see that the inventory is taking shape. The one from here is almost completed and will reach you in a few days.

It has made a very disagreeable impression on me that the old wigs in Mexico City have so little deference as to refuse payment to the few servants still left over from the former court. This is the eternal result of a system of official lies, based upon falsely understood national pride. If people would only honestly acknowledge having no money, I would be content if necessary to make do with one servant and to go on foot. I have already written to Fischer about these improper proceedings and will further write today to Lares. It is understandable that you could not send *sub seperatim* the objects which Dr. Basch has requested. Their delivery was calculated on the eventual departure of the hussar regiment.

Write to Herzfeld that I am overjoyed with his intelligent and diplomatic proceedings in connection with the volunteers, and that he and Leisser will receive instructions for dissolving the commission. Write to him that I recognize again all his talent and his old energy in the current endeavors.

[†]Apparently Basch prefers army rank, while Maximilian uses naval titles.

It is necessary to end the matter of the volunteers as quickly as possible. . . .

The few Austrians still loyally at their posts win honor and respect. It is desirable for Leisser and Herzfeld to act together energetically and not await my problematic departure, about which I am allowed and able to think less than ever. Be so good as to write Herzfeld about the present situation and tell him that I stand at the head of an army which is only six weeks old and is composed only of Mexican elements. . . .

You are completely wrong in describing yourself and your position as useless furniture. This is very easy to forgive you under the present circumstances. If only I had more such furniture, my house would be well decorated, and I would be permitted to live quietly and well. Under current abnormal conditions it was most urgent that you remain in Mexico City in the first moments of my absence. Without Fischer in the secretariat, you in the Palace, and Khevenhüller and Hammerstein in the barracks, the whole operation would have broken up in the first twenty-four hours.

I well understand that staying behind was very unpleasant for you. It was, however, one of those sacrifices which I believed I could demand of your constantly manifested loyalty and devotion.

Attributing your current difficult position to your candid public remarks is the hallucination of a depressed mood. No one loves the truth as much as I, and the more naked and free it is, the better I like it. If I sometimes opposed what you said, I constantly distinguished between telling the blunt truth and discouraging useless alarm in difficult and severe times.

I would gladly welcome you here as it is always valuable to know that you are by my side. Only now it is completely impossible to come here without a convoy. As you know, we had to fight our way through. Time brings wisdom, and perhaps in a few weeks I can have the pleasure of seeing you with us at headquarters.

I hope you receive good news from your wife and son. What do you hear from Professor Bilimek? Did Lanyi* arrive safely in Veracruz and continue to Europe *sin novedad?* . . .**

Yours with kindest regards,

Maximilian

*Formerly the Emperor's valet.
**Without mishap.

Chapter Twelve

The third of the Emperor's letters is addressed to Professor Bili-mek, who, even before our departure from Mexico City, had traveled to Orizaba as appointed director of the museum at Miramar. From there he was to go to Europe after receiving instructions from Maximilian. The letter is dated March 2 and best characterizes His Majesty's ability to distinguish Fischer the man from Fischer the secretary. The sovereign valued the talents of his cabinet secretary and gave him his trust, without thereby in the least letting this influence the judgment of human weakness which he had formed with a dispassionate eye.

Querétaro, March 2, 1861†

Honored Professor!

Although not a line from Orizaba has reached me yet, a situation which I attribute to the irregularity of postal service, I shall nevertheless try to give you news of us.

As you will have learned from the newspapers, after the endlessly longed-for withdrawal of our enemy-friends from Mexico City and after obtaining freedom of action because of this, we have exchanged the flyswatter for the sword. Instead of buck beatles and insects, we now pursue other goals.

Twice on the road between Mexico City and Querétaro we were in action. There were dead and wounded. One of the latter fell three paces in front of my horse and immediately was operated on under fire by Dr. Basch, the sole European to accompany me.

In the second action, during which they shot right at us like targets, our Hungarian cook, who is well known to you, was on horseback behind us with Grill and was wounded on the lip.

Everywhere there were no dissidents, the populace greeted us more cordially, longing for peace and cursing the French.

After long and difficult marches in which I took part only on horseback or on foot, we arrived February 19 in beautiful and interesting Querétaro.

The welcome by the populace was more enthusiastic than

†The year in the date is obviously incorrect.

I have seen even in the best of times.

I have now assumed command of this poor, young army which was only drummed together six weeks ago.

In the days that follow we will try out our luck. If we succeed I hope we will meet again soon in Mexico City or at some point in the interior. If we do not succeed, we shall have at least fought as honorable men. We will have held out some weeks longer than the world-famous, glorious Frenchmen.

To go down with sword in hand is fate, but not disgrace.

How I regret that the peaceful sciences cannot bloom and thrive by the side of Mars. Honored friend, you would find the most magnificent things on the whole way here and in warm and beautiful Querétaro. In the interesting forest of Calpulálpan, while the bullets whistled around us, I saw the most beautiful butterflies calmly fluttering about. Here in Querétaro we have discovered a species of insects, *Cimex Domesticus Queretari*, which appears to have double the usual number of stinging and suctorial organs and astonishes all who approach it. Had I been able to take along phials I would have preserved some samples of these remarkable animals for you, despite the incidents of war.

I have left your bosom friend and spiritual colleague Fischer behind in Mexico City, where he is the victim of the most painful anxiety about his life and those of the statesmen remaining there. On the other hand, on my present trip I have stumbled upon something of Fischer; I mean, the often mentioned household of the pious herdsman. To speak more clearly, I have finally come upon the track of the Fischer family. It is no dark rumor, no picture of phantasy; the Fischers exist in flesh and blood; *verbum caro factum est.* Only there is a serious hitch in the matter. . . . A friend of the household, a witness to the cheerful story who knows the facts in greatest detail, told us here in Querétaro the comic truth. I do not know whether even more American Fischers exist here from the antediluvian time when your friend and colleague was still an American lawyer. For an explanation of that, you must examine his past.

Schaffer watches the house in Mexico City. I have left the Austrian troops behind at the Palace to give events in the capital a firm footing. The climate of Querétaro is almost like that of Cuernavaca. From that you can imagine that I feel well since my fever has also entirely left me. As usual, hardship does me uncommon good. Now, at the height of spring, you will certainly take the richest catch, leaving untouched scarcely an old tree trunk around Orizaba. Entreating you to greet Boteri,* I remain

Yours with kindest regards,

Maximilian

In view of the significant role which Father Fischer played in the last months before the Emperor's expedition to Querétaro, the reader will permit me at this point to recapitulate my judgment of this personality.

In my criticism of the father's activities I have boldly and straightforwardly accused him of pretending loyalty to His Majesty while working for partisan ends. As harsh as my judgment sounds, I am convinced that with full objectivity I have made no false accusations of him. I have not charged that when he induced the Emperor in Orizaba to give up abdication and return to Mexico City, he did so with full knowledge of the circumstances. What I accuse him of is lack of candor and political honesty. I need only allude to his behavior in Orizaba and at the last meeting in Mexico City, to justify my conclusions. Isolated as we were in Querétaro, I cannot say whether, after Maximilian had marched away from Mexico City, Fischer was faithful to his mission of presenting the sovereign's wishes to the government.

On March 2, the Emperor also issued a handwritten letter to Minister of Public Worship and Education Aguirre, who was accompanying him. In this message, which appeared in the *Boletín de Noticias* in Querétaro, he analyzed in detail the reasons for the expedition there and his intentions for the future. And again he designated the congress as his final goal. The handwritten message to Aguirre read:

My Dear Minister Aguirre!

My expedition to Querétaro, when I put myself at the head of a newly organized army, could be falsely explained by malevolent people in this country as well as abroad because of ignorance as to my motives. I therefore consider it necessary to answer a few of the slanders which our enemies

---

*A Dalmation professor of natural sciences at the secondary school in Orizaba.

111

eagerly take pains to circulate against the retention of our government. These observations should clarify and expose the present difficult situation.

The program I announced in Orizaba after listening to the free and loyal expression of opinion by the advisory bodies has changed in no way. Still predominant with me is the idea of a congress as the only foundation for a lasting future and the basis for a rapprochement of our severely afflicted Fatherland.

I announced this idea of a congress, which I already supported at the time of my arrival in the country, once I was certain that national representatives could assemble free from foreign influences.

With the French ruling the heart of the country, a congress with free deliberation was inconceivable. My journey to Orizaba accelerated the departure of the troops of the intervention, and so the day came when we could speak openly for a constitutional congress.

The very strong opposition to the plan evidenced by the withdrawing French authorities proved that such a step was impossible earlier.

A congress elected by the nation—the real expression of the majority, provided with full free power—is the only way to end the civil war and check the sad bloodshed.

As sovereign and ruler chosen by the nation, I wanted to submit myself a second time to the expression of its will. I was motivated by a fervent desire to end the desperate struggle as soon as possible. I did even more. I had access personally, or through trustworthy and loyal agents, to different leaders. According to their claims they are fighting in the name of freedom for progress in order that they, as well as I, might submit to the lawful vote of the majority of the nation.

What was the result of my endeavors?

These men, who speak of progress, were unwilling or unable to submit to such a judgment. They answered by shooting loyal and excellent citizens. They rejected the fraternal hand which sought peace among brothers, or better said: As blind partisans they want to prevail only with sword in hand.

Where then is the will of the nation? From which side comes the desire for freedom? The only excuse for them is their own lack of vision. The sad actions committed under

112

their banner which cry to heaven, stand as evidence.

Therefore, we cannot rely on these people. We have the duty to act energetically to return freedom to the people as soon as possible so that they may then voluntarily and openly express their will.

This is why I myself came to this city, why I endeavor in every way to restore peace and order to our unfortunate land, so as to protect it a second time against pernicious foreign influences.

The bayonets of the intervention are withdrawing to the east. With armed influence no longer directly or indirectly threatening our independence and the integrity of our Fatherland, we must achieve the goal we desire.

We will negotiate to the last minute, and precisely for this reason we must do everything to remedy this critical situation and free Mexico from pressure from any quarter. Then, finally, a national congress will determine Mexico's fate, its institutions and form of government. Should this reconciliation fail to materialize; should we who aim for reconciliation be defeated in battle, the judgment of the country will give us our due. It will be said that we have been the real defenders of freedom, that we have never sold the national territory; that we wanted to protect it from pressure from intervention from two quarters; that we have taken this step in good faith to insure triumph of the national principle.

Be assured of the benevolence with which I send my kindest regards.

Maximilian

Querétaro, March 2, 1867

Our army in Querétaro totaled 9,000 men. As I already mentioned, at the time of our departure from Mexico City, there were only 50,000 pesos in the war chest, and no later influx worth mentioning was sent from Mexico City. Of this sum, the Emperor reserved only half the monthly quota of the civil list to maintain his household and the court, that is 10,000 pesos, and even this amount was not supplemented during his stay in Querétaro. In the first days after our arrival, procurement of needed money already presented the principal problem. As I have mentioned, the order had gone to Mexico City that the hussars and Hammerstein's infantry were to leave for Querétaro, bringing along money and munitions. These orders were not carried out by the ministry. If His Majesty did not want to find himself stopped in action due to a lack of necessary war materiel and money, it was absolutely essential to seize upon a solution. Indeed it had to hit the inhabitants of Querétaro hard, but in the emergency of the moment it could not be avoided. A forced loan was decided upon, and General Méndez was entrusted with executing relevant measures. The rich townsmen of the city had to pay and the army to receive, whether they liked it or not. However, they submitted with goodwill to the inevitable. Querétaro was well disposed to Maximilian, and its citizens willingly tolerated the sacrifices laid upon them.

The state undersecretary in Mexico City, financial wizard Campos, did not concern himself further with the Emperor and his army in Querétaro. Abandoning both without pecuniary resources, he proved true to his promise: After the New Year, there was no deficit. Moreover, since the ministry acted as a completely independent government, the sovereign was forced to name General Vidaurri finance minister. This was naturally of the gravest importance now that the army was in the field and no help could be expected from the government in the capital. We had to introduce a regulated administration of expenditure of our slight resources.

His Majesty could have made no better choice when he entrusted this important office to Vidaurri. The general justified his old reputation for administrative capabilities, and the army could only be content with his efforts. He skillfully solved the complex problem of furnishing the troops with all the necessities without too heavily burdening the populace. After all, it was difficult for a city of forty thousand people to support an army of nine thousand men. He brought order to payment and feeding. The officers, to be sure, received only half their wages, but this regularly; the troops received their daily gold.

At this time Maximilian himself became extraordinarily active in military affairs. He regularly attended the generals' councils, visited the barracks and hospitals, held reviews, and by open participation and cooperation he made himself the army's idol. Troop morale was excellent. The men's confidence, based on the unity of command and the recognized ability of most of our generals, grew with every day, and final victory was certain.

Besides the affection which Maximilian gained among the troops, he also quickly won the greatest popularity among the citizens of Querétaro. Day in and day out he went through the city, usually without escort. In the streets and on the *alameda* he could be seen: when in uniform—without sabre, in a simple blue tunic bearing no insignia of rank, his walking stick under his arm. On horseback excursions he wore the Mexican national costume—the gigantic *sombrero* (hat), the picturesque *chaqueta* (jacket), and the *calzones*[†] (trousers) richly inlaid with silver buttons. Often he mingled as an onlooker among the crowd at military exercises and reviews, conversing good-naturedly with his neighbors, exchanging lights, and smoking cigars.

His way of life in Querétaro was very simple. He lived in two rooms in the casino, one of which was the bedroom; the other was the office in which he received visitors and held audiences. After constant work during the day, he relaxed for an hour in the evening by playing ninepins and usually, when important business was not awaiting completion, went to bed at around nine o'clock, to get up again at five in the morning.

† Calzoneras.

CHAPTER XIII

Querétaro—Events, March Fifth through Thirteenth.

For the reader's easier orientation I want to sketch here briefly Querétaro's topography as an introduction to the following description of the siege.

Querétaro, a city of about 40,000 inhabitants, forms a rectangle facing in a direction slanting from northeast to southwest. The length of the city is around 2,400 meters; its width, 1,200 meters. Along the northern, wide side flows the Río Blanco, a small river streaming out of the Sierra Gorda mountain range. This range lies northeast of the city. Only towards the west, Querétaro ends in a wide, extended plain cut off in the distance by the mountains of Guadalajara.

In a pointed arc around the city, broken only in one spot where the Río Blanco has widened its bed, from south to northeast are located: the Cimatario, the Cuesta China, the Loma de Garreta, and the Cañada; north and west, La Cantera and San Pablo. Nearer to the city and parallel to San Pablo is San Gregorio Hill; Jackal Hill, at whose foot a hacienda of the same name is located, also forms a direct continuation of the Cimatario.

The Cerro de las Campanas rises on the western end of the city in the middle of the opening in this mountain arc. From here, facing north, one looks out over San Gregorio, San Pablo, and La Cantera. On the right is the city, with the Cruz Convent rising on its outermost end, and behind this, the Cuesta China, the Loma de Garreta, and the Cañada. On the left lies the wide plain of Guadalajara; at the rear, the Cimatario and Jackal Hill.

The enemy occupied all of these heights during the siege. We only held the Cerro de las Campanas, and this and the Cruz Convent, built on an elevated cliff on the eastern end of the city, were our only strong points. Otherwise the city lacked any natural or artificial fortification.

An aqueduct running out of the Cañada—a massive construction originally built at the time of Spanish rule—supplied the city with drinking water.

117

March 5 approached amid military preparations. At four o'clock in the afternoon Miramón's division held a large review and exercise under fire. The same afternoon arrived the first certain reports that the enemy was approaching from the north and west. On the road from San Miguel de Allende moved a force of seventeen thousand men under General Escobedo, composed of battalions from Nuevo León, Coahuila, Durango, Zacatecas, and San Luis Potosí. A second corps farther back, comprised of troops from Sinaloa, Sonora, Jalisco, and Colima, advanced under General Corona with an alleged actual strength of eighteen thousand men.

Escobedo's troops had already reached the intersection of the road from San Miguel and Celaya in the valley of Querétaro, around three miles from the city.

Immediately the Emperor assembled Generals Márquez, Miramón, Mejía, Méndez, and Castillo in a war council which he presided over personally. Here it was resolved not to attack the enemy, but rather to await his expected attack in protected positions. We now took up prearranged posts: our right wing rested on the Río Blanco; our left, on the Hacienda de la Casa Blanca and the Garita de Celaya; the center held the Cerro de las Campanas, later to become famous. Our reserve stood in front of the *alameda* (promenade).

The enemy attack was already expected for March 6 (Ash Wednesday). At four o'clock in the morning Maximilian rode out in front of the city to inspect the troops standing at full readiness in battle lines. The evening before I received from him the order to be ready to follow immediately when weapons fire and cannon thunder gave proof that the action had begun. The expected attack failed to take place. At eight o'clock the Emperor returned, and at five o'clock in the evening he rode out again in front of the forward lines with Márquez and the general staff. Around eight o'clock His Majesty's ordance officer, Lieutenant Colonel Pradillo, came to notify me that I was to hold myself in complete readiness to depart for headquarters at daybreak the next morning. Two hours later, a direct order reached me to go immediately to the Cerro de las Campanas with full field pack.

The Cerro de las Campanas (Hill of the Bells), allegedly an old

Indian temple mountain, is a hill thickly grown with cactus, located around ten minutes from Querétaro. Only gradually rising on the side facing the city, it falls away rather steeply on the north towards San Gregorio Hill and west towards the road from Celaya. There was located our headquarters. When I arrived on the Cerro, everything had become quiet for the most part. Men, horses, mules lay in the most motley disorder across and next to each other among stones and prickly briers. The sleepers were constantly in danger of being awakened from their dreams by a horse kicking or stepping on them.

Maximilian had brought nothing for himself but a traveling rug and a coverlet, and on this night as well as the following ones, he slept as a soldier among soldiers, camping on the bare earth, under the open sky. I also tried to win a free spot for myself and, rolling up in my coverlet, went to sleep earlier than I had expected in this unusual situation.

I now include here what is left of my diary kept during our stay in Querétaro and saved from the catastrophe of May 16.

March 7, 5 A.M.

We have been expecting the attack for three hours. It is the Mexican custom to attack at the *madrugada* (daybreak). The sun is already high above the mountains; still there is no trace of the eagerly awaited attack. We hear nothing but individual rifle fire, exchanged between our outposts and the enemy's. At nine o'clock in the morning the Emperor makes an inspection on horseback of our right flank, composed of Castillo's division. From the Cerro we hear the soldiers' enthusiastic cheers; we can also see Maximilian riding in front of the lines.

His Majesty devotes particular attention to the provisioning of the troops, and the soldiers are spirited and inspired by the highest courage. The populace of Querétaro shows itself to be very sympathetic and helps us as much as it can. Citizens voluntarily lend a hand to pull cannon up the Cerro.

The prince shares with me what he calls a wonderful discovery made on the Hill of the Bells. On its northern slope he had come upon a niche hewn in the rocks, whose primitive comfort was heightened by a stone bench. Protected from the blaze of the sun, surrounded by

119

high cactus shrubs in which beautiful hummingbirds flit about, and with a view towards the dark-blue mountains of the Sierra Gorda, this spot is as if chosen for a spirit in need of calm. "Do not tell anyone about this treasure," exclaims Maximilian, enchanted. "I should like to be alone here." But others had already found it and put it to good use. His Majesty tells me that today at noon, when with his servant he climbed down into the grotto for his noon meal, he bumped into a couple sunk deep in love. They also had sought solitude and now, embarrassed by this disturbance, slipped away with downcast eyes.

At nine o'clock in the evening a deserter comes over from the enemy camp, half naked and totally miserable. He is brought before the sovereign and, speechless with fright, throws himself to the floor, begging for his life. Local custom is well known to a Mexican. His Majesty commands him to stand up and assures him that nothing will happen to him. The man then explains that troops in the enemy camp are very badly treated and most of them are fighting against their will.

The enemy's campfires inform us of his exact position.

March 8

Morning. Again no attack. Small-arms fire at us from the outposts. We can hear the enemy trumpet signals distinctly.

On the sovereign's instructions, the Hill of the Bells will be cleared of cactus bushes and fortification begun. At eight o'clock in the morning he makes an inspection tour of the left wing on horseback and rides to the farthest outposts. Without his asking them, the soldiers call out: "somos satisfechos de todo, tanto paga que comida." (We are satisfied with everything, pay as well as food.) As he says to me, it is probably the first time since Mexican Independence they have cause to be so. This is primarily due to the excellent management of war supplies by General Vidaurri. Actually the *rancho* (ration) for the men is very good, much better than what the Emperor has at his table. Parenthetically, his cuisine is really ridiculously bad.

During this inspection tour Maximilian presents the Second Battalion with a banner and gives a short address which is received with enthusiasm. He even visits the heights of Santa Cruz, the location of

120

our hospital and artillery depot.

New deserters bring us a more detailed report about enemy movements. We have been expecting him to attack since the day before yesterday. His long delay makes everybody in the camp impatient, from the prince down to the last soldier.

Today there is a council in camp. His Majesty confers with Minister Aguirre, General Vidaurri, and Márquez. He tells me he is very indignant about the negligence of the government in Mexico City. Only nineteen thousand pesos have been sent for the entire month we have been in Querétaro. Even with the extensive economies introduced by Maximilian in cooperation with General Vidaurri, this sum scarcely lasts nine thousand men six days. The monarch works a great deal with Vidaurri, who enjoys the popularity of the whole army. Fortification of the Cerro continues. The order is given to organize a civilian convict brigade for embankment work so that our strength, very meager in comparison to the enemy's, is husbanded and can be applied to action.

The night of the twelfth the Emperor is awakened. Enemy movement against our right flank is reported; against Río Blanco and San Gregorio. We are afraid of having our flank turned. A council of war is convened, the result of which is a lateral displacement of both our flanks corresponding to the enemy's movement. In this new position our center is still the Cerro de las Campanas.

March 9

Nothing but skirmishes on the outposts throughout the whole day. To date we have not lost a man. Eleven of the enemy have been killed, among them a major whose horse our soldiers brought back as booty. Our diversion today was observing this skirmish from the Cerro. Mexican battles of this kind are really unique.

Thirty or forty horsemen armed with long flintlocks stay in range opposite each other as long as it suits them. Now begins a very loud conversation before hostilities are started by one side or the other. Each side lustily insults the other; one group surpasses its opposite in verbal abuse. At that point is heard a peculiar sound—vibrating, shrill, and far carrying—a kind of battle cry, as the Emperor remarked to me, like that made by nomadic Arabs. After they have engaged in these insulting screaming exercises for a while, the most stouthearted among them hurries twenty or thirty gallops forward, fires his weapon, wheels his horse around and gallops back again. The same maneuver is repeated over and over in the course of one or two hours, until finally one side tires, or one of the people is accidently injured by careless playing with weapons. However, as soon as one side looks as if it is beginning to pull back, the others immediately hurl themselves on the defeated foe, and scarcely has this occurred when the attackers also withdraw to their own lines. The best illustration of shooting during these skirmishes is the fact that the bullets of the combatants flew over the spectators' heads, even on the high hill.

March 10

Still no attack. At nine o'clock in the morning a council of war. His Majesty tells me that he himself spoke out for advancing to the attack. However, the generals are against it. At ten o'clock he takes an inspection ride along our entire line and visits the outposts.

At ten-thirty, from the Hill of the Bells we see the entire enemy army drawn up as for a parade and watch them pass muster. This lasts more than three hours. Individual gusts of wind carry the sound of enemy trumpets to us.

The Emperor, who has been informed, comes to the Cerro after his inspection ride in time to see the spectacle. Smiling, he remarks to the generals standing around, "I see this enemy review only as the expression of their duty-bound respect towards me as sovereign."

It is improbable that the enemy will attack at this advanced hour. At one-thirty Maximilian holds a large council of war, for after this demonstration we certainly expect an enemy advance. After the council, a deputation of the generals comes to ask the prince not to expose himself to unnecessary danger and to go back tonight into the city where the reserve corps is located.

General Mejía says in his impressive manner: "You must protect yourself, Your Majesty, for if something happens to you, one of us generals will want to become president."

Maximilian receives the deputation in a very friendly fashion and, as he told me, answers that under the present circumstances a fainthearted ruler would be of little use to the cause. He remains on the Cerro.

Pictures of saints are sent to him from local convents.

At two o'clock in the afternoon, a deserter comes over from the enemy camp. He is alleged to be a farmer from Celaya who only shortly before was conscripted by Corona, along with many people from his district. The munitions he shows us are very bad. He also says that the enemy soldiers are pitifully paid and receive only a medio a day (around ten kreuzer). In addition they suffer poor treatment. Our soldiers receive two reales daily (about fifty kreuzer).

Imperial General Olvera with a force of 1,200 is some miles distant from us in the nearby Sierra Gorda. He is supposed to push through to us tomorrow or the day after.

Quiroga, colonel of the cavalry, goes on a reconnaissance mission and captures two hundred oxen.

Today for the first time the Emperor does not sleep on the bare earth. He has finally accepted Almonte's tent which General Mejía has offered him repeatedly. Miramón and Márquez also have big tents put up for themselves on the Cerro. Headquarters more and more resembles a fortified camp.

March 11

Morning passes as usual with skirmishes at the outposts. The aqueduct leading to Querétaro, an old structure from the Spanish period, has been cut off by the dissidents. Maximilian has provisions brought from the surrounding area by flying columns. The enemy shows himself on all the heights ringing the city. It seems to be his plan to surround us without fighting. Our army is full of enthusiasm. For the first time in Mexican history, the generals are in agreement, at least to outward appearance.

At eleven o'clock in the forenoon General Méndez reconnoiters San Pablo with the Empress's Regiment and the hussar squad. He runs into an enemy superior to him on the heights of San Pablo. The republicans do not attack but send forward only a skirmishing cordon. After this reconnaissance Méndez returns to the reserve.

At three o'clock in the afternoon the battery on the Cerro fires off its first shots. The Emperor has withdrawn into the cliff grotto, his favorite resting place notwithstanding the small adventure he experienced there shortly after its discovery. General Márquez sends for him to observe the effect of our fire from the Cerro.

The artillery shoots superbly. From the Cerro we see a column of several hundred enemy horsemen, dashing at us at full speed. The second well-aimed shot brings them to a halt, and a salvo of three cannon directed at them—we see how the shells fall into their ranks —scatters them completely.

Shortly before this small affair the brave cavalry colonel, Quiroga, who had run into the enemy on a second reconnaissance, also threw him back. Quiroga's horsemen capture an enemy captain, who is brought before Maximilian. He is recognized as an individual twice punished for pillage and twice pardoned by His Majesty.

In the evening around five o'clock Miramón makes a sortie to the Cañada, where the guerrilla leader Carabajal is located. Carabajal immediately takes to his heels when Miramón approaches. Two of the enemy are killed and two horses captured. Besides that Miramón brings back with him as booty sixty oxen, one hundred goats, twelve thousand tortillas (flat corn cakes), and a large quantity of corn.

March 12

At nine o'clock in the morning General Castillo's division, composed of the Cazadores Battalion and the Seventh-Line Regiment, and supported by the Empress's Regiment, makes a reconnaissance of the village of San Pablo. A brisk, small battle develops. Our cazadores storm the hill, but our cannon fire is not returned. It seems that the enemy has no artillery in San Pablo. The reconnaissance has achieved its purpose, and Castillo returns to his old position on our right flank. Our losses are seven dead. Villasana, Colonel of the Cazadores Battalion, is wounded. The Emperor transfers command of the battalion robbed of its leader to Colonel Prince Salm-Salm, who until now has only been in Vidaurri's suite in Querétaro without any particular employment.

Around three o'clock in the afternoon is reported a wheeling of enemy columns towards the back of the city and the Cuesta China. At six-thirty there is a session of the council of war.

The campfires we see at night show clearly that the enemy has significantly changed his position. The fires in front of us which on earlier nights lit up the whole plain of Celaya have now become scarce, while bright flames flicker in new positions on San Pablo Hill, on the Loma de Garreta, the Cañada, and the Cuesta China.

The bulk of the enemy no longer stands opposite the Cerro, which has now lost its importance as the center. Since our flanks remain the same, our center is moved in a diagonal direction towards Mexico City. The Cruz Convent, a solid, rambling structure originally built in the Spanish period stands on a rocky plateau. Already its position or, more exactly, its strong stonework, makes it a natural fort. These monstrous premises will be turned into a barracks and a hospital; the large *huertas* (kitchen gardens), surrounded by strong walls, are so many outposts. Headquarters is to be moved here tomorrow.

CHAPTER XIV

Siege, March 13-22—The Attack on March 14—Márquez Goes as a Lugartenient to Mexico City—The Emperor's Letter.

March 13

Still no enemy attack. At ten in the forenoon headquarters are moved to the Santa Cruz Convent.

Quiroga's reconnaissance of the Cuesta China convinces us that the enemy has assembled a considerable mass of troops at that point—according to Quiroga's estimate, about eight thousand—and has weapons which include cannon.

The Emperor takes up residence in the Cruz with his whole entourage and the general staff. Near His Majesty, I obtain a room on the second floor which opens on a corridor with a view towards the Cuesta China. No noteworthy steps are taken to fortify the convent, which lies in range of the enemy batteries. The structure's outermost point is the pantheon with a small chapel. Between this and the high ground of the Cuesta China and the Loma de Garreta, the terrain is deeply slashed and thickly overgrown with cactus. Protected by this underbrush the enemy can approach us unnoticed up to the closest range. Many different people advise Maximilian to fortify and occupy the chapel and pantheon as hurriedly as possible and to cut down the cactus bushes so favorable to the enemy. But Márquez does nothing.

From the pantheon we look out on the enemy batteries on the Cuesta China and the enemy flag on its ridge.

At five-thirty in the afternoon, the enemy brings his cannon into play for the first time, plastering the Cruz with a goodly assortment of grenades, roundshot, and conical projectiles.

March 14

At nine o'clock in the morning, the Emperor visits the great courtyard of the convent. The embrasures of the outer walls are manned by soldiers of the Emperador Battalion. I accompany the prince. Enemy movements this morning make an attack beyond question, and Maximilian exhorts the troops and calls upon them to be brave.

While he is there, the enemy attack begins on three sides simultaneously: from the Cuesta China at the Cruz, defended by General Méndez; from San Pablo at Castillo's line on the Río Blanco; from the Cimatario against the Casa Blanca and the Alameda, occupied by Mejía.

We leave the kitchen gardens under a hail of grenades. His Majesty goes to the great square in front of the convent (on the side towards the city) and stays there throughout the action.

Adjutants dash back and forth from the lines. An Austrian officer of the general staff, Captain Baron Fürstenwärther, armed with a good telescope and stationed in the tower of the Cruz, immediately reports the movements to the monarch and General Márquez, standing below in the square.

Maximilian's position is less than safe. He is continuously in a rain of grenades and rifle bullets. Toward noon, while Generals Márquez, Méndez, and the officers of the general staff stand grouped around him, a grenade lands six to eight steps in front of them. It explodes; everyone ducks; only the sovereign remains on his feet. Luckily no one is injured. The only damage is caused by a fragment which bends the sabre of General Méndez's adjutant, penetrating his clothes.

Around one o'clock reports arrive from our two flanks that Castillo and Mejía have repelled the enemy. On both lines he is fighting only to make an ordered retreat. Our generals, officers, and troops have fought at both points with bravura and without fear. Colonel Prince Salm-Salm, who stood with his battalion on the bridge at the river, made a brilliant sortie and captured a cannon.

Numerous prisoners are brought into the city, among them even an American officer, who is presented to the Emperor. His Majesty asks him: "Why do you fight against us?" "Because I am a republican," he answers. "If you are really a republican," Maximilian replies, "you ought never to stand up for Juárez, only for Ortega." During this conversation the American calmly keeps his sombrero on, perhaps because under the circumstances he forgets his place, or from a desire to show his republican defiance. General Méndez, standing next to him, removes his hat, observing that he is in the Emperor's presence. His Majesty, not at all pleased that the officer spoke to him with covered head, smiles at the general's courteous indignation and dismisses the prisoner.

Around five o'clock in the afternoon, fighting ends on both flanks. The enemy has withdrawn from all points. Only in the center do hostilities continue without interruption. Despite a direct imperial order, the pantheon has been left unoccupied by Márquez. All he did was post maybe forty Austrians on the chapel roof under the command of Linger, Captain of the Municipal Guard (likewise an Austrian). These few people understandably could not prevent the enemy's taking the pantheon. After a brave two-hour resistance and after Captain Linger had fallen, the imperial troops were forced to evacuate the chapel lest they be cut off from the convent by the enemy pressing on in ever larger numbers.

Our men are forced back from the outer courtyards, and the danger increases with every minute. At this critical moment the Second Battalion, under its daring colonel, Juan Rodríguez, makes a brilliant sortie. It is personally led by Márquez, suddenly overcome with a fit of bravery. The attack is strongly supported by the effective fire of a cannon mounted in the inner courtyards and served by Artillery General Arellano himself. Finally, towards six o'clock, after an hour's murderous struggle, the Cruz is again completely cleared of the enemy.

At six o'clock the Emperor inspects the lines, with General Márquez, several officers of the general staff, and myself in his suite. All along the lines from the Río Blanco to the Cerro de las Campanas the enemy pursues us incessantly with his grenades. It is a very small group indeed on which he lavishes his powder, but in it he rightly suspects choice prey. This is clear to him from the cheers and exultant trumpet calls showing the enthusiasm of the troops when Maximilian rides past. Bullets hit the sand in front, behind, and beside us, but luckily not between us. Under this obstinate fire His Majesty and, naturally, also his suite ride at a slow trot down the lines. Only when we have returned behind the Cerro and over the Casa Blanca and the Alameda into the city, only out of range of enemy fire, does he urge his horse to a gallop.

The day's result: Although we have thrown back the enemy from all the lines, he has come closer to our main body and occupies San Gregorio Hill, north of the city, left out of our defense perimeter due to lack of men. Today we are more narrowly hemmed in than yesterday.

Principally for military readers, I supplement these comments from my diary with the official report from the April 12 *Boletín de Noticias* about the fierce fighting on March 14.

At nine-thirty in the morning enemy cannon from the Cuesta China signaled the beginning of battle. Their cavalry advanced in strong rows on the road from Pueblito and almost gained possession of the Hacienda de Jacal, immediately adjacent to the Garita de Pinto. In this latter building was the general staff of our cavalry division. The first brigade of this division, under the direct command of the brave General Mejía, rushed at the enemy without delay, stopped his advance, and quickly dislodged him from the terrain he had captured. The attack was a brilliant one, and our cavalry reached the outermost enemy line near the estancia. Sixty prisoners and more than double that number of casualties resulted from the first battle. While this column reoccupied its old position, the city was attacked anew from the northern side, where the enemy had assembled considerable forces. He had taken possession of San Pablo and San Gregorio Hills without opposition and stationed his heavy artillery there. From there, he now made a movement towards the Río Blanco to take the bridge dividing the city from the suburb of San Sebastián. For many hours a heated battle raged on this line. Enemy columns were thrown back repeatedly, and still they reassembled on the heights to renew their attack with fresh strength. Neither their number nor their spirited attack was sufficient for them to take these important posts defended by Generals Castillo and Casanova. After throwing back the enemy, our brave soldiers made a sortie over the entrenchments, pursued the attackers, and captured a cannon and a great number of wounded and prisoners. During this bloody affair the battery posted on the Cerro de las Campanas kept up an unbroken fire with remarkable precision.

Meanwhile, the enemy stormed the Cruz Convent where the Supreme General Staff was located. By using terrain favorable to them, they succeeded in taking the pantheon and the adjoining chapel. On the enemy side this attack was supported by a battalion with two cannon positioned on the heights of San Francisco and by four strong columns of cavalry with an equal number of cannon posted on the even slope of the Garreta. Thus the Alameda and the whole south of the city seemed gravely menaced. The enemy, continuously attacking the Cruz, deployed a column of cavalry from the men stationed at the Garreta against the Cimatario, to stop our attack threatening their left flank from the Casa Blanca. General Miramón immediately understood this difficult situation. Taking advantage of the moment with characteristic sharp-sightedness, he occupied the Alameda with his division —infantry and artillery—supported our cavalry attack, and at the same time struck the enemy reserve at San Francisquito.

In the meantime, three brilliant sorties, one after another, were made from the Cruz. The enemy was thrown back from the pantheon. He had to leave the kitchen gardens and the buildings adjacent to the convent and was forced into open retreat. The day was over.

The enemy fought back to his lines. He himself admits he had suffered great losses. Our soldiers returned to their positions with trophies of victory. Glory to the Emperor, whose admirable sangfroid in danger astounded even those least afraid. Honor to the brave soldiers who took part in this magnificent defense. Even according to enemy reports we have taken 750 prisoners.

March 15

The day passes without disturbance. From time to time the monotony is broken by bullets fired from the Cuesta China. In the evening the Emperor gives me a direct order to make myself ready to march between two and three o'clock early the next morning.

March 16

At four-thirty Maximilian goes up to the Cerro de las Campanas. Our army had planned a decisive combined attack to be led by Miramón's division. According to His Majesty the attack did not take place because Miramón overslept. In the meantime dawn broke, and we could not expect much success from an attack on the already prepared enemy.

Enraged over this negligence, the Emperor orders two high-ranking officers on Miramón's staff placed on twenty-four-hour arrest because they did not [awaken their commander]. There is a gap here in the rescued portion of my diary, but I can well complete this

131

sentence from memory.

The days until March 21 passed without any occurrence worth mentioning.

Before noon on the twenty-first a large council of war met. On the same day the prince told me under the seal of silence that he had decided to send Márquez to Mexico City.

Until now the behavior of the ministry in Mexico City had been entirely suited to fill the sovereign with displeasure and distrust. The Austrians did not follow us as ordered, and it appeared that the ministry had completely given us up. State Undersecretary Campos undisputably played the worst role. Because of this Maximilian decided to call together a new ministry. First of all he named General Vidaurri, who had already proved to be so excellent, as Finance Minister and Minister President. Iribarren was designated Minister of the Interior.

Márquez, furnished with the most extensive authority, was to go to Mexico City as the Emperor's representative. There he would disband the old ministry, establish a new one, and raise money in the shortest possible time. No matter what happened he was to return to Querétaro with relief.

There are many who try to defend Márquez by saying he did not overstep his authority since His Majesty gave him carte blanche. That is just not so. Márquez was to return with relief to Querétaro in any event. His Majesty merely left to the general whether to march the whole garrison out of Mexico City and entirely abandon the capital, or to hurry to Querétaro's relief with some of the troops, leaving the rest to protect the metropolis. The Emperor personally told me so.

On this occasion I will analyze in general the accusations raised about Márquez's conduct before his departure to Mexico City, some of which are apparently justified. First of all, it is certain that he deserves most of the blame for the monarch's leaving Mexico City and going to Querétaro. It is said that he acted with the serious intention of destroying his sovereign. Actually, if he really did have this plan, he could have devised nothing more diabolical or better executed.

There is no doubt that the general persuaded Maximilian to quit Mexico City without troops, without money, and without ammunition.

Chapter Fourteen

If he did so on purpose, the charge of betrayal is entirely well-founded. If that was not his intention, one must still accuse him of a lack of principle in inducing the prince to take such a step under false pretenses. He will never be able to defend himself against this indictment. Even if the withdrawing French had destroyed much war materiel, there was still an abundance on hand. Moreover, at the time of the march from Mexico City to Querétaro, the best troops were left behind, along with all the cannon.

Over and over again Márquez played the old song with which the conservative ministers tried all along to lull the Emperor to sleep. To cover up our own lack of resources, he referred to the dissidents with the greatest contempt. He refused to concede that they were a consolidated force rather than a conglomeration of separate disorganized bands. In a letter to Lares from Querétaro, which I still partially remember, Márquez promised the greatest success for the expedition to Querétaro, especially since Maximilian could personally get to know his enemy—a band of criminals. However, His Majesty retained full confidence in the general. He had a reputation as a good soldier and as one of the few who had always been faithful to one banner, a rare recommendation among Mexicans.

Márquez, supported by his sovereign's favor, had the strongest voice in the council of war. His word counted for everything, and when he was not able to make his judgment prevail, it was still certain that only his wishes would be actually carried out. For he knew how to maneuver so adroitly behind the generals' backs that in the end the ruler always did what the chief of the general staff thought was good. I know directly from the source that this is how he thwarted the march against Escobedo's army towards San Luis Potosí, scheduled for February 26. At that time Escobedo and Corona's armies were fifty leagues away from each other, and under the circumstances an energetic blow to one side would have also paralyzed the other. In a council of war shortly before the siege, after both armies already had almost joined, Miramón reproached Márquez for this mistake in front of the Emperor and the generals. He accused him of transgressing all the rules of war by his behavior. Márquez could not vindicate himself and, giving no reason at all, only answered that he was justified. When

133

both enemy armies were completely united before Querétaro, the general again advised in the council of war that an aggressive course of action would fail.

On March 10, in a council of war on the Cerro de las Campanas, he even proposed that Maximilian and his army retreat to Mexico City. Beyond a doubt, carrying out this proposal would have led to disgrace and ruin for the sovereign and his troops. Since the enemy had strong cavalry at his disposal, an army of nine thousand men pursued by more than thirty thousand inevitably would have been annihilated—especially a Mexican army, which never is so unreliable or fights so poorly as when showing its back to the enemy. His Majesty emerged a hero from the events at Querétaro. Had he then followed Márquez's advice, history, to be indulgent, would have had to suppress his memory. But he did not listen to Márquez. Already he had resolved to fight and to fall if fate so wished, and he said so firmly to his generals.

If we brilliantly beat back the attack on March 14, no honor is due Márquez. Rather, it was his fault that greater results were not achieved on this day. Had we thrown back the enemy from the Cruz, the Río Blanco, and the Casa Blanca at the same time, a sudden massive breakthrough could probably have lifted the siege. And even if, as some assert, Márquez did not directly betray us on that day, he was at least a terrible general who should have paid for his mistake.

A sortie in the direction of San Juanico and Jacal was planned for the morning of the twenty-second to distract the enemy from Márquez's intended breakthrough. This was to be led by Miramón, who, however, was unaware of the Emperor's plan for Márquez. At four o'clock in the morning His Majesty went up to the Cerro de las Campanas to observe the action personally. I was in his suite. Miramón marched past the Garita de Celaya to the Hacienda de Jacal and San Juanico with a detachment of two thousand men. The enemy, surprised, abandoned his baggage and provisions and bolted as hurriedly as possible. Miramón succeeded in capturing twenty-two carts with food and munitions, sixty more oxen, and nearly two hundred head of sheep and goats. After this successful strike and after a cavalry unit which had just advanced was hurled back, Miramón led his troops back into the city at around nine o'clock.

The road into the city ran nearly three hundred paces south of the Cerro. The enemy was irritated and overwhelmed by need of provisions. Unable to take any other revenge he fired an endless number of shells at the column passing by us from his battery on San Gregorio Hill. Attentive observers saw not less than 219 shells land in a half-hour.

An imposing military spectacle offered itself to us on the Cerro: San Gregorio with its batteries on one side; our "richly laden Greeks drunken with joy over the plunder of the Trojans" on the other. In addition, there came shot upon shot, salvo upon salvo from the enemy cannon, continuous lightning and crashing, and the whistle of shells, which flew over our heads to the other side of the hill, kicking up dust and burying themselves deep in the ground.

In reality these shells were a gift from the enemy. Since we already had a considerable shortage of munitions, the projectiles salvaged by Querétaro children were a welcome present. Lucky finders were rewarded with two reales per piece.

Deserters who came over to us on the following day declared that the enemy was to hold a great victory celebration on the evening of the twenty-second. Like earlier deserters they told much about demoralization in the enemy ranks. Their detailed information about dissident strength and location coincided very closely with what we had observed.

On March 21, the Emperor dictated to me the following letter to Colonel Schaffer, which Márquez was to take to Mexico City, along with a similar one for Father Fischer.

Querétaro, March 21

Dear Captain Schaffer:

Since the great question which now preoccupies Mexico is a purely military one and the ministry in Mexico City, as seen from its communications, does not seem up to it, I have resolved to dissolve the ministry and to name General San Iago Vidaurri minister president, to deal with the situation.

The previous ministers remain: Aguirre for justice, education and public worship; Portillo for war; and the loyal, honest Murphy, until further notice, for foreign affairs and the navy. The new minister of the interior, who at the same time has to take over *fomento,* will only be announced later. Vidaurri is to take over the finance ministry as well as the presidency.

In addition to these measures I am sending General Márquez to Mexico City as my deputy, with unrestrained authority to restore order among the old women and raise lowered morale, while supporting and protecting my true friends. It is naturally understood that you belong to the latter group. In this matter Márquez has oral instructions from me concerning your person; you can turn to him directly for all concerns and wishes.

.Since military eventualities might make it necessary for Mexico City to do without complete army protection for some time, in such a case, Márquez is to bring you and Knecht with him in the center of the troops in the field. Under such circumstances I want to know that the archives are saved. What is too voluminous or insignificant will be burned under your supervision.

Unfortunately, since my orders given months ago for the sale of silver, wagons, horses, harnesses, the wine cellar, etc., have not been fulfilled on schedule, you, Sánchez Navarro, and Fischer must deliver these objects along with a validated inventory to the English Legation for safekeeping. In the unlikely event of the latter's refusal, commit the objects to the Austrian or Prussian Legation.

Márquez, Sánchez Navarro, and you too must sign this inventory. The legation concerned will be instructed to issue a validated receipt.

When the case arises, pack those objects of my private property which could be necessary for a longer campaign and different climates and seasons and send them here in the midst of the troops.

Since we suffer from a total lack of books here, I wish you would take along a few select works. You should not forget the brochure by State Councillor Martínez, with its different translations, as well as several copies of the volumes of my speeches and letters which I have had Boleslawsky print in the secretariat printing house. Also do not forget: the compilation of imperial laws, the military and civil code, the almanacs, the almanac of those decorated, the collection of official newspapers from the Regency assembled by Blasio, a good map of the country from the French collection presented by Pierron, and a very good telescope; all decorations, military and civil medals, medals of Guadalupe, medals *pro literis et artibus* still stored in the Chancellery of Orders and all castings of the different medals, in the blue strongbox next to the ministers' table in my private apartment in the Palace. In such a case it would be desirable to bring along the new castings for all kinds of coinage and to have the old republican ones destroyed.

Knecht must not forget the small collection of charts and annotations. Dr. Basch's trunk either has to be taken along or delivered to the legation concerned. Likewise, with the remaining private baggage.

God be With You.

We here are content and in good spirits despite all difficulties. We only grieve bitterly about the actions of the old weak wigs in Mexico City, who miserably engage in open treason out of sheer anxiety.

Hoping that we are allowed a happy reunion, I remain

Yours with kindest regards,

Maximilian

P.S. For three weeks we have received no news at all from Mexico City, from other points, including Veracruz, or from Europe. This is due to the egotistical betrayal by the old mandarins, but none of this distracts us from our path.

It is clear that by now the Emperor's eyes were partially opened; he already judged the conservative ministers according to their correct worth. Nevertheless, he still placed his fullest confidence in Márquez, to whom he had again entrusted a very important mission. To be sure, there exists no written evidence of how His Majesty's judgment of Márquez later changed. I will, however, find occasion to show that his opinion altered considerably during the siege.

At the same time, in the foregoing letter lies direct proof, as I have explained earlier, that Márquez was supposed to return to Querétaro.

Towards eight o'clock on the evening of the twenty-second, I took the general the letters destined for the capital. Márquez was lying on his bed when I entered the room, as if sunk in deep reflection, and started up alarmed when I told him I was delivering the sovereign's letters for Mexico City. At that moment Márquez's mission was still a deep secret. According to Maximilian's instructions, even I, though completely informed of it, was not to show the general that I knew he was the actual forwarding agent of the letters. I gave them to him, requesting that they be delivered by the ostensibly departing courier.

To this day it has remained a riddle to me that Márquez was startled. At the time I attached no meaning to it at all, and only later, when his behavior made him suspect, did I again remember the strange reaction. Perhaps he was surprised in one of those moments when, brooding over private thoughts, one believes himself overheard and betrayed by the sudden entrance of another person.

At eleven o'clock at night Márquez and Vidaurri and the officers of their staff left Querétaro, escorted by eleven hundred horsemen, and passed unnoticed through the enemy lines.

CHAPTER XV

Querétaro, Siege—Castillo as Chief of the General Staff—Fighting, March 24 and April 1—Fragment from One of the Emperor's Letters — Letter to Herzfeld — The Emperor Is Decorated — Hospitals in Querétaro—Letter from a Captured Officer.

The new chief of the general staff named in place of General Méndez was Severo Castillo, one of the most excellent military supporters of the conservatives and recognized as a trained and cultivated strategist. With Miramón and Arellano he was one of the few generals who had received their education in the military school at Chapultepec and held their rank in the army in accordance with real performance. This deserves special stress since most staff officers owed their advancement to repeated *pronunciamentos*. Many young commanders did not possess even a paltry academic education, and—I do not exaggerate—even generals looked at a situation with wondering eyes and naively asked what the lines and points on the paper meant. Castillo aroused particular astonishment as an educated military man. Rumor had it that he even studied books.

Apart from his theoretical knowledge, Castillo was an exceptionally composed and contemplative general. The endurance he could display when circumstances warranted could scarcely be foreseen in this small, weakly man with the soft, timid speech, who was, moreover, as deaf as a post. Even his deafness bothered him less in action that might be supposed. When he did not see the enemy fire, information from his adjutants as to its existence and location was completely sufficient for his orientation. Moreover, he was the Emperor's loyal and honorable servant, devoted to him to the very last, through and through a soldier. Unfortunately, he was a procrastinator and lacked initiative. He did bring considerably more organization to the defense, and the fighting after March 22 showed greater circumspection in leadership.

The twenty-third passed without disturbance, and we reassured ourselves that the enemy, discouraged by the rough lesson of the fourteenth, would refrain from attacking for the present. We certainly had no hope that he would withdraw and lift the siege, but we thought perhaps he would leave us in peace long enough for Márquez to return with relief. This would have to occur within fourteen days. In the meantime we could fortify the city properly to make our position more tenable for an offensive after Márquez's arrival. The numerical disproportion would then be less, and our young troops—who already were acquainted with the enemy and had brilliantly withstood the baptism of fire—joined with the elite corps from Mexico City would clearly be superior to the enemy.

But we were not to have quiet. On the twenty-fourth, the enemy, considerably reenforced by troops from the districts of Mexico, Puebla, and Guerrero, attempted a new assault. General Ignacio Martínez had added 5,000 men; Riva Palacios had brought 2,800. According to their own reports, these two corps swelled the dissidents' army to more than 40,000 men. General Escobedo, the general-in-chief of the enemy forces, had stationed his new troops, as yet unacquainted with our way of fighting, in the forward battle line. Prisoners subsequently stated they had been told that battle was safe and victory sure. In enemy reports the March 14 attack was passed off as a simple reconnaissance, thus masking their defeat.

By four o'clock in the morning strong enemy troop units were moving towards the south side of the city against the Alameda.

The enemy attempt at a combined attack on the fourteenth had failed, and he thought he could easily take the city from its most exposed side. We had not yet fortified at all the line between the Alameda and the Casa Blanca. Defense was solely and completely entrusted to our cavalry.

At eight o'clock in the morning, numerous infantry columns were plainly seen advancing on us from the Cuesta China. Following them were strong cavalry units and a considerable number of field guns. They deployed along the Cimatario, almost up to the Garita de Pueblito, where the general staff of our cavalry division was located. The enemy's movements convinced us first of all that he intended to gain a footing between Jacal and the Cimatario, where Márquez had broken through, thus cutting off our sole remaining communication with Mexico City. However, it could also be viewed as an attack on

140

our extended and exposed southern line.

The Emperor immediately grasped the importance of this crisis. Measures were taken to oppose the enemy, who incontestably wanted to storm the Garita de Pueblito from the Cimatario.

The attack was not long in coming. Around noon several strong infantry columns, bolstered by cavalry and supported by the fire of twenty cannon, attacked Mejía's division at the Casa Blanca. Between there and the Alameda, other columns advanced against Miramón's troops.

Both Mejía and Miramón let the enemy column approach peacefully. Only when they were within our range did our side open intense fire. The enemy, who until now had hurried forward on the double, immediately came to a full stop in the attack. Now Miramón's troops marched out of the Alameda, and Mejía's cavalry advanced from the Casa Blanca. Miramón's success was instantaneous, but the cavalry hesitated for a moment before the furious enemy artillery and rifle fire. Then General Mejía and his staff officers rode in front of the ranks, calling "Muchachos! Asi muere un hombre." (Boys! This is the way a man dies.) The bold cavalry general dashed forward, and after him followed the troops, enflamed by his heroic example.

The enemy fled both points. The same day Prince Salm-Salm led a brigade, whose command he had received from Maximilian because of his brilliant performance on the fourteenth. Major Malburg of the cavalry took fifty prisoners—we had more than four hundred, among them fourteen officers—and captured a banner with his own hand.

During the battle the Emperor was stationed on the roof of the Cruz with Chief of the General Staff Castillo, and Swoboda and Fürstenwärther, two staff officers. At around three o'clock in the afternoon the Cruz was also attacked by a column supported by the battery on the Cuesta China, but this attack also failed. One of the grenades pelting the convent exploded a few feet in front of the prince, but, miraculously, neither he nor any member of his entourage were injured. Three of the soldiers posted on the azotea were seriously wounded.

On the twenty-fifth and twenty-sixth of March, the enemy repeatedly attempted to storm the bridge over the Río Blanco leading into the city from San Sebastián. He was repulsed every time.

Among my papers I found the following fragment of a letter dictated to me by the Emperor and addressed to the prefect of Miramar. It dates from the period after the twenty-fourth.

> All my old sea comrades will be amazed to see me at the head of a real army.
>
> For the moment the admiral must take a rest. Now I am an active general-in-chief with high boots and a gigantic sombrero. All that is left of an admiral's trappings is a telescope, which never leaves my side. I pursue my new task with real passion, especially because of the enthusiasm and bravery of our young troops. In the navy I once made inspections night and day and liked to surprise ships and barracks. Now I inspect outposts and make nightly surprise visits to the outermost trenches. The enemy already knows us so well that every day when I appear at the outposts or outworks on horseback or on foot, he aims grenades, shells, and rifle bullets directly at me and my staff. During the action on the twenty-fourth, a grenade exploded three paces in front of me, fortunately wounding only three men and killing none. I shall send you a piece of the grenade for our small museum in Miramar.
>
> I must especially stress the fact that in this campaign I am by choice surrounded only by Mexicans and that, at this time in Querétaro, the only Europeans at my side are my physician, Dr. Basch, and a servant, Grill. There are no foreign troops in the garrison, while my opponent Juárez is richly supplied with North Americans. We have captured some of the latter officers.

On subsequent days the enemy left us generally unmolested. On each day's agenda stood shelling of the Cruz; morning and evenings for two hours at a time we were regaled with enemy shells.

The Emperor spent the interim working constantly with the general. Day in and day out he surveyed the fortifications which were now zealously accelerated by our side as well as the enemy.

In the midst of military pursuits, Maximilian formulated a plan to be implemented in case of victory after the arrival of General Márquez. The idea of a congress still uppermost in his mind, the sovereign intended to move the seat of government to Nuevo León, there convoking the legislative body. He told me he had long cherished the thought of moving the capital into the center of the country. Nuevo

León, a city of around 130,000 inhabitants and capital of the industrious state of the same name, seemed to him the most suitable choice.

After March 26 the enemy launched no further serious attacks. He restricted himself to thrusting his parallels forward and tightening the siege. Provisions in the city became very scarce thanks to sins of omission by our former chief of the general staff. Only the last meager ration of meat and corn was on hand. But we were in good spirits, for Márquez had to appear within eight to ten days at the latest.

The Emperor carefully watched the care of the sick. He visited the hospitals daily, comforting casualties and giving them presents out of his privy purse.

On March 29, at Maximilian's instructions and partially from his dictation, I wrote the following letter to State Councillor Herzfeld in Vienna.

March 29

Toward the end of February, I sent you a longer, detailed letter from Querétaro describing events from the thirteenth, the date we marched out of Mexico City, to the nineteenth, our arrival in Querétaro. We cannot depend on the delivery of letters which must pass through enemy territory. Therefore, first of all, I forward the duplicate of my first letter from Querétaro.

The French, pleasing all the world, have finally left Mexico City, as you no doubt know. As I write these lines, they are probably already in Veracruz. They are withdrawn without ceremony—less like someone who can contemplate with satisfaction what he leaves behind, than like someone who dares not look back because he fears getting in his face the dirt which marks his tracks. And in fact they have left very much dirt behind. Their marshal certainly was an honorable man. Before departing, he sold the government's furniture. Santa Anna's coach—which he had borrowed and which not even Juárez had confiscated—he converted to clinking coins. It is no secret that he negotiated with Porfirio Díaz and sold weapons and munitions to the dissidents. As if this were not enough, honorable Marshal Bazaine ordered destruction of as many weapons and munitions as possible forty-eight hours before his departure. He even engaged in direct betrayal by leaving four hours earlier than promised. This whole time the outer walls of the city were unoccupied.

After it was certain that the great cavalcade had left the

Valle de Méjico, His Majesty resolved to put himself at the head of his troops. Surrounded by the most tested generals of the Mexican national army, he would lead the thrust which would conclusively decide the perpetuation or annihilation of the Empire. Full of confidence, the Emperor committed himself this time to the Mexicans. I was the only European, let alone Austrian, in his entourage. Therefore, since I was a direct participant in the campaign and, at the same time, the only person who has the honor of knowing you, I have the task of faithfully reporting it to you.

[Here follows the description of our march.]

We reached Querétaro on the nineteenth. Generals Miramón and Mejía rode out to receive the Emperor. His Majesty's entry into the city was truly dazzling, and the popular reception was enthusiastic, joyful, and cordial. Cannon salvoes saluted our arrival at the city's outer walls. The city streets teemed with an exultant, cheering crowd. A local poet, capitalizing on the occasion, had voiced his inspiration in a hymn to the Emperor. Down from the rooftops, the loose sheets drifted among the crowd in the streets, which scrambled for them as if they were treasure. When he reached the Spanish Casino, designated as his Palace, His Majesty was greeted by the generals and the highest civil authorities and conducted to the cathedral for a solemn *Te Deum*. Afterwards, he received the generals, the prefects, and the Alcalde. General Miramón and the prefect, General Escobar, addressed His Majesty, the latter concluding with the words: "Dios os bendiga Senor y a nosotros tambien y que la posteridad Usted proclame con justos titulos de gloria: Maximiliano el grande."*

[Private messages follow.]

Now, however, the last two mails have been intercepted and destroyed by the withdrawing Frenchmen. All His Majesty's efforts are in vain as long as the ex-allies remain in the country. Since so many of his letters have been destroyed, His Majesty has temporarily ceased writing and has commissioned you to please send a copy of my letters which reach you through Davidson-Rothschild & Company to . . . .

[Private messages follow.]

*God bless you and us, Sire, and may posterity call you with the just title of glory: Maximilian the Great.

His Majesty also communicates indirectly because all important addresses and even his well-known handwriting attract the attention of French agents. At the same time, I will tell you that an order and authorization concerning the volunteers accompanied my letters for you and Colonel Leisser.

I write these lines in Querétaro where for a month we have been besieged by the enemy, who in the meantime his assembled forces out of the . . . .

[Here again pages are missing from my diary.]

On March 30, during the customary enemy cannon thunder and rifle fire, a solemn military ceremony took place on the square in front of the Cruz. The Emperor personally decorated the officers and men who had distinguished themselves in the actions on March 14 and 24.

However, the climax of this celebration was a surprise prepared by our young army for its imperial leader, a surprise designed to express the army's love and enthusiasm. After Maximilian had distributed the decorations, the generals stepped forward, led by Miramón. In a stirring speech the latter requested His Majesty's permission to decorate him with the bronze medal for general military merit. This medal, without distinction of rank, had been founded by the prince two years before. To be sure, during the siege of Querétaro he wore the Knight's Cross of the Guadalupe and Eagle Order, of which he was the Grand Master, but he had never wanted to wear the bravery medal. From the moment the army expressly bestowed it upon him, he wore it daily. He even gave it precedence over the other decorations on his chest.

On April 1, we made a sortie directed at San Gregorio Hill, from which, if possible, we sought to dislodge the enemy.

At three o'clock in the morning one thousand cavalrymen were posted below the northern slope of the Cerro de las Campanas to support the movement of our infantry. At this hour Miramón, who personally led the action, ordered the Salm-Salm brigade—comprised of the cazadores and the battalion from Celaya—to advance towards San Sebastián. The advance guard led by Pitner surprised the enemy, who immediately fled. The ease of victory merely tantalized Miramón and enticed him to advance farther. Pitner stormed San Gregorio with his battalion and took two cannon, but he had to withdraw because he had encountered a superior force. He did succeed in bringing the captured cannon to safety.

The day's success was the same as that of our actions up to May 15. Each time we drove the enemy from his positions, but with our extremely limited forces (at this time scarcely seven thousand men) we could not use our advantage. In all the action, victory consisted only of inflicting losses on the enemy; killing, wounding, or capturing many of his men; reducing his military supplies. But the rebels could easily stand such losses, while they only weakened us. They were true Pyrrhic victories.

April 1 through 11 passed without any significant military activity. But because food stocks in Querétaro were dwindling, our impatience for Márquez was growing by the hour. For this reason, the situation appeared increasingly critical.

The munitions supply had improved since we tried to overcome our original shortage as much as possible. A powder factory was set up in the Carmen Convent. Likewise, we made percussion caps with paper husks and cast shells by turning the metal of the church bells into grenades and lead from the theater roof into musket balls.

In the meantime, I was entrusted with a new office in addition to my personal service to the Emperor: general inspectorate of military hospitals in Querétaro. The disorder I found was difficult to eliminate. The Mexican physicians left the care of the sick entirely to inexperienced male nurses, at most, from time to time inspecting critical cases. Therefore, it was no wonder that these honorable colleagues plotted against me from the outset. They felt slighted by me as a foreigner and immediately tried to go on strike. The previous chief physician announced that he was ill, and a few threatened resignation. However, I refused to be intimidated and calmly continued my work.

Without endangering the sick, it was impossible to deal severely with those who passively resisted progress. Instead, I decided the best strategy would be to set up a model standard field hospital in the casino to prove the practicality of my instructions. The Emperor had his apartments there—two large rooms and two bedrooms with space for forty beds. These he made available to the clinic which I managed myself, assisted by a German physician, Dr. Prantl. Arrangements in this field hospital were in every way equal to those of a European institution. I also introduced my innovations in hospitals operated only by Mexican doctors and insisted that they be accepted since I myself had submitted to carrying them out. My Mexican colleagues could not object that as manager it was easy for me to arrange and command. They had no alternative but to accept the norms I had introduced.

It was well known that the war chest was empty and could furnish no money for the hospitals. So, at Maximilian's instigation, a charitable committee was formed from some of the wealthy citizens of Querétaro, the curate, and two other clergymen. This was the *Junta de Beneficia,* which I joined at the wish of the leaders.

Through generous contributions from the populace, we obtained mattresses, linen, wine, and lint. But because of the great number of casualties—not only our own but also the captured wounded—what we raised was insufficient, and the mortality rate was high.

The Emperor's concern about treatment of the sick evoked astonishment and bewilderment among the Mexicans. That he took care of prisoners provoked secret opposition from many who misunderstood such generosity.

The following letter, forwarded to the dissidents' camp from a captured captain, and of which I have a transcript, shows how well we treated prisoners.

Querétaro, April 26, 1867

Captain George W. Green of the Legion of Honor.

Dear Friend:

Through the Emperor's kindness we have obtained permission to inform you and General Corona that we are alive and well. I use this permission supposing that you believe us all dead. On the contrary, we are all alive, and I cannot commend His Royal Highness the Emperor and all of his officers enough. The French officers especially have spared nothing for our convenience and welfare. We have good quarters—comfortable, clean, and cool. Our living place far exceeds anything we expected, anything I ever thought they would provide prisoners of war. We can say the same about our treatment. I must also give the names of two Americans who are here: Mr. Clark and Mr. Wales. Mr. Clark is a reporter from the *New York Herald;* Mr. Wales has been here for some time. He was kind enough to help by buying us a few things usually forbidden prisoners of war. Our quarters were inspected by General Castillo, and every officer was asked whether food and lodging were satisfactory. Our comfort is not neglected. Have the kindness to ask Captain Bellon and Lieutenant Bailey what has happened to the things I left in camp, as well as to my saddle. Greet all our comrades. We hope to be exchanged soon. If possible, answer this letter, for which we will be very thankful.

Yours,

Captain John Brady

Lieutenant Joseph Pluke

General Corona:

Señor Miguel Ximenes is a prisoner of war here.

The above letter was originally drafted in English. On their own initiative the captured Mexican officers addressed a similar letter in Spanish to their troops in the enemy camp. Originally also among my papers, it was later lost.

CHAPTER XVI

Querétaro, Siege—Anniversary of Ascension to the Throne—Address by Minister Aguirre; the Emperor's Answer—His Majesty's Decoration Diploma—Two of the Emperor's Dictations—False Reports—Letter to the American Consul Otterburg—An Officer from the Enemy with a White Flag—A Communiqué in the Boletín de Noticias.

April 10 was the anniversary of Maximilian's ascension to the throne. On this day three years ago he received the second deputation at Miramar, bringing him the Mexican crown. This day was also celebrated in Querétaro. At ten o'clock a deputation composed of the highest military and civilian authorities and led by Justice Minister Aguirre entered the Cruz headquarters, bringing His Majesty their wishes for success.

On this occasion the minister gave the following address:

Your Majesty!

The memory of April 10, 1864 will never be extinguished in the heart of every Mexican filled with pure love of the Fatherland. For on this day Your Majesty deigned to accept the crown of Mexico, by this memorable deed forever opening the gates of hope for this unhappy land—gates which seemed closed to it by the unmerciful hand of revolution.

Half a century has raged the fratricidal struggle under the battle cry of order and freedom, in which opposing parties have fought each other for life and death. This quarrel could only have one sad result: choked by the blood of civil war, the vital principle autonomy would collapse.

By accepting the crown and by your pledge so to rule the nation that order and freedom might walk side by side, Your Majesty has derived a happy solution to the dangerous crisis. True to this solemn promise, all of Your acts as sovereign testify that Mexico was not deceived in adopting a monarch and in choosing You as its ruler.

Sire, I say this considering the facts and in the name of my fellow citizens.

The real epoch of individual and social guarantees; the epoch of just equality between the oppressed and the oppressor; the epoch of supreme efforts toward progress; the epoch of prosperity—such has been the Empire until now.

Sire, I have no doubt that I express the real opinion of the nation, even if these words are uttered in the midst of a city besieged by numerous armed troops who do battle with the Empire. I believe I have grasped the meaning of both contending principles.

The revolution is weak despite its mighty external appearance since it attacks the dearest interests of society. Basically speaking, it stands for nothing but the will of a few, who would subjugate the will of the nation.

In contrast, the Empire, reflecting the will of the nation, is based on justice.

Gentlemen! Emperor Maximilian was worthy of the enthusiastic homage our fellow citizens extended him as sovereign on behalf of the Mexican people, in the official statement sent to Miramar April 10, 1864. Today he is a thousand times worthier of this greeting, for he has shown greatness in misfortune and steadfastly proves fidelity and love of his adopted Fatherland. So much more must we love the nation—we who since birth have been its sons.

The Emperor answered this address with the following words:

Gentlemen!

Surrounded by dangers and hindrances of every kind, I receive you with goodwill on the day which begins the fourth year of My reign. I receive you as loyal representatives of the healthy and honorable part of the nation and of our brave and steadfast army.

Three years of hard work and great difficulties have passed. The fruit of this troublesome period is that I have been in a position to show My fellow citizens the constancy and loyalty of My government's views.

On the day I accepted My present position, in My distant native land, I voluntarily took an oath—to sacrifice myself in defense of Mexico's independence and integrity and to advance its welfare, as far as I am personally able.

For three years I have fought a painful battle against important and mighty influences destructive to our country. I have struggled and finally triumphed without a single stain on Our glorious national banner.

150

I could fight with perseverance and spirit, for I found the source of My duties and the basis of My legality in the numerous documents brought to Miramar by loyal citizens and in the historic expressions of majority opinion which established and maintain Me as chief.

At the moment the foreigners left our territory, thus fulfilling one of My highest goals—preservation of the integrity and the threatened independence of our Fatherland—I believed that remaining at the head of the nation perhaps might be a hindrance. Because of this doubt I convoked the legitimate advisory bodies, comprised, in accordance with My precautions, of people of every political complexion, in order to place in their hands the free determination of this question so delicate and important for My conscience.

The ministers and state councillors immediately expressed the almost unanimous opinion that under existing critical conditions it would be a serious violation of duty on My part to give up the post to which the nation had called Me. I therefore agreed to sacrifice Myself a second time and to tread the hard path which unfortunate obstacles daily made more difficult. At the same time, following My own inner impulse, before returning to the capital I called the nation from Orizaba to a free constituent congress. I wanted to submit Myself willingly to definitive scrutiny by My fellow citizens and at the same time to present them with all the deeds, documents, and accounts which, with the cleanest conscience, I can lay before them and the whole world.

You gentlemen know why the congress cannot yet freely come into existence. Our opponents obstruct it, probably because they cannot submit to the national will as We can. It is true; there are matters, already history, which only with difficulty can stand unpartisan examination by a free congress.

As a result, Our duties and present paths are very clearly defined.

Even as We do independence, We must defend national liberty and restore to the nation, at any price and as quickly as possible, its own free action and worth, which today suffer under the absolutist terrorism of social revolutionists.

On September 16, 1865, I told you: "Every drop of My blood is now Mexican, and if God wills it that new dangers menace our beloved Fatherland, you will see Me fight in your ranks for its independence and integrity."

Those who surround Me in the difficult and danger-filled days of Querétaro see that I have kept My word.

One year later on the same memorable day I declared: "Without struggle, without blood, there is no triumph for the state, no political development, no lasting progress," and I added: "I still stand where the will of the nation has called Me, despite all difficulties, without vacillating in My duties, for a true Hapsburg never leaves his post in the moment of danger."

Here I stand and fight joyfully beside you. Let us then faithfully persevere in our duties. God will reward our efforts and, as recompense, vouchsafe peace and freedom to our Fatherland.

And so may our cry forever be the unsullied motto: "Long live independence!"

On the same day a deputation of generals presented the Emperor the diploma of the bravery medal bestowed upon him by the army on March 30. The award reads in verbatim translation:

Sire!

The Mexican army, defending the city of Querétaro under Your Majesty's immediate command, represented by the undersigned generals, requests of Your Majesty the one additional honor: Your Majesty's wearing the medal for military merit on his breast henceforth.

Your Majesty, reward with this noble token of distinction the excellent services of the generals, commanders, officers, and soldiers, who in fulfillment of their holiest duties today only imitate the heroic bravery, the constant modesty, and unique self-abnegation of Your Majesty.

Never did a sovereign under such circumstances as Your Majesty descend from the height of the throne to live so in the midst of danger.

Sire, you have united with your soldiers, whose privations and hardships are unlike anything in the world, and to whom Your Majesty sets the lofty example of patriotism and sacrifice.

The nation Your Majesty endeavors to save and to strengthen—as well as strictly impartial history—will soon confer upon the sovereign of Mexico complete vindication.

For its part, the army, relying on Your Majesty's kindness, decorates you with the Medal for Military Merit.

Chapter Sixteen

Querétaro Headquarters, March 30, 1867.

Major General of the Infantry
Miguel Miramón

Major General of the Cavalry
Tomás Mejía

Brigadier General of the General Staff
Severo Castillo

Brigadier General, Chief of the
Second Division of the Infantry
Pedro Valdez

Brigadier General, Chief of the
Second Infantry Division
Ramón Méndez

Brigadier General, Director of the Artillery
Manuel Arellano

Brevet General, Chief of the
Corps of Engineers
Mariano Mejes

After three o'clock on the morning of April 11, we attempted to storm the Garita de Mexico. Miramón issued dispositions for our advance. However, the operation miscarried, thanks to the truly Mexican *mise en scène*.

The cazadores under Pitner again formed the advance guard, and the second battalion of Méndez's brigade followed under its brave Colonel Cevallos. These worthy troops advanced at double time up the garita under violent enemy cross fire. But here they had to take a wall in which there was no breach, no gate to force open. According to the vague notion of the Mexicans on the general staff, there was supposed to be a hole our men could forcibly penetrate. Fighting lasted a full hour. Only after heavy losses and after Pitner sustained a head wound, did our men withdraw.

The enemy remained passive even now. Avoiding attack, he continuously harassed us with cannon shells, from which both the soldiers and the people of Querétaro suffered greatly. Almost daily, men, women, and children were wounded or killed by projectiles in the streets of the city.

Our situation darkened with every day, and privation became extreme. Flour, corn, and meat were in scarce supply. We already began to content ourselves with horse meat, and the Emperor ate the same food as the rest of us. Even our financial situation was deteriorating. The forced loan was insufficient to cover requirements, and we needed money all the more because the price of the very few provisions still at hand had risen almost ten times. We imposed a head, window, and balcony tax, at the same time issuing an order that male inhabitants must help build fortifications. Those who balked were fined.

I still have two small fragments of Maximilian's dictation from those days, intended for my reports to Colonel Schaffer in Mexico City. I include both here in context:

> The Emperor very frequently visits outposts and the outermost trenches at night. This is disagreeable for the generals, because they are morally compelled to undertake similar nightly excursions. Most honored friend, you would be unable to suppress a melancholy smile if, remembering the old navy days, you saw His Majesty daily passing the communication trenches in the midst of the army, carrying a gigantic navy telescope in order to be a lookout everywhere in old seaman's fashion.

> . . . The minister of justice, accompanying Maximilian as countersigning minister, grimaced today when the Emperor announced to him his new earthworks project. Our friend . . . almost became sick with fear at this news. . . .

Meanwhile there still was no trace of Márquez, no certain information about him at all. We sent courier after courier, but none returned. One day a woman entered our camp, reporting that Márquez and his army had been seen near Cuautitlán. As it later developed this was a lie, incontestably invented by the enemy to reassure us.

Soon, more than three weeks separated Márquez's departure from his projected arrival date. Now, with a cavalry detachment, Mejía was to force a breach towards Mexico City and hunt up Márquez, or push on to the capital for relief. But Mejía was sick and therefore incapable of undertaking the mission. For that reason the sovereign assigned it to Prince Salm-Salm, who had proved his bravery, loyalty, and reliability repeatedly during the siege. He would be furnished with credentials granting him broad powers, and Major Malburg would accompany him as adjutant. During a feigned attack by our side, the prince was to escape and fight his way through to Mexico City with the hussars and a small cavalry detachment, the so-called *Exploradores del Valle de Méjico.*

Among the notes discovered in prison, I found the twenty points dictated by His Majesty concerning the Salm-Salm mission. These read as follows:

1) Three points for the diplomatic corps:
   a) Invite several men to come with Márquez.
   b) Use influence on the Juaristas to act humanely.
   c) Publicize that the Emperor will not yield if he cannot hand over his mandate to a legal congress.

2) Letter to Minister Murphy.

3) Tell only Generals Márquez and Vidaurri the real situation—that we have been eating horse meat for six days.

4) Good news for the public.

5) Order General Márquez to put the whole cavalry at the prince's disposal.

6) Prince Salm-Salm must obtain a definite answer from General Márquez within twenty-four hours. If not, he departs with the whole cavalry after twenty-four hours have elapsed.

7) If the prince leaves with the cavalry, he is to bring along at least 200,000 pesos and the Emperor's private moneys.

8) Send couriers with as much news as possible for as high a price as 1,000 pesos.

9) Prince Salm-Salm will announce in Mexico City that all generals urged the Emperor to leave Querétaro with the whole cavalry.

10) Prince Salm-Salm influences the foreign and domestic press. He takes along all editions of the *Boletín de Noticias.*

11) Mexico City will be abandoned entirely if there are enough troops there to relieve Querétaro, but not enough to leave a garrison in Mexico City as well.

12) Newspapers, domestic and European: domestic from February 20 on; cuttings from foreign newspapers beginning January 1.

13) Prince Salm-Salm brings along all stamped civil and military medals, the Medal of Guadalupe, some order decorations, and order and medal ribbons.

14) The prince will arrange with Father Fischer or Vidaurri secret funds for sending secret couriers.

15) Prince Salm-Salm brings some good books of historical or other subjects, according to the selection of Baron Magnus.

16) The prince brings especially a copy of the brochure by State Councillor Martínez and of the volume of the Emperor's speeches and writings printed at the secretariat press.

17) Prince Salm-Salm will not forget to ask General Márquez his news of General Negrete.

18) The prince delivers either to Márquez or Vidaurri secret documents with instructions concerning General O'Horan.

19) The prince is authorized to negotiate with the opposition party.

20) Prince Salm-Salm inquires about the yacht.

Maximilian informed me that Prince Salm-Salm was also to bear authorization to arrest Márquez if necessary.

At His Majesty's instructions I wrote the following letter to Marcus Otterburg, the American Consul in Mexico City, for delivery by Salm-Salm.

At His Majesty's request, I permit myself as a complete neutral to convey some data which you will possibly want to use at a suitable place.

As personal physician to the Emperor, I am at the camp of the imperial troops in Querétaro. Before us stands an enemy who, to be sure, calls himself liberal. But judged by his past actions, present ones, and, according to prisoner reports, those he proposes in case he wins, this claim—which will be heeded by civilized Europeans and Americans—reveals itself to be a complete lie. I will not speak about the well-known fusillade after Miramón's defeat and the shooting of the general's wounded brother. I want only to show recent evidence: The so-called liberals have hanged the corpse of a newly intercepted and killed courier in the sight of our people—an act one would expect of Comanches and Apaches.

At the head of our army stands a European prince; this

in itself completely guarantees that we conduct the war in a European manner. Nearly six hundred prisoners, among them sixty-two officers, are now in our camp at Querétaro. To be sure, they are not at liberty on their word of honor, as is the custom in Europe. But, as you see from the enclosed letters, they are treated in a way which must cultivate their respect and gratitude towards us.

Moreover, the fact that two American officers, a day after their capture, requested in writing the Emperor's permission to serve in his army, proves that the noblest Americans do not fight for Juárez. It would be impossible for me to say "fight for freedom." It is doubtful that their conviction suddenly changed only because of seeing the Emperor. It would be good if in some way you made our opponents aware of the difference between their conduct and ours. In view of the behavior of those Mexican generals now surrounding the sovereign, the fact that he alone is responsible for our army's humanity is self-evident. I stress this because, if our opponents do not change their methods, even Maximilian may be influenced by pressures for revenge from his generals and his officers.

Our enemies might observe that we have shot no prisoners, not even deserters, and that we hold six hundred hostages. Hoping you will take appropriate steps in the name of humanity and civilization, I remain, etc.

At two o'clock on the morning of the twenty-second we tried to break through enemy lines. But ground obstacles built in the meantime by the enemy—ditches and earthworks—hindered our cavalry's advance. After a two-hour struggle our small band had to yield to the hostile cross fire. The attempt and the Salm-Salm mission had failed.

Around eleven o'clock in the forenoon, a parley took place between Miramón and Arellano on one side and an enemy negotiator on the other. On the northern line where they met, hostilities temporarily ceased.

Maximilian told me that the enemy negotiator, Colonel Rincón Gallardo, proposed we surrender, promising the sovereign freedom to leave. In accordance with his instructions, Miramón could not accept these proposals, but he remarked that we were not at all compelled to capitulate; our possibilities for rescue were far from exhausted. Miramón questioned Rincón Gallardo as to why the liberals declined participation in a congress in which the national will would prevail;

why they followed Juárez's banner when his presidency had been legally terminated for two years; why they did not grant power to Ortega, who, according to the constitution, as president of the supreme court, should occupy the national presidency. Rincón Gallardo ansered he had no other instructions from the general-in-chief who had ordered him to these negotiations, that he must limit himself to the stated proposals, and that he could not answer the questions.

As was predictable, negotiations remained a complete failure, and after their termination hostilities began anew.

In the official daily newspaper *Boletín de Noticias* of April twenty-second appeared the following account by the general staff:

> A courier arriving yesterday from the capital brought a message from the Minister of the Interior addressed to the Emperor. Under the circumstances great importance must be attributed to its contents.

> In the message His Excellency Minister Iribarren reported to the Emperor that a detachment of dissidents which had reached the immediate vicinity of the city suddenly withdrew the following daybreak upon learning that strong columns had been called up against them in the capital. Our troops strike out through the environs of Mexico City, clearing them of all enemy hordes.

The article was accompanied by the following characteristic reasoning:

> This report, which seems so insignificant, nevertheless is of the highest importance. Conclusions can be drawn from it about His Majesty the Emperor's latest measures and about the people connected with them. One of these decisions was to change the personnel of the ministry in Mexico City as the situation required. General San Iago Vidaurri was named Minister President by the Emperor, and Don José María Iribarren who prepared the communiqué, was named Minister of the Interior.

> From this report derive consequences which the public will doubtless evaluate correctly:

> 1) The Emperor's appointments are approved by the new ministers, who are already in office; their acceptances prove that the situation is neither extremely difficult nor compromising.

> 2) Mexico City has nothing to fear, and reports circu-

lated by enemies of the country are worn-out attempts to deceive and blind the credulous.

3) Moreover, most important for the population of Querétaro is the fact that General Márquez has already left Mexico City. Were this not the case, the same courier who delivered the message from Iribarren would certainly have delivered a similar one from Márquez.

Without a doubt General Márquez will stand before this city within a few days, and the patriotic and meritorious populace of Querétaro will soon see the day when its suffering will end. Out of the generosity of our noble sovereign, they will receive most just recompense for sacrifices of every kind which they have brought and still bring to the altar of the Fatherland.

Like earlier and later reports included in my book, this one was falsified by the enemy and delivered to us by his own people. Without my adding anything, this fact clearly illuminates our situation at that time.

However, the reader might overlook one circumstance, to which I therefore will call especial attention. True Mexican sophistry characterizes the commentary on the short, completely meaningless communiqué from Iribarren.

Point one says that because the ministers accept their appointment, the situation in Mexico City cannot be difficult and compromising. Contributors to the *Boletín de Noticias* well knew their readers and could judge the degree to which this kind of interpretation corresponded to their general expectation.

The other arguments need no further commentary. However, concerning the last passage, I must still mention that Maximilian had promised the thoroughly pro-clerical population of Querétaro that in case of a victory he would immediately repay the forced loan and donate a golden crucifix for the main altar of the church in the convent of the Sanctissima Cruz.

CHAPTER XVII

Querétaro, Siege (Until May 13)—My Diary, From: April 23 to May 5—The Battles of April 27, May 1 and 3—Falsified Reports about Márquez and Vidaurri—The Soldiers' Women—Demoralization of the Troops—López—Preparations for the Breakthrough.

I can report the events after the twenty-second from my diary.

April 23

The hussars make a small sortie from the Cerro at a unit occupied with earthwork and bring back twenty-three prisoners, including one officer. With great suspense we watch enemy movements, hoping to draw a conclusion about Márquez's approach from them. Reportedly, he is in Salva Tierra, two days' march from Querétaro, and his advance guard under General Tavera has already engaged the enemy cavalry.

April 24

Fortification of the Cruz is completed, and the batteries mounted there should today make their debut with a cannonade at the Garita de Mexico. We open fire at seven o'clock, and the answer is immediate. Now begins an artillery symphony unlike any I have heard in a long time.

During the bombardment the Emperor is in the tower of the convent with Miramón, Salm-Salm, López, and Major Malburg. A round shot pierces the spire but fortunately injures no one. Maximilian and his suite descend from the tower covered with rubble.

A courier who left here ten days ago returns, but his statements are carefully hidden. It seems that he has nothing comforting to report about Márquez. His Majesty is outwardly pleased and reassured that things go well.

April 25

The day passes undisturbed except by the continuous bombardment. In conversation with me the monarch mentions the possibility of capture. "Nothing will find me unprepared. In case I am captured, my resolve remains firm to entreat Juárez immediately in writing, if he still wants blood, to take mine and be content with that."

This evening a surprise attack on San Gregorio is to occur. This hill is crucial to a possible breakthrough because it commands the entrance to Sierra Gorda. The latter is also commonly called the Sierra de Mejía because Mejía was born there and there has his greatest following.

Battle plans are as follows: The French captain, Curié, with volunteers from the cazadores battalion and other units, will surprise the enemy with an unexpected attack. The Salm-Salm brigade will support him. General Valdez, with the seventh and twelfth battalions, is to await the result near the garita and in case of success occupy San Gregorio. If the attack fails, he is to cover the withdrawal.

April 26

Because of a misunderstanding, the projected sortie did not take place. Miramón, who was to lead the action, did not oversleep again, but he misconstrued an announcement. He was supposed to break camp at twelve o'clock at night, *a las doce* (in Spanish), but he understood it to be *a las dos*—at two o'clock. However, a surprise attack could scarcely take place at this hour; reveille had already sounded in the enemy camp.

Prince Salm-Salm is named honorary adjutant in place of Colonel Ormachaea, who obtained a regimental command.

The Emperor tells me, "Márquez will attack tomorrow, and we will do likewise at the same time as he." I receive instructions to be completely ready to march.

In the evening all bells ring and reveille is sounded, ostensibly because favorable news has arrived, but really to revive and raise the people's sinking confidence.

April 27

At six o'clock in the morning occurs the attack Maximilian mentioned to me. I am not the only one to whom the action is described as a combined movement with Márquez. His Majesty also has General Méndez in the dark. Only Miramón and Salm-Salm are certain there is not the slightest trace of Márquez.

At five o'clock in the morning, Méndez moves against the enemy's extended parallels on the Cimatario. General Morett leads the advance guard, while Méndez attacks the Cimatario. Threatening the Garita de Mexico from the Cruz, Castillo will take it if possible, and General Gutiérrez will support Méndez with the cavalry. Command of the reserve and supervision of the whole action is under General Miramón.

The initial success is brilliant; the contrast between our soldiers' bravery and the enemy's cowardice is more apparent than ever. Our advance guard, again led by Major Pitner with his cazadores, encounters little resistance and quickly takes the first parallel without any losses. Immediately the enemy begins to flee en masse making no attempt at resistance. He leaves everything in the lurch, his cannon and his wagon train. Our attack column pursues as fast as the enemy flees, capturing booty of twenty-one cannon—among them, thirteen mountain guns. In addition, we take more than five hundred prisoners. Without great exertion, victory is ours within one hour.

In the Cruz the Emperor scarcely learns of our success when, accompanied by Salm-Salm, Arellano, and the hussars, he rides forward to the battlefield, amidst the vigorous cheers of the soldiers. Jubilation over the quick triumph momentarily causes us to forget our breakthrough, the true purpose of the attack.

The horses have been saddled in the Cruz since four o'clock; everything is packed so we can follow Maximilian at any moment.

Two full hours pass without the slightest incident and without our massing the necessary strength against San Gregorio. There, by exploiting the enemy's confusion, we could perhaps fight our way through most quickly.

Thus we leave the enemy time to assemble and organize. In the meantime, the uppermost parallel of the Cimatario is occupied by fresh troops, the enemy's elite units.

To show off in front of his prince, Miramón orders a new storming of the Cimatario. But this time the enemy stands fast; he receives us with intensive fire from his eight-shot guns, forcing our cavalry to retreat.

During this last action, His Majesty is on the battlefield in the midst of a deluge of bullets. Followed by his staff, he dashes with drawn sabre in front of our cavalry, who are discouraged by the furious fire, and tries to stir them to advance. But even his presence can bring no renewal of the attack. At one o'clock in the afternoon we retreat into the city. The day is lost despite the morning's victory, despite the captured cannon and prisoners.

Our goal is not attained; the intended breakthrough, not accomplished. The disillusionment of those who this morning still believed Márquez would come is bitter, and only a few still hope for relief.*

April 28-30

During these three days hostilities ebb, a natural result of exhaustion from the twenty-seventh. All the while, both sides maintain a lively artillery fire.

May 1

In the early morning there is another attack on the Garita de Mexico and the Hacienda de Callejas. As always the advance guard is led by Pitner, and this time also the first victory is ours.

The Hacienda de Callejas is taken by assault, and our men move at double time up the heights towards the Garita. Here, although the enemy has considerable forces at his disposal, our men press their way in after a short fight. A murderous struggle follows inside of the Garita. The enemy mounts increasing support at this point, but our men offer stubborn resistance and hold their ground in the building. At the critical moment the brave commander of the *Guardia Municipal,* Colonel Joaquím Rodríguez, falls. His battalion, which has always fought well, now loses courage without its leader and yields to the enemy.

Our losses are eighteen wounded, two dead, and thirteen missing.

May 2

Solemn burial rites for Colonel Rodríguez are celebrated in the Congregación Church. The Emperor attends the funeral with his entourage.

At four o'clock in the afternoon, on the request of Field Chaplain

---

*In due time after I had left the prison in Querétaro, I spoke a great deal with officers of the liberal army about both of these attacks on the twenty-seventh. All admitted to me that the panic among their soldiers and the disorder shortly after the evacuation of the Cimatario were so great that undoubtedly, if we had used our advantage without delay, we could at very least have escaped with our whole army.

Father Aguirre, His Majesty is photographed at headquarters. At this time he jokes that the priest is cleverly using the opportunity to obtain a memento of him while he is still alive.

Rumors of approaching relief again begin to circulate. This time word is that Generals Chacón, Olvera, and Márquez are approaching. However, we are no longer optimistic.

May 3

We make another sortie—this time at San Gregorio—but our side soon stops fighting and begins retreat.

During the battle Maximilian again stays in the tower of the Cruz. Once more a round shot penetrates the spire and lands between the sovereign and General Arellano, grazing the latter lightly on the shoulder.

The Emperor informs me that Márquez is certainly in the vicinity. I reply that in Querétaro victory news about the general is hardly believed, expressing the conviction that we will have to help ourselves.

Reports in the city seem not to surprise him, for he calmly answers that ultimately we shall know whether or not Márquez has arrived.

May 4

Quiet at all points except for constant enemy bombardment. Our line facing the Cimatario is now safer; the capture of twenty-one enemy cannon has naturally left a serious gap in the battery posted there.

May 5

Exceptional quiet this whole day. The dissidents celebrate the anniversary of their 1862 victory over the French at Puebla, under the command of Zaragoza. This celebration seems to occupy them completely, allowing us a day to recover.

Suddenly at seven o'clock in the evening—I am just returning from a visit to General Mejía, who is ill—in the course of a few minutes, they open upon us a truly murderous fire from all sides. It is the heaviest of the whole siege, and the rifle fire is so intense that through the rattle of the salvoes we scarcely hear the cannon thunder and the bursting of grenades.

With blind faith in this day's lucky star and stirred by the day's liquor consumption, the enemy pushes forward impetuously on all fronts, deploying his main force against the bridge over the Río Blanco. But the initial spirit soon subsides after some well-aimed grapeshot sobers them up. Firing lasts around an hour, and we have no more than two slightly wounded on all our fronts, while our cannon, served by artillery men who have not been drinking, wreak havoc in the enemy ranks.

Here ends the salvaged portion of my diary, and I present the conclusion of the siege from memory and from official documents at hand.

After this the enemy stayed quietly in his entrenchments and responded rather passively. But want in Querétaro concerned us more than the enemy in front of our lines. Hunger plagued our soldiers, and its pernicious effects—physical weakening and debilitation—undermined confidence and combat capability.

In the meantime, the enemy was not as idle as he seemed. His activity was not military, however; he regaled us with false reports.

In the May 7 *Boletín de Noticias,* edited at headquarters, appeared two such falsified dispatches. The introduction—"Since it is unnecessary to hide from the enemy the communications from Generals Márquez and Vidaurri which have finally reached His Majesty" —furnishes evidence that headquarters was fully aware of the nature of these writings. We knew the dissidents were too well served by their secret police in Querétaro for us to guide them with such meaningful news if it were true.

I repeat here the document in question:

Long Live Independence, Long Live the Emperor, Long Live the Mexican Army!

Since it is unnecessary to hide from the enemy the communications from Generals Márquez and Vidaurri which have finally reached His Majesty, we publish them to insure peace of mind to the army and the inhabitants of this admirable and so hard-afflicted city. Defenders and friends of the national cause will read enthusiastically the favorable reports which the worthy sovereign has received from Mexico City. Doubters and anarchists must finally believe that only a short time of privation for the army and the people will yet suffice successfully to repulse the Juaristas and to free our society from the horrors of demagogy.

His Majesty received the following reports:

"Your Majesty

As I had the high honor to inform Your Majesty by my messages of the sixteenth and nineteenth of this month, I marched from Mexico City on the seventeenth with an army organized as follows:

I.	Infantry Division
Command:	General Rosas Landa
1. Brigade:	General Ruelas
2. Brigade:	General Oronoz

II.	Infantry Division
Command:	General Zerez
1. Brigade:	General Vega
2. Brigade:	Colonel Pozo
Artillery:	2 batteries

III.	Cavalry Division
Command:	O'Horan

Hussar Regiment, 6 and 9.
Cavalry Regiment, 1 squadron of the Empress's Regiment.

IV.	Reserve Division
Command:	General Vidaurri
Infantry Brigade:	General Piña
Cavalry Brigade:	Colonel Quiroga
Artillery:	2 batteries of mountain guns and 36-pounders.
Army train:	90 Carts

The commissariat has sufficient funds.

His Excellency General Vidaurri marches by a different route than my troops.

He intends to join me at the Hacienda Jordana. An adequate garrison remains in Mexico City under the command of General Tavera.

I assure Your Majesty that there is no need to worry about protection and preservation of the capital and that the garrison there is sufficient to last a long time.

I have the honor of enclosing a message to Your Majesty from His Excellency General Vidaurri.

Signed

General-in-Chief

Márquez"

"Monte Alto, April 27, 1867.

Your Majesty!

Uncertain whether the present message will reach Your Majesty's hands, I present relevant details concerning the army in the field and the natural and unforeseen hindrances with which I and General Márquez have struggled in order to follow Your Majesty's orders. I am satisfied to inform Your Majesty that operations will begin against the besiegers of this city. As in earlier dispatches, I am honored to inform Your Majesty that the cabinet has been organized according to Your wishes and that during my absence His Excellency Iribarren, whose respect and energy are well-known to Your Majesty, will be its president.

Morale in the capital and its current defense posture are supremely gratifying.

Signed: Finance Minister

San Iago Vidaurri"

Istlahuaca, April 23, 1867.

No longer could we expect relief by Márquez. It puzzled everyone, why after a six-week absence not even the slightest credible news about him had arrived. The Emperor himself now considered his conduct betrayal.

One day when he was walking back and forth with me on the plaza in front of the Cruz, he commented that he was now really beginning to believe he had been betrayed by Márquez and Vidaurri. No one should wonder that such circumstances severely shook our soldiers' endurance; desertions, until now a rarity, became frequent. Considerable blame for this flight belonged to the soldiers' women, who accompanied our troops in large numbers. The common Mexican soldier generally endures hardships and privations with ease if he is spared the lamentations of his woman. It is characteristic of the Mexican military that all its units include women and children. On the march and in the field this peculiar addition to the train is often advantageous, for to some extent the women replace our European quartermaster. As soon as a campsite is chosen, they hurry ahead of the troops and collect foodstuff with a business-experienced eye, carrying out the most abundant forage in the shortest time. Naturally, in

168

a city under siege they are merely a troublesome burden, helping consume provisions all the faster. The dissidents, at any rate, enjoyed a richer diet than we. We had no more *tortillas* and *frijoles* (black beans, the favorite Mexican dish). Hollow-eyed hunger had not yet called at the enemy camp, and the short way to the other side was quickly crossed.

What was it worth after long deliberation to serve further a cause to which one had dedicated oneself and shown goodwill in better times? Why bear need and privation when a good reception was likely from the enemy, who had the clear advantage? No Mexican is capable of sacrifice; whoever offers him the greatest material advantage gains his convictions and his services.

Every day desertions mounted. Even the Empress's Regiment, which, if not brave, was exceedingly trustworthy, proved susceptible. The Emperor asked López, organizer and former commander of the regiment, for an explanation. By all sorts of evasions, López avoided a definite answer. He told me at that time that he himself would prefer to be back in Orizaba or better, to completely leave Mexico— "Que a mi me pesa como Mexicano con tanta canalla y picaros"— which depressed him with its rabble and its scoundrels.

I did not suspect that these words expressed López's own guilt-laden conscience. At this time he was already negotiating with the enemy about his betrayal, and this comment reflected the judgment that his conscience told him the world would make.

Mexican by birth, with unimpressive blue eyes and blond hair (rare among Mexicans), López had a blemished past. He had repeatedly betrayed his own countrymen, earlier to the Americans and recently to the French, and counted few friends in the army. However, the Emperor liked him; he had been one of the first to offer his services after the landing at Veracruz. His modest appearance, his skillful ways, impressed Maximilian. In addition, López was an officer of the Legion of Honor and most highly recommended by the French. Thus he won his sovereign's trust and obtained from him the Empress's Regiment (cavalry). As its commander he succeeded in assuring His Majesty's favor.

On the whole his unit conducted itself well and because of good behavior and excellent equipment was a sort of ceremonial regiment. It had never proved itself at Querétaro, but during the siege López played a significant role. He was commander of the Cruz and, even if not in title, was in fact adjutant to the Emperor. Maximilian entrusted him with secret orders, with providing couriers, etc., and López accompanied him on inspection tours which he made unarmed in the earliest morning hours. He appeared in every respect the monarch's clear favorite.

May I be allowed to insert here a small episode which I recall involuntarily when talk turns to López. The prince also mentioned it repeatedly in the prison at Querétaro. Maximilian was always fond of dogs. As a result, during the siege he was presented a pretty spaniel. Originally the pet of an imperial officer, the dog had fallen into enemy hands at San Jacinto, returning to us across the lines during the siege. It attained a certain fame in camp, taking to the ruler with remarkable devotion and showing friendliness to everyone who came to see its master. It was only bad tempered with López. To the latter's great anger the dog lunged and snapped at him as soon as he appeared. The explanation might have been some injury he had caused the animal. Nevertheless, this chance coincidence is still strange, and the Emperor often spoke of his loyal "Bebelle" and its hatred of López.

Our situation in Querétaro was now clear. We realized we could no longer remain in the city; we had to break through at all costs. Even if he had already left Mexico City, we no longer could await relief from Márquez.

The question now was where to turn. Under no circumstances could we dare escape toward the capital. We were too weak to continue the march after breaking through enemy lines. In this case Escobedo's and Corona's armies, far superior to ours in number and means, would be at our rear, while in front would stand the army of Porfirio Díaz, presumed to be besieging Mexico City. Caught between these three bodies of troops, our small force would be wiped out instantly. There was only one route open—the road to the Sierra.

The enemy could not follow us there. If we could reach the pass to the Sierra, nearly six leagues (three miles) from Querétaro, a general levy of the populace would supply a force sufficient to repel the dissidents. Indians of the Sierra Gorda, as I have already mentioned, clung to Mejía with body and soul. They called him their "Don Tomasito." Once he was in their mountains, they responded to him as true leader.

Sierra inhabitants are a real mountain people. Strong in defense of their passes and gorges, they only needed the right commander. If he understood them and treated them in their own peculiar way, he could tear them from their passivity. By this time liberal units had already been bloodied in the Sierra Gorda, whose villagers consistently remained loyal to the conservatives.

As planned, the Emperor would wait in the Sierra for further developments, especially for information about the fate of the capital. He would decide from that.

In case of the worst, the way from the Sierra to the Gulf of Mexico was open. The Austrian corvette *Elizabeth,* commanded by Captain von Gröller, lay in the harbor of Veracruz, and it would have been easy to have it sent to Tuxpan, the port most accessible to the mountain.

Therefore, we decided to fight our way out towards the Sierra. Preparations were made, and Salm-Salm took over formation of the Emperor's escort: Colonel Campos's troops, mostly collected from Vidaurri's men and other completely trustworthy units; Khevenhüller's hussar squadron, originally a complement of fifty, expanded in Querétaro to one hundred by addition of eighty men from the Exploradores del Valle de Méjico—both units commanded by Major Malburg; the Empress's Regiment; the Fourth Cavalry Regiment, under a new commander selected for this purpose, Lieutenant Count Pachta. López was given supreme command of these combined units, a demonstration of the extensive trust His Majesty invested in the traitor.

In view of the sad situation one should examine the closely related question of why the monarch was still in Querétaro. This is chiefly traceable to his preoccupation with the mistaken belief that his duty was not yet completely accomplished. After demonstrating his courage, endurance, and capacity for self-sacrifice; after sharing privations and hardships with his soldiers for months; after facing the most disgraceful betrayal, even by the conservatives, he still hesitated to leave this unlucky place of ruin. He did not want to damn that party which had induced him to remain and could not believe they also cheated and deceived him most disgracefully. His sense of nobility made him prey to their low selfishness. And he still nourished the hope that Márquez would bring victory.

There was also Miramón, who advised holding Querétaro. I do not want to accuse this man who atoned for his mistake with his life; I only report his comment to Maximilian on this point. Shortly before the sortie of April 27, the Emperor told me after a long discussion with the general: "Miramón has just convinced me that he can hold the city for three to four months with the means at hand."

All the foreign officers in Querétaro, including the sovereign's adjutant, Prince Salm-Salm, and Pitner, now a lieutenant colonel, were already convinced that the only solution was to fight our way through.

Now naturally everyone united to get us out of the city. But circumstances had completely deteriorated. The cavalry, from which Márquez had carried off the best forces, weakened daily, and most of the men were unfit for combat because of the loss of horses to starvation and slaughter.

Moreover, possibilities of a breakthrough decreased with every day because the enemy in the meantime had been actively entrenching and had encircled us in an almost impenetrable wall. But we had no other way out; this was our last hope.

Most preparations were now directed by General Mejía, who to his bitterest regret had lain sick in bed for weeks. Despite fierce pain he now aroused himself to revitalize headquarters. Grief-stricken, the sick general had followed events in the city, and he expressed particular indignation over Márquez's disgraceful behavior.

One forenoon I visited Mejía and ran into Colonel López who had come on an errand from Maximilian to discuss finding a trustworthy courier. Mejía commented, "I do not understand Márquez. If we had sent a sergeant to Mexico City, it would have been better."

Once he had alluded to failure, the general expounded at greater length, accurately observing that the present emergency was merely a consequence of the mistake begun at Matamoros (June, 1866). In

172

Chapter Seventeen

Matamoros, not in the capital, lay the key to the Empire. There at all costs we needed a strong garrison to stop American intervention. The general finished excitedly—"How I then asked only for men. I wanted to arm and feed them myself, but I was ignored, and with Matamoros we gave up everything."

Mejía concentrated primarily on organizing a national guard from the citizens of Querétaro, among whom he was already very popular. They would support us in the escape and undertake the defense of the city. There was a massive turn out for the civilian corps, and we could still hope the breakthrough set for the morning of the fourteenth would succeed.

CHAPTER XVIII

Querétaro, the Night of the Fourteenth-Fifteenth—The Morning of the Fifteenth—Capture—López's Betrayal—José Rincón Gallardo— May Fifteenth.

Around eleven o'clock on the night of the thirteenth, a council of war met and postponed our departure from two-thirty the next morning to the following night.

With the strong rush of citizens to the municipal corps, Mejía had not yet succeeded in completely organizing it, so he requested extra time to properly arm, distribute, and position volunteers. He urgently needed their energetic cooperation for success in the action. Thus we set departure for twelve o'clock on the night of the fourteenth.

We were all ready to march, having packed only what could be taken along on horseback.

The Emperor himself was full of confidence in the undertaking. On the afternoon of the fourteenth, he said to me, "I am very pleased that it is coming to an end once and for all, and I have high hopes for success. My luck has not left me yet. Tomorrow is my mother's name day, and, even if you consider me superstitious, I believe it will bring me good fortune."

His Majesty's baggage was divided up among the escort; documents, records, and writings among his entourage. His private funds were distributed the same way: among Salm-Salm, the ordance officer, Pradillo, the sovereign's secretary, Blasio, the commander of the special escort, Colonel Campos, and me. Even López received a portion.

At ten-thirty (on the night of the fourteenth), López came for the money, complaining that he did not receive gold like the others, but a lesser sum in silver.

After ten o'clock a council of war convened. For reasons unknown to me—this time at the wishes of General Méndez—we again postponed departure until the next night. At eleven o'clock His Majesty once more summoned López to discuss the sortie.

In prison Maximilian told me about this conversation: "On that evening," he said, "I pinned the medal for military merit on him with

175

my own hands, instructing him that, in case I were wounded during the breakthrough and he saw I could not escape, he was to end my life with a bullet."

The sovereign did not go to bed until one o'clock despite the fact that the renewed postponement had been decided by eleven. Excitement robbed him of sleep. At two-thirty, he had me awakened. A deep nocturnal stillness enshrouded headquarters as I walked across the corridor.

He was suffering a severe colic attack. Bad food and endemic influences after the rainy season had bred dysentery in both camps, and now even the monarch was afflicted. I stayed nearly an hour until the pains were quieted and then lay back down on my bed fully dressed.

I was suddenly awakened before five o'clock. Into my room stormed two men, one of whom I recognized as Lieutenant Colonel Jablonski, the accomplice traitor. Both shouted, "Where is Prince Salm-Salm? He must be awakened at once." With these words they disappeared, and I jumped up. It was clear that something extraordinary must have brought them both into headquarters at this hour. I did not waste much time in thought. Hurriedly awakening my servant, who slept in the same room with me, I ordered him to saddle my horse quickly and rushed into Salm-Salm's room. He was already awake and dressed, and I asked him what was happening. "Hurry! we have been taken by surprise," he answered. "Tell Fürstenwärther (an Austrian captain in the general staff) to have the horses saddled immediately."

I had just instructed Fürstenwärther when the Emperor's Mexican valet, Severo, came to inform me that his master wanted to speak with me. I stepped into his room, to find him already dressed. "Nothing will happen," he said to me with great calmness. "The enemy has broken into the *huertas* (kitchen gardens). Take your pistol and follow me out onto the square."

As the head steward Grill later informed me in prison, Maximilian did not for one moment lose his composure after Salm-Salm informed him the enemy had broken in. While dressing, he had his drawn sabre put at the door to have it ready for defense. Grill went on to say that he suspected the ruler expected to defend himself against a direct, personal attack.

Following His Majesty's order, I went to my room to fasten on my revolver. There my servant told me he was prevented from saddling the horses by an officer unknown to him, who took away the saddle blankets. I had personally relayed the instructions for hussars to mount up, and since I assumed I was to accompany the Emperor on horseback, I tried to get my horse. Therefore I ordered the servant to follow me and point out the officer who had hindered his obeying instructions. In the entrance to the convent courtyard, we found him wrapped in one of my blankets; the other was over his shoulder. Since the sovereign had reported only a forced entry into the kitchen gardens, I could only think that an officer inside the convent itself was one of our men. With him, wearing the uniform of the enemy regiment, were about ten men—*Supremos Poderes*—whom I assumed to be imperial soldiers. We had captured quite a few of them who now fought in our units in their old uniforms, so I felt no surprise at their clothing. Besides, neither our side nor the dissidents had an exact uniform; my mistake was quite natural.

I requested that the officer return my blankets and asked him if he did not know who I was, that I was court physician to Maximilian. He sought an excuse and, pointing to a staircase to the roof of the convent, said: "Your blankets will be up there." I still did not understand. Angry at the useless delay, I reached for my revolver. Then I heard him call to his soldiers: "Desarme lo." (Disarm him.)

I saw a row of bayonets lowered at me and heard bolts cocking. Now the situation was clear. It would have been lunacy to resist. Accompanied by the officer and his soldiers, I climbed the stairway to the roof of the convent and found to my astonishment everything already thickly occupied by enemy soldiers of the same Supremos Poderes. "I now declare you my prisoner," the officer told me. (His friends later informed me that his name was señor José María Pérez.) "I am aware of that," I growled. My revolver was taken away immediately, and Pérez began to rummage through my pockets with the skill of an expert. Naturally, my watch and the money belt filled with gold coins did not escape his sensitive fingers. He took everything.

Moreover, it appeared that the unexpected booty made him more charitable towards me.

I was greatly alarmed at my situation. As I stood there completely plundered, I could not help offering the surgical case I had been allowed to keep. However, this he refused. I also retained my notebook. In this land where there are no bank notes, naturally no one looks for papers.

Whether I carried papers or important documents did not interest the officer of the Supremos Poderes. He wanted only what clinked and was materially valuable. He would have left an entire archive undisturbed in my pocket.

I was now led into the tower where the Emperor so often had braved enemy bullets, and given a two-man guard. I thought I would die of rage and inner shame. It was not only my being a prisoner that aroused this feeling. What provoked me most was fury that I had practically invited my capture. I found solace in the one thought, that surely Maximilian and his entourage had left the Cruz in time.

Before long, I was led down from the tower to the square of the convent. Here stood a crowd of prisoners, and we were all transported together through the Cruz kitchen gardens to the Hacienda de Garreta.

On the way, several fellow sufferers joined us. My illusion that I was the only one of the attendants taken prisoner was soon dispelled when I discovered all the servants in one carriage. They also had been captured even before they could follow their master, some in the Cruz itself, some on the square. En route to the hacienda, we halted by a small church. There the prisoners were divided into two groups: one, mostly common soldiers, was led off separately; the other, many officers and myself, had a long wait before continuing on our way.

We now met His Majesty's ordance officer, Lieutenant Colonel Pradillo, who galloped past, holding a white banner and accompanied by several enemy riders. As I later learned, the sovereign had sent him to Escobedo with the message often expressed during the siege, that he required no indulgence himself, that they should be satisfied with his blood and spare the others—especially his entourage.

The watchful eye of an officer in our escort fell on the last article of value I wore: a signet ring given me by a good friend as a memento before my departure from Europe. "Would you like to give me what you have here?" he asked, in the usual friendly Mexican fashion. "Let me keep that," I answered. "It has little value and is only important to me as a gift from a friend." "So what?" he blurted out. "I am also your friend." And he took the ring.

Around eight o'clock we reached the hacienda, where we were brought into a courtyard whose exits were carefully guarded. Once there, I demanded to speak to the commander. I was presented to him, and, identifying myself as the Emperor's physician, I voiced concern that he had been captured. I urgently needed to reach him because he was sick and required my help. The commander, a polite man, promised to fulfill my wishes if possible.

What I report in the following paragraphs about Maximilian's capture I learned from Prince Salm-Salm and Lieutenant Colonel Pitner, who were forced to surrender on the Cerro de las Campanas, along with the ruler.

Immediately after ordering me to follow him onto the square, His Majesty had left the Cruz with General Castillo, Prince Salm-Salm, Lieutenant Colonel Pradillo, and the secretary, Blasio. Reaching the gate, he ran into enemy sentries, who let him and his party pass on orders of the enemy colonel, José Rincón Gallardo. Standing there with López, with whom he had a few whispered words, he called to the soldiers: "Que pasen, son paysanos" (let them pass, they are civilians).

From the square of the Cruz the sovereign went towards the Cerro with Castillo, Salm-Salm, and the others. On the way there and on the Cerro itself, General Mejía, Lieutenant Colonel Pitner, Count Pachta, Major Malburg, and Captain Fürstenwärther joined him.

By this time, all our lines were completely in enemy hands; only a small group of cavalry stood at the foot of the Cerro. Even this shrank by the minute as deserters, overcome with fright, fled to the dissidents. The latter now swarmed en masse from all sides and bombarded the Cerro with a hail of grenades, mostly from our own guns.

The Emperor turned to Mejía and asked if a small group of

determined people could break through, but the general denied the possibility. Maximilian remained calmly on the Cerro, hoping that one of the many grenades exploding there might end his life. "Ojala" (If God wills), he said, turning to Castillo. He had enough composure to dispose of two pieces of writing: a new political and military arrangement of the country and a simplified settlement for the imperial household, which he had worked out shortly before, during the siege. These he ordered Captain Fürstenwärther and Secretary Blasio to burn. Five times more he asked Mejía if a fight through were possible, but the general's answer was always no. Finally, he ordered the white flag put up on the Cerro. Nonetheless, bombardment of the hill lasted without interruption a good while longer. Suddenly the firing stopped, and the enemy general, Echeguerray, was the first to come galloping up on the Cerro. General Mirafuentes immediately followed and took His Majesty's sabre. General Riva Palacios then led him back to the Cruz, to the same room which two hours previously he had occupied as reigning monarch.

For details of the capture I must rely on descriptions by eyewitnesses—that of Lieutenant Colonel Pitner, which has already appeared in Vienna in *Sport,* and the one by Prince Salm-Salm, soon to be published.

Command of the Cruz and supervision of the prisoners was entrusted to General Pancho Velez. Around ten o'clock, one of his adjutants came to the Hacienda de Garreta for me and the imperial servants.

Only with difficulty could I master the deep feeling which had overcome me on the ride back to the Cruz when, climbing the steps, I saw the changes since midnight. With a heavy heart I approached the monarch's room and remained a moment spellbound on the threshold. He spotted me, walked up to me and put his arm around me in tears. But he quickly regained his self-control, pressed my hand and turned away with a deep sigh. There was a gloomy pause.

Only then did I notice that Salm-Salm, Blasio, Pachta, and Pradillo were also in the room. Maximilian walked a while, submerged in thought. Finally, he broke the silence. "I am happy," he said, already in a calmer tone, "that everything has happened without more bloodshed. I have done what I intended to do. I have cared for you all." He told me he was very content with the behavior of the enemy officers, especially with that of Escobedo and Riva Palacios. "They are better than I had imagined," he remarked. "Moreover, I am proud that I have educated them by my methods during the siege. They see the results of my clemency towards our prisoners."

Until now, the great excitement had kept the sick prince on his feet. But with the return of relative calm, a vigorous reaction set in. He had to be put to bed. I had no means at hand to ease his fierce pains. Then, to my surprise, he showed me a small box of opium pills that I had put on the bedside table the previous night. He told me smiling: "You see, you must never lose your head. This morning, when I already knew that we were betrayed, I did not forget also to bring that with me."

The bed where he now lay—his traveling bed—and an armchair from Mejía's tent were the only furniture left him. Otherwise, all effects disappeared from his room in the course of the morning's plunder. Laundry, clothing, books, writings, toilet articles, decorations —in short, everything—had disappeared. Much of this López had taken over as souvenirs of the Emperor.

That forenoon several enemy leaders came by, driven mostly by curiosity, to meet "Maximilian de Habsburgo." Among these were General Vega, Colonel Smith, and the two brothers, José and Pedro Rincón Gallardo, the first of whom had helped Maximilian leave the Cruz. They told in detail how, led by López, they had gotten into the convent, describing the traitor in the blackest terms. José Rincón Gallardo ended his drastic report with the words: "Such people are good as long as they are needed. Then one turns them around, gives them a kick, and shoves them out the door."

His Majesty told me that even Altamirano, one of the most gifted republican politicians, had visited him earlier. "I was very gratified," he commented, "and it particularly pleased me to hear from Altamirano that he hopes the republican government will accept many of my laws, which he himself praised." With the exception of a few still in hiding, most of our generals were in the adjoining room, which during the siege had served as General Castillo's quarters and the secretariat of the general staff. Miramón was not in the Cruz. That morning on the way to the Cerro, he had been shot in the face by an enemy officer and lay wounded in a private house.

Accompanied by an escort I went at the Emperor's request to see General Mejía, who was ill.

The contrast between today and yesterday in the Cruz was gloomy. Yesterday, there was still a bustling life, the noise of weapons, the general excitement preceding any action, and cannon thunder from the lines; today the greatest calm, no loud word, the whole building in the somber stillness of the grave.

We prisoners remained the whole day in total uncertainty about our fate. We were not severely mistreated at all; nor could we possibly surmise from the way they dealt with him what the victors had decided about Maximilian. It seemed as if the enemy himself were surprised and stunned by a success which surpassed his wildest hopes. He could never have dreamed that after a string of battles in which he had consistently fared badly he would succeed completely and unexpectedly in capturing the sovereign, the generals, and the whole garrison without striking a blow. Yet, the satisfaction of victory was lacking. The expressions on the enemy generals' faces revealed no excitement. In fact, they could feel little pride at this feat of arms. They must have been filled with shame when they found in Querétaro a small band of only five thousand men who had so successfully opposed their sevenfold superiority for seventy-two days. They had estimated our army to be at least ten thousand and learned with dismay that treason alone had delivered this handful of exhausted soldiers.

I have mentioned how disrespectfully enemy generals described López's treason in front of witnesses who are still alive—Salm-Salm, Blasio, myself, etc. I would go no further into what he did were it not for the traitor's well-known written defense. With false and shameless testimony, he tries to justify and refute the accusations against him, imposing on me the obligation to publish my evidence of his crime. López's guilt is as clear as day. Counterallegations in his defense— that at midnight the Emperor sent him to the enemy camp to begin negotiations, and others of the same ilk—are gross untruths. They are refuted in the most fundamental fashion by the replies of the imperial officers in Morelia, as well as by all other true facts of the case.

We were taken by surprise while asleep. Without any noise, without even a shot fired, the enemy gained possession of the city and the convent.

Both his position as commander of the Cruz and the indolence often bordering on imbecility of the Indian soldier helped López carry out his task. Through a breach in the outer walls, he led the first detachment of Supremos Poderes; he accompanied them to the imperial sentries, whom he ordered to leave their posts, yielding their positions to the infiltrators. The commander ordered it. Why should the Mexican soldier have thought about it twice? Moreover, the darkness of the night obscured the enemy uniform. The ability to understand what was happening surpasses by far this race's native intelligence. Among other things, López ordered an artillery post to direct its cannon against the Cruz on the pretext that some of the troops had revolted. In this manner he succeeded in taking the building without the slightest disturbance. Thus, at five o'clock in the morning when I was brought as a prisoner to the roof of the convent, it already teemed with enemy soldiers whose presence had not been betrayed by noise. We were in enemy hands when, around three o'clock in the morning, I was called to the sickened Emperor.

During the Cruz's capture, even after we had been led away, eyewitnesses repeatedly testified that López spoke freely with enemy officers and was never taken prisoner.

The López defense was drafted under the direct influence of General Escobedo and the Juárez government. They wanted to justify murdering the monarch by invoking the law which condemns to death anyone caught with weapon in hand. This was particularly abominable since the heroic prince had come into their hands only through betrayal, not honest fight.

They are not ashamed to let López lie that he was captured the night of May 14. Colonel Yeppes, commander of the Supremos Poderes, gave one such report. I can comment about it through the remarks of enemy colonel Mayer, a native Argentinian I came to know in Mexico City after the catastrophe. He too entered the Cruz on the fateful night. By chance, in a conversation about the lies in Yeppes's testimony, he asserted in his rough military manner: "I have just spoken to Colonel Yeppes and called him to account about how he could give such testimony. 'What do you expect? Escobedo ordered me to do it,' was the colonel's simple answer."

Moreover, the Juárez government had to struggle to disguise the fact of betrayal because this would undermine Escobedo's pompous falsehood that he had stormed fortified Querétaro, taking it in less than half an hour. Confirming betrayal would also have weakened the pretext for a speedy conclusion to the trial: namely, the Emperor was captured on the Cerro de las Campanas with weapon in hand. This description of the situation was of great service to Juárez and Escobedo. Capitalizing on the magnanimity of José Rincón Gallardo, who, not wishing to be a traitor's accomplice, let Maximilian out of the Cruz, they both made disgraceful use of the inherently noble deed to support their lies.

Colonel López's act has found its fittest estimation in the eyes of the world. His name will be mentioned in history only with disgust.

CHAPTER XIX

Querétaro, Prison—My Prison Diary.

On the afternoon of May 15, the crowd in His Majesty's room decreased. We were disturbed less, and since señor Pérez had left me my notebook, I could resume writing my diary. I continued this throughout imprisonment and here reproduce its contents *in toto*.

May 15

Toward evening General Mejía enters the Emperor's room. "I am prepared for anything," says Maximilian to Mejía, "and have already completely settled accounts with myself." The general answers, "Vuestra Majestad sabe muy bien que nunca he tenido miedo de un fusil." (Your Majesty knows very well that I have never been frightened by a gun.)

I am most anxious about the prince's illness, which has become much worse.

May 16

Both servants and I sleep in the room with the prince, who has a restless night.

This morning a decree is issued that anyone who does not surrender within twenty-four hours will be shot. Consequently, Generals Escobar, Casanova, Valdez, Morett, and Minister Aguirre, until now hidden, gradually appear in prison one by one.

The sovereign is suffering greatly but remains amazingly calm—this, despite the fact that at any moment the execution order may arrive. He says to me, "I will not give my enemy the satisfaction of showing him weakness or fear."

Today after General Pancho Velez marches towards Mexico City, General Echeguerray will take over command of the Cruz and supervision of the prison.

Since I am a prisoner myself and cannot contact the outside world, I propose to His Majesty that the chief physician of the liberal army be called in as a consultant. This suits the Emperor very well because it will eliminate the enemy's suspicion that he only feigns illness. Dr. Riva de Nejra, chief physician of the republican army, visits Maximilian, accompanied by an officer. The preliminary effect of my proposal is that the republican doctor urgently recommends better living quarters. Supposedly, we will move today. However, we know the usual outcome of Mexican promises.

A merchant named Rugio sends the ruler's food. The rest of us must for the moment be satisfied with the remains of his meal, because the republicans are not remotely worried about our care. If it depended upon our jailers, we would quietly starve.

Today, passing my former room, I find the diary fragments and other notes among shreds of paper scattered in the corridor.

Around seven o'clock in the evening we are alarmed by the sound of shots, and our guard has his men take up arms. A second officer comes for me and immediately reassures me that he only wants my medical help. He leads me to a fatally wounded republican officer. Only now do I learn the cause of the noise. In the large church of the Cruz, where were confined all captured officers—four hundred in number—cigar sparks had set off several cartridges. Frightened by the explosion, everyone ran to the gate, and the officer of the guard, fearing a revolt, had his men fire into the crowd. Three officers were wounded, including the one to whom I was called.

His Majesty summons Colonel Margaño, and in connection with this incident he guarantees his own behavior and that of his entourage but refuses responsibility for what the other prisoners do.

May 17

Tonight I again sleep near Maximilian, along with Grill and Severo. His Majesty has another bad night, scarcely sleeping two hours. At one o'clock in the morning we move into a new prison, the former Santa Theresa Convent.

A coach, in which I ride with General Echeguerray and his adjutant, transports the Emperor, accompanied by a mounted escort. All other prisoners, even generals, have to walk. As we cross the square in front of the Cruz, a man comes out of López's house bringing the sovereign his general's hat.

During this drive through the city, the populace behaves with utmost tact. The streets are deserted; no curious spectators. The faces of the few people we see bear expressions of sympathy. Windows of the houses are shut, revealing no one. In the immediate vicinity of our new prison, by the Alameda, most of the prisoners catch up to us. All respectfully uncover their heads. Laughing, Maximilian comments, "No monarch can boast of a larger court."

The quarters made available to the prince and his entourage consist of two large rooms with a view of the courtyard, and His Majesty enjoys the fresh greenery of the trees.

The enemy generously supplies some easy chairs which, along with the bed and the stuffed chair from Mejía's tent, comprise the furnishings of the Emperor's room. Adjacent to him live Prince Salm-Salm, Minister Aguirre, General Castillo and his adjutant, Colonel Guzmán, former adjutant to the prince; Ormachaea, the ordnance officer, Lieutenant Colonel Pradillo, Imperial Secretary Blasio, and I. By Maximilian's special wish, we are left near him.

To the courtesy of Dr. Ciuró, a physician I befriended after the siege, the Emperor is thankful for some bed linen.

We in the second room make ourselves more comfortable. We have made mattresses out of *cocos.** Maximilian secures *sarapes*** for blankets and necessary personal effects such as combs, brushes, soap and hand towels.

His Majesty's health is somewhat better. In the evening captured officers have to fall in for *lista* (roll call); their names are read off.

A proclamation from Escobedo has appeared in which he has the effrontery to boast of his feat of arms. The first list of those captured is published. On it the sovereign appears as "el Emperador Maximiliano gefe del ejercito sitiado, Austriaco"; Minister Aguirre, Secretary Blasio and I, as second lieutenants.***

May 18

Surveillance of prisoners again transfers to a new person, General Refugio González, formerly a famed bandit.

No one is allowed to see us, although other prisoners in the nunnery are permitted to receive visitors. From the door I speak to Dr.

*Mule saddle blankets made of maguey fibers.
**Mexican shoulder blankets.
***On the twenty-fourth appeared a second official list on which "el Archiduque" instead of "Emperador" stood as the Emperor's title.

Prantl, who is just passing the corridor to visit the prisoners. Like all doctors he is free to move about and is busy in the hospital of the republican army. Prantl informs me that a republican officer who had been our prisoner has described me to General Escobedo in unflattering terms. This officer, by the way, was formerly my patient, and the manner in which he expresses his thanks is truly Mexican. Such are they all without distinction, regardless of party: a hypocritical, malicious, spiteful breed.

Although still in bed, Maximilian receives several enemy officers.

At midday, lista again. We in the entourage are not called, but lista will also be held for us. An officer checks us and the prince against a piece of paper bearing our names. It seems that my medical activity is also being watched. At least, my prescriptions are detained at the pharmacy, while those signed by Dr. Riva de Nejra are filled.

Today two of the trunks stolen on the fifteenth are returned to the Emperor, and he is pleased to find some books in them.

At eight o'clock in the evening—I am in the room with the sovereign, who is already asleep—Pradillo softly opens the door and startles me with the news: "ya se han llevado el principe" (they have taken the prince [Salm-Salm]). They reportedly asked for me. Salm-Salm returns after only half an hour; they merely wanted to see his identification papers.

May 19

His Majesty feels significantly better. The disturbance by Pradillo did not awaken him, and he slept calmly all night.

Yesterday evening General Méndez was discovered in his hiding place, and this morning he is shot—victim of Escobedo's latest law.

Major Gorwitz (a fellow prisoner) has received a letter from a German merchant in San Luis Potosí, who claims to know from reliable sources that, since all the European powers and North America are interceding with Juárez, he will abstain from shedding blood.

In the forenoon, the sovereign receives several women who offer their services and promise to do his laundry. Once again, enemy officers also visit him. His health is noticeably improved. The dysentery has slackened; the pains have stopped.

Despite the report about Méndez, some hope stirs in us today. It is already the fifth day, and Mexicans usually expedite this kind of justice.

Until today only higher officers have asked permission to visit the prince, but now general curiosity increases. Two ragged junior officers come to see "Maximiliano." Finding their demand very peculiar, we want to prevent their admittance, but they show a pass from General Escobedo, allowing them to do this. Nevertheless, these republicans firmly believe they are treating the Emperor and the rest of us with perfect chivalry. In our helpless state, they let us breathe and starve and waste away in filth; that is their highest conception of humanity and consideration.

The ruler is indignant about this demand which he cannot protect himself against in any way. "This kind of curiosity is completely improper," he remarks excitedly. "What can we do about it? They will never force me to anger or displeasure!"

In the afternoon General Escobedo, accompanied by General Díaz de León and Colonel Villanueva, visits the Emperor.

We are all intensely expectant and at the same time thoroughly worried. What can the visit of Escobedo and his adjutants mean? Possibly they will announce a death sentence. Perhaps, and this is the hope we cling to, it means the beginning of negotiations. Simultaneous hope and anxiety increase as the discussion continues. Not only we, but all the captured officers who know of the visit are full of anticipation and tension. Large groups assemble in the corridor outside our door.

The visit lasts a half-hour and is nothing but a formality; Escobedo also visits General Mejía.

This evening the rumor spreads that they have mustered out twelve of our former guerrilla leaders to be shot tomorrow. This is the kind of daily news that keeps us occupied.

Tonight, our watch makes a horrible noise; every ten minutes all the sentries—there are around ten posted—scream their *centinela alerta** at the top of their lungs. The Emperor, who needs so much quiet because of his illness, is unable to close his eyes.

*All is quiet.

May 20

Today is our sixth day in prison. Our captors speak to us as friends, but they treat us as enemies—the Mexican way. Always "á la disposicion de Usted" (at your service). Then they are enraged if you hold them to their word.

Lista at ten o'clock in the forenoon. There is no trace yet of any decision. It appears our captivity will last a long time.

His Majesty's health is rather good; his unshakeable calm is admirable. Through Pitner's good offices, I have obtained Heine's *Romanzero* for the sovereign, who feels the need of occupation and distraction.

Since yesterday our guard has been strengthened. The republicans are alarmed by a rumor that the imperial general, Olvera, is approaching Querétaro and that already individual bands of his men have shown up in the surrounding area. There is talk of taking us to Mexico City, even of ransoming Maximilian.

At eleven o'clock, Princess Salm-Salm arrives from San Luis Potosí. I am told that she entered Escobedo's camp during the last days of the siege, asking permission to come into Querétaro. "She heard her husband was wounded and thought they would allow a wife to take care of her husband." "If it is true that he is wounded," they had given her to understand, "we will allow you to go to Querétaro. If not, this will remain forbidden to you." As the betrayal showed and as they themselves told us, the republicans always maintained excellent secret police in Querétaro. From these agents they learned that the prince really was wounded, and yet they rejected his wife's request, as if this were not so. As a result she immediately departed for San Luis Potosí, the seat of the republican government.

According to Prince Salm-Salm, the information the princess brings completely contradicts hopes we have held in recent days. Juárez, the Indian, thirsts for blood. He wants to make full use of the law of January 25, 1862, and the life of His Majesty hangs by a thread. "Where there is nothing, even the Emperor has lost his rights," he said to me this morning. Princess Salm-Salm converses at length with the sovereign, informing him of the mood in San Luis Potosí; the siege of Mexico City; Márquez's contemptible betrayal.

190

After talking with Maximilian, the princess goes into Escobedo's camp, and at four o'clock she returns with Colonel Villanueva. A while later, another of Escobedo's adjutants, Colonel Palacios, appears with instructions for His Majesty to come to headquarters. Palacios recognizes Pitner as a prisoner from Santa Gertrudis and guarantees he will not escape unharmed this time. Pitner explains how he became active again but remarks in closing to the spiteful Palacios: "I can die no more honorable a death than that in the company of the Emperor."

Salm-Salm tells me that the situation is much more serious than they had thought and that, as things stand, it would be very difficult to save the monarch's life. From conversation with Villanueva and Palacios I hear that the law of October 3 is the main charge against him. Palacios says the republicans have communications from Bazaine, reproaching the prince for reluctance to abdicate at any price. This is direct provocation by the person most responsible for undermining the Empire and most instrumental in its downfall.

Villanueva comments, "Actually, I must admit, you are a great burden to us."

Despite his weakness Maximilian leaves his bed to answer Escobedo's summons. He drives to camp, accompanied by Prince and Princess Salm-Salm, Colonels Villanueva and Palacios.

Before leaving, he gives me two more papers. One is a letter from General Arellano, who is still free and had written to the sovereign from his hiding place. The second is a poem which a captured French officer had dedicated to His Majesty. Handing me the papers, he says, "Store them for the time being. If I do not return, a strong possibility, destroy the letter from Arellano." Well-acquainted with thoughts of death, he calmly leaves the prison with a firm step, greeting the officers with a friendly smile.

Three long excruciating hours pass, filled alternately with anxiety and hope. Care dwindles and hope grows the longer his absence lasts; if there were cause for concern, rumors would have already reached us.

At eight o'clock we hear the rolling of a coach. The Emperor is returning, his moral strength once again having triumphed over his body in this hours-long conversation with Escobedo. He collapses exhausted. He reports that Escobedo was exceptionally amiable, and he conversed with the general in his usual manner, walking back and forth.

From Salm-Salm, who acted as mediator during this parley, I hear that His Majesty made the following proposals:

1) The Emperor declares himself ready to order the surrender of both cities still occupied by the imperials—Mexico City and Veracruz.

2) He is ready to declare that he will no longer interfere in Mexican affairs.

3) He concedes that he and his entourage should be brought to Veracruz under escort. As for the Mexican officers, he requests the new government to spare them.

It appears that the republicans intend to engage in negotiations.

May 21

The Emperor had a peaceful night. Our hope revives. Today the sentries are less strict. They let me see the generals without a guard, and they also permit General Morett to visit His Majesty. Even the centinela alerta was screamed less loudly last night.

I see the main obstacle to a favorable outcome of negotiations in the Mexicans' sense of distrust. False and disloyal themselves, they fail to grasp the meaning of a word of honor. Limited in judgment and completely in the dark about the inviolability of Europeans' promises, they really believe the desire to return might still come over us once we are out of the country. Both parties—ours, as well as the enemy's—have surely done enough to forestall the remotest thought of that kind.

Princess Salm-Salm is back in Escobedo's camp. Until now, she has been the only non-Mexican mediator between Maximilian and enemy headquarters. At five o'clock in the afternoon she returns, accompanied by Villanueva. Nothing is decided yet, but Villanueva says that in two days will arrive detailed orders concerning the prisoners.

It seems the United States is intervening, and Juárez is insisting that North America itself guarantee the future.

The Emperor's physical condition is excellent.

May 22

Today is the eighth day of imprisonment. The Supremos Poderes, already well-known to us, have the watch again and parade their mock valor in front of the prisoners. Last night they screamed so their lungs almost burst, managing to keep all of us awake.

It is strictly forbidden to come and go. The chivalrous Mexican nature is again in glorious evidence.

The Emperor tells me that yesterday Princess Salm-Salm went to great lengths to secure him better quarters with a garden, for his convalescence. The fear she showed on the battlefield never leaves her, and spectres of escape and abduction haunt her constantly.

At one-thirty Princess Salm-Salm returns from camp. When she tries to enter, she is insulted by two officers. The officer of the guard today is particularly crude. This man who is scarcely capable of being a doorman criticizes the number of His Majesty's servants. He is not the only limited soul among the republican officers. One of their generals, Blanco, on visiting Maximilian today, tells me with the greatest naiveté, how modest and popular their General Corona is. "Imagine, señor," he tells Maximilian, describing Corona's inspection of the Rubio cotton factories, "during this whole time, he walked around with his head uncovered."

"Aren't these Mexican democrats laughable?" the Emperor asked, after Blanco had gone away. "These people call taking off their hat making themselves popular. Apparently Blanco intended to show me respect in front of the republicans; they are really so pitifully small."

At three o'clock this afternoon, we are supposed to be brought to still another convent, this time the Convent de las Capuchinas.

At four-thirty the move occurs. His Majesty, the generals, and Prince Salm-Salm are led away. Meanwhile, the rest of us are supposed to wait here. We are promised an escort very soon.

Two German merchants from San Luis Potosí—Bahnsen, the Vice-Consul from Hamburg, and a Herr Stephan—visit the prisoners. They say that among the populace of San Luis Potosí, there is profound regret over the sovereign's tragic fate. Apparently Juárez was initially determined to have the generals and the Emperor shot immediately. Detailed information about the betrayal at Querétaro is said to have changed his mind. Yesterday, he ordered a stay on all executions.

The hours stretch out endlessly. Night is coming on, and still the promised messenger has not arrived to fetch us and reunite us with Maximilian. Our hope of seeing him again starts to dwindle; possibly, they have taken him and the generals to San Luis Potosí.

Finally, at eight o'clock, an officer appears with the longed-for message that he has come to reunite us with our prince.

Salm-Salm is the first person I speak to at the Capuchina Convent. "Where is the Emperor?" I ask him. "He is in a crypt." Noticing my terror over these words, Salm-Salm adds: "Calm yourself; he is alive, but he really is in a crypt. I will show you to him." I open the door; the cold smell of decay assails me. Deep in a corner of a great gallery, the pantheon of the convent, stands a bed; in front of it there is a table with a candle. On the bed Maximilian lies, reading Cesare Cantù.

Calmly smiling, he remarks, "They have not had time yet to prepare a room, and so temporarily they have had to give me a bed among the dead." They have outdone themselves with this brutality, confining a prisoner who expects to die in a crypt among the dead. It is a vestige of the Inquisition; it is the thumbscrew refined by culture.

That night I sleep alone in the crypt, with the Emperor, on a large table where apparently bodies are laid in state. Next to me stands a coffin. But after the hours of uneasiness I have undergone this afternoon, the dead will leave me alone.

May 23

The sovereign did not have a bad night. He slept quietly with very few interruptions. He moves his quarters from the crypt to a tiny, dark, damp cell, which, like all the other cells assigned us, overlooks a small courtyard. Since there are only two exits, the watch is relaxed. We enjoy relatively more freedom now and can see and talk with each other undisturbed. Our cells, like His Majesty's, are real dungeons, but the courtyard expands them, at least by day.

Maximilian points out to me that an officer of the guard—a boy of about sixteen—plays with a small doll, wearing a crown on its head and costumed in a blue dress coat and red pants. On its face is a removable mask, under which appears a death's head.

They are still in constant fear that one of us will get away, and a lista for us is drawn up again.

May 24

The Emperor had a restless night. Today is the tenth day in prison. The monarch's serenity startles the enemy officers. He told me that even the cross-eyed cat, Palacios, became tame and told him that he wished he had his trust; he was acting in good faith. Peculiar chivalry. They give His Majesty a damp hole to live in; for themselves, they have sought out airy and sunny rooms in the convent.

This evening very bad news must have arrived. I deduce this from the dismayed expressions of Bahnsen and Stephan, who visit us, as well as in Salm-Salm's dejection. Although hope of saving the Emperor is fading, Herr Stephan suggests that it might be easy to escape from here.

The order to start Maximilian's trial has arrived, but we are unsure about the type and makeup of the court. If it is a court-martial, things are hopelessly bad. Assigning the final decision to such a court expressly shows they intend to murder the defendant.

As of now, only His Majesty and the two generals, Miramón and Mejía, will come to trial.

At five o'clock in the afternoon, the prince is separated from us and taken to the second story of the convent with Miramón and Mejía. Through the mediation of Bahnsen, the vice-consul from Hamburg, we obtain permission for me, as his physician, to attend the sovereign.

Around six o'clock in the evening, Bahnsen informs me, much to my relief, that I can remain with Maximilian, but I am to contact no one during the trial. The same restrictions apply to His Majesty and both generals. I am now resigned like the monarch.

In the meantime, Bahnsen has already spoken with Vázquez, a lawyer in Querétaro who advised the Emperor that in case of trial, he would stress the court's incompetence and demand defense attorneys. Of these I was to give Maximilian the names of Vázquez in Querétaro, Martínez de la Torre and Mariano Riva Palacios in Mexico City.

I hid the scrap of paper on which Bahnsen had wisely made

195

these notations and immediately went up to the second story of the convent where His Majesty and Generals Miramón and Mejía occupied three small cells.

The monarch's cell is a small, gloomy hole with one door and one window but, more important, with a large rectangular opening in the wall. The window has neither panes nor shutters. In front of this hole the Emperor hung a sarape, obscuring the guards' view. Furnishings are as before, except for a table.

I could not enter immediately because the prosecutor, who had brought the indictment against Maximilian, was speaking to him. As he withdrew, I entered the cell. The door was half open, and a guard stood constantly looking in, observing our activities. By suitable maneuvering I succeeded in blocking the door somewhat, and quickly I slipped the paper Bahnsen had given me to His Majesty.

I could not give him the message orally, because I didn't want to arouse suspicion by naming the lawyers, thereby jeopardizing the possibility of further dealings with the prince.

He read the slip of paper and told me: "I have already done exactly as the consul advises me here. I am something of a lawyer myself. They will have a hard fight with me; I do not give up so easily."

Speaking of the first judicial hearing, which had already taken place, he elaborated:

> The indictment is so laughable, clumsy, and spitefully made that, if it came before a congress, I would choose no defense attorney at all. Moreover, I had a very good conversation with the prosecutor. Above all, before he brought the indictment, I explained to him that I am not able to answer any political charges, because I am completely without necessary documents and pieces of evidence for this and that in such a serious affair, I could not speak knowledgably without them. He then introduced personal history, and I explained who I am, who my parents are, where I was born, what I have done previously, etc. The prosecutor did not get a word from me related to the indictment. When he had read the first charge he asked whether I had a reply. Since my answer remained the same, and he knew it in advance, he himself finally dictated it to his stenographer.

So that my dealings with Maximilian will be undisturbed, he

196

asks the prosecutor, who has just ended a judicial hearing with Mejía, to inform the officer of the guard that I am the imperial physician. The prosecutor guarantees me free interchange with His Majesty, but I must speak to him only in Spanish. This restriction little influences our conversation, for the Indian at the door indeed does not know what language we speak. If he hears a Spanish word only occasionally, his scruples are completely satisfied. The Emperor is in a very good mood as a result of the intellectual activity at the beginning of the trial.

May 25

Today is the eleventh day in prison and the first day we have been incommunicado.

After yesterday's excitement, the quietness of complete isolation is painful. The embargo on messages is very strict, not lifted for anyone. Miramón and Mejía are allowed to deal and communicate neither with Maximilian, nor with each other. Even food reaches the sovereign indirectly, through a sentry who picks it up from the cook.

On a nail in the sovereign's room hangs a crown of thorns. He shows it to me with the words: "I have a claim to this; they will not dispute it with me. When I leave here, I shall take it back to Europe as a souvenir."

I visit him infrequently, to avoid arousing the suspicion of the officer of the guard. Most of the time I spend alone in my room, a cell similar to Maximilian's, only completely without furniture. I spend hours pacing diagonally across the space that is the longest distance.

The prosecutor was due this morning at ten o'clock. Instead, he appears at six in the evening and remains a full three hours with the defendant.

The thirteen counts of the indictment are formulated precisely, read aloud twice, and signed at the bottom.

His Majesty is very weak; he spends most of his time in bed. I can allow him to get up only at midday.

His food consists of soup, hash, chicken, tea, coffee, and some red wine.

197

May 26

The twelfth day in prison and the second incommunicado.

They have now decided to try the sovereign before a court-martial. According to him, the indictment is drawn up in a completely spiteful way, based largely on open lies. Truly Mexican!

At eleven o'clock in the forenoon Escobedo visits Maximilian. The conversation is brief but sufficiently long to reassure us about the death sentence. How we cling to everything; to time, to place, to expressions and gestures!

Finally the cook is allowed to bring meals personally to the Emperor. We find ways to contact the outside world. Aguirre, our field chaplain, has sent His Majesty a message in a cigar, offering his help. Maximilian communicates with Salm-Salm by slips of paper stuck in bread.

Today Dr. Riva de Nejra, who has been in Mexico City, returns again to visit the monarch. Since it is in the latter's interest to postpone the trial as long as possible, I vividly describe the critical nature of his illness. In reality, despite the constant excitement, he is in relatively good health. Riva de Nejra goes along with my intentions.

A swiss officer, Charles Benaut, who has the watch today, reassures me that as far as he knows, and as far as he can interpret public opinion, the prospect is good that we will soon gain our freedom.

This evening, Miramón and Mejía are questioned at length by the prosecutor.

Tonight I sleep again in the same room with the Emperor.

Before ten o'clock in the evening, Vice-Consul Bahnsen, who is traveling to San Luis Potosí, takes leave of Maximilian, who gives him a long letter to Juárez.

May 27

Those who obtain a specific pass from the prosecutor may now speak with His Majesty. At his request even Salm-Salm has such a pass; it reads "The prisoner Salm-Salm may talk with Maximilian."

Father Aguirre brings a lawyer, a liberal from Querétaro who has offered his service to the defense. He and Vázquez, the lawyer chosen by the sovereign, will collaborate.

Telegrams to Mexico City were sent off the day before yesterday, summoning the diplomats here—especially Magnus and the two law-yers Martínez de la Torre and Mariano Riva Palacios. This means that Márquez did not want to let anyone through.

Miramón and Mejía are now allowed to communicate with each other, but not yet with His Majesty.

May 28

Colonel Gagern, the enemy commander who on April 27 had fled before us on the Cimatario with his whole battalion, visits the Emperor and generals. Not using his title of baron, he introduces himself to me as a nobleman so I might inform Maximilian that he is the brother of the Baron von Gagern. The latter had served His Majesty in Austria as an officer in the Uhlan regiment. "We are not as bloodthirsty as you think," Gagern says to me. "Qui s'excuse, s'accuse." The Juaristas know very well what they are and what they are considered to be.

A court-martial, comprised of a lieutenant colonel and several captains, is to make the final decision about the monarch.

For two days the public pleadings are postponed on behalf of the defense. Gagern also says that a commission which has reportedly left America is expected in San Luis.

The accused works at length with his lawyer, Vázquez. Still—this terrible uncertainty.

May 29

The fifteenth day in prison. Today Maximilian points out to me that three years have passed since he first stepped on Mexican soil.

News from San Luis bodes no good.

This evening will be the first session of the court-martial. Un-heard of! Boys who can scarcely read and write are entrusted with the task of judging international questions.

In the afternoon a telegram from Princess Salm-Salm comes from San Luis Potosí. She reports she is returning tomorrow with gratifying news. Bahnsen will not leave until tomorrow; he will also personally use his influence with Juárez. The telegram from the princess kindles great hopes.

May 30

Everything looks black to Prince Salm-Salm; perhaps he is right.

In the afternoon, the princess arrives, accompanied by Wilhelm Daus, a German merchant from San Luis Potosí. The news that she promised is only that a postponement has been granted. However, under the circumstances this is also a gain since each delay enhances efforts to save the Emperor. Daus tells me that the enemy general, Treviño, indignant over the betrayal, left immediately for San Luis Potosí.

The delay for the defense is temporarily extended, pending arrival of defense attorneys from Mexico City.

Bahnsen leaves. He will make every possible effort in San Luis, overlooking nothing in urging the government to change its mind.

May 31

The seventeenth day in prison.

A decision must come soon. One of the main drawbacks is the childish Mexican jealousy of foreign interference. According to what I know of these people, open intervention is useless, can in fact greatly strengthen their obstinacy. Such influence should only be exerted in a secret and confidential manner.

Márquez remains in Mexico City. The Emperor is furious at him, commenting several times to the enemy officers: "Suppose I were offered Márquez and López. Left free choice between the two, I would release López, the cowardly traitor, and hang Márquez, traitor out of cold-blooded calculation!"

The behavior of the republicans openly reveals weakness. If the government were strong and confident of permanence, Maximilian would have been released instantly. But weak and afraid of its own soldiers, it may be forced to provide the army the victim it desires.

Even captive, the ruler inspires their respect. They delight in calling him Maximilian behind his back, but in person they address him as "señor Vuestra Majestad," even "señor Emperador." They are too cowardly to take the crown from his head while he lives, and they show the same indecision in their official documents. Alternately he is called: "el Emperador"; "el Archiduque"; "el titulado Emperador"; "el Principe."

In addition to the princess, Prince Salm-Salm and the American lawyer Frederic Hall are in communication with His Majesty.

Chapter Nineteen

June 1

The eighteenth day in prison.

The princess and Daus leave for Mexico City this morning to get Baron Magnus and the lawyers.

It is certain that the republicans intend nothing but harm for the Emperor. They seem to severely regret not having shot him the first day.

Gagern revisits the sovereign, but this time he is not as optimistic. To my question about how matters stand, he answers: "Undoubtedly Maximilian will be shot."

About his talk with Gagern, the monarch says, "He wanted to prove to me that the Mexican and American governments follow the same standards of conduct. That was too much for me, and I asked him how he could equate the two. There, law rules; here, nothing but partisan caprice."

Salm-Salm tells me he has asked twelve enemy officers their assessment of the situation. All concurred with Gagern's ominous forecast.

His Majesty speaks about a trip to San Luis Potosí, instructing me to prepare medications. In case he has to travel without me, Salm-Salm will take them. I understand the reasons behind all this. "Nothing will come of today's trip," the Emperor says to me in the evening.

June 2

The nineteenth day in prison.

The princess, Daus, and Bahnsen are away. We are waiting, and the situation gives rise to a feeling of hope.

Maximilian works with Vázquez and Hall. He is well enough again to spend several hours of the day out of bed. The embargo on messages between him and the generals is lifted.

Back and forth go the lawyers; the sovereign confers with them and the generals. In the forenoon he plays dominoes with Miramón, Mejía, and me.

Besides the defense the Emperor still has other things to consider. Notes are exchanged between him, Salm-Salm, and Miramón, with me as go-between. Daily I bandage Miramón, who still has a small

201

wound on his face, and I take these opportunities to pass him the slips of paper.

June 3

Today Magnus and the two lawyers, Mariano Riva Palacios and Raphael Martínez de la Torre, are expected from Mexico City.

Maximilian's cause seems to be faring somewhat better. The prosecutor comes to see him several times today and behaves in a friendly manner.

The following episode, like everything of potential damage to the prisoners, is sketchily described in my diary for obvious reasons. But my memories of that day are vivid and accurate.

In the evening Maximilian informs me in the presence of Prince Salm-Salm that all is ready for an escape, probably tonight. He describes how, according to their plan, I was also to have joined them. But after long and careful deliberation, this was judged impossible because it would complicate the escape. Announcement of the plan does not surprise me; I knew of it the day before yesterday when the Emperor asked me to prepare medications. I show him the appropriate passage in my diary, and he sees I have not been deluded; I have understood why I had to sleep in my cell in recent nights. The escape attempt has been postponed this long because the sovereign under no circumstances will abandon Miramón and Mejía. The plan is now for all three to flee together.

Within an hour, they will decide whether escape is still possible today. The horses stand ready, and the exact route is chosen. It will entail six hours of uninterrupted riding. "I still wanted to ask you," the Emperor remarked, "whether I can stand this ride." My answer is reassuring; I myself am in full accord with this sole means of salvation. Attempted escape is, in any case, more certain than believing in the government of San Luis Potosí.

At seven o'clock the guard is changed. For three days it has been the same unit *(Cazadores de Galeano)*. Both officers, who had been won over completely, are replaced by complete strangers. This change arouses our suspicions of betrayal to Escobedo. In that case there can be no escape today. There is still another possibility: the new officers might have been won over to us by their comrades, and the plan might still be carried out. I go to my cell, lying on the *cocos* completely undressed, to give more plausibility to my confusion when they discover the Emperor's absence. I spend a sleepless night. The slightest sound nourishes my hope that the escape is underway. But the night slips away without incident.

June 4

This evening Baron Magnus should certainly arrive with the lawyers and four other people.

Today, a member of the court-martial visits Maximilian. He tells me he recognized him as the man who several months before had successfully begged pardon for the life of a General García in Cuernavaca.

Salm-Salm is permitted to occupy the same wing as His Majesty. He will sleep in a cell with me.

The sovereign expects the visit of Baron Magnus and those accompanying him around noon. To show his composure to the new arrivals, he arranges a domino party in which he, the generals, Salm-Salm, and I take part.

In order to cheer up General Mejía, he tells him of his estates at Miramar and Lacroma, and he guarantees that if the trial has a happy ending, he will take him along to Europe. "I will not be a burden to Your Majesty in Europe," replies Mejía.

June 5

Tonight Magnus arrives with his secretary, Scholler, the lawyers, and Hoorricks, the Belgian chargé d'affaires. We have now two hopes: successful escape and good results from the new defense attorneys. Mariano Riva Palacios is the father of republican general Vicente Riva Palacios and is known as a strict republican and a friend of Juárez. His taking on the defense speaks already for the probability of success.

At eleven o'clock in the forenoon, Baron Magnus visits the Emperor and converses with him for hours. After he leaves, he says to me, "I hope things will improve now. At last someone is here who understands how to handle them properly."

Suddenly at one-thirty the order arrives to take all prisoners except His Majesty and the two generals from the convent to the casino.

Unquestionably, they are on the scent of the escape attempt. It has been postponed too long, and the people around us would have to be deaf to miss what has been going on.

I am separated from Maximilian only a short while. I stay in the casino just two hours, then am led back again. "We have only the women to thank for that," declares the Emperor. "I believe Miramón's wife must have talked too much."

In the meantime, our guard has been significantly strengthened. A whole battalion encamps on the street in front of the prison. The monarch comments: "It is only right for those below to tremble, when the lion stirs in his cage."

Also in the afternoon both lawyers, Mariano Riva Palacios and Martínez de la Torre, come to see the defendant. It is decided they will go to San Luis Potosí, confer with the government, and obstruct the court-martial so as to change the course of the trial.

In the meantime, here in Querétaro, the lawyers Vázquez and Eulalio Ortega—the latter also from Mexico City—are to work on actual defense.

Our lawyer, a young man from Querétaro recommended by Father Aguirre, visits the Emperor, and I discuss his views with him. He disagrees with Vázquez's defense strategy, explaining to me that his brief focuses on the question of the government's right to try a man who was sold out and betrayed. They could not claim the sovereign was captured, knowing he was bought out by Escobedo.

Eight officers keep watch. Among them, both colonels, Palacios and Villanueva. During the night while His Majesty is sleeping, they inspect his room and even put a candle on the ground to facilitate their checking.

The Emperor is very ill, feels extremely weak.

June 6

Today Baron Lago, the Austrian chargé d'affaires also arrives. He tells His Majesty that Márquez is still keeping up his farce in Mexico City. Only recently he issued a proclamation informing the populace that the sovereign was nearby with seven thousand horsemen.

Surveillance becomes increasingly strict. Now they even forbid us eating utensils. This is the way to treat galley slaves. Yet, if questioned, they would call it chivalry.

We still lack direct information from San Luis Potosí. Envoys visit Maximilian daily, but even for this they need a special pass from Escobedo.

June 7

The twenty-fourth day in prison.

Things go from bad to worse. They isolate us even more, and tomorrow all foreigners must leave the city.

A one-thousand-man guard, and still this worry!

I have called six doctors in for consultation. Among them are the head doctor of the republicans, Dr. Riva de Nejra and my friend, Dr. Ciuró. At ten o'clock the doctors meet and agree that a change of quarters and strictest calm are indispensable for the Emperor's recovery. He will never regain his health in this damp cell.

With my encouragement these findings are drawn up into an official report for presentation to Escobedo. Maximilian hopes this will result in assignment to better quarters, with a garden if possible— altogether more space in which to move about.

How hypocritical these Mexicans are. Dr. Nejra, ardent spokesman for securing the improved living conditions fears compromising himself by signing the report. He does so only after receiving Escobedo's permission.

Due to the cunning of the boy who brings my food daily, I now have eating utensils and am no longer compelled to cut meat with my fingers like a savage.

June 8

This evening all junior officers are released. It seems the others, captain to general inclusive, will be interned from three to six years in different locations. This reassures me greatly. There is quite a difference between that and the death penalty. Imprisonment and internment, even if for so many years, mean little in Mexico. It is only a matter of time until the government falls and with it the punishment imposed.

Today Curtopassi, the Italian chargé d'affaires, also arrived from Mexico City.

June 9

During the night there is again a frightening uproar. More brazenly than ever the guards scream their centinela alerta, and at four the noise of trumpets awakens us.

Today the junior officers leave Querétaro. Escobedo addresses them before they march away, reminding them that this is the way a government treats traitors.

High officers, until now confined in the casino with the generals, will also be moved. It is said that some will go to Piedras Negras on the northern frontier; some to Acapulco. Their sentence reads: Imprisonment from four to seven years.

For the present, despite his being only a lieutenant colonel, Pitner remains in the casino, along with several generals; also, Castillo, Salm-Salm, and Minister Aguirre.

Pitner's situation is very bad. Those left in the casino are also to be tried by court-martial.

Rumors reaching us are favorable. They do not speak of execution for the Emperor; perhaps he and the generals will also be interned in Acapulco.

June 10

The twenty-seventh day in prison.

Yesterday evening Daus came from Tacubaya. He brings little comforting news and describes the army's attitude towards Maximilian as very bad. This horde of deserters, for that is what they are primarily, demands the sovereign's death.

The colonels are sentenced to seven years and today will be removed from Querétaro; the generals reputedly face the prospect of ten years in prison. Since he only ranks as colonel on the republican list, Salm-Salm displays his general's commission and remains in the casino.

Escape no longer seems possible as our captors are uncommonly observant. In the evening we are always guarded by Escobedo's adjutant.

The day of decision moves ever nearer. His Majesty's health is somewhat better. However, we must delude the others into thinking that he still suffers a great deal and is very weak. Perhaps this will divert attention from an escape attempt; perhaps they will believe that because of his physical condition, he can no longer consider it.

The Emperor has worked out a codicil with the Austrian chargé d'affaires. He asks me to look it over and see that he has forgotten no one and to make any comments I might have.

At two o'clock in the afternoon a telegraphic dispatch arrives from both lawyers in San Luis. It reads "all our efforts are fruitless."

Maximilian summons Baron Magnus, who after a short conversation goes straight to San Luis Potosí to intercede with the government. It is impossible to tell from his appearance the effect of the dispatch on His Majesty. The lawyers in Querétaro and Baron Magnus are much more upset than he.

As usual the sovereign is in bed by five o'clock in the afternoon. "How do you think things will end?" he asks me. "Tell me your honest opinion." "Your Majesty, I still consider the whole trial a comedy designed to show Europe how merciful they are. I believe they will carry through to the end, but I am not afraid of the outcome. If I may say so, I consider all this merely a game that is played too hard and has lasted too long." He answered me with complete composure.

> No, I do not believe that; they will simply shoot us. It is a mathematical problem you can calculate on your fingers. Colonels are sentenced to seven years in prison; generals ten. The only higher penalty under Mexican law is death. Moreover, I will admit to you that, even though no one ever said so to me, I have conceived of no other outcome. I did not want to alarm you before. Therefore, I have behaved as if I expected rescue. The only escape is still flight. Already on two occasions I have expected to die: The first time, you will remember, was when they took me to Escobedo; the second time, when I was brought here from the Teresitas. Both times, I had completely come to terms with myself.

I try to refute him, but inwardly I must acknowledge the truth of what he says.

June 11

Today is the twenty-eighth day in prison. From San Luis have come telegraphic instructions giving me my freedom. Colonel Palacios notifies me about the telegram and says I may claim my pass and depart at any moment. I explain that, despite my freedom, I will remain in prison with the Emperor.

The day after tomorrow, the court-martial is to begin its sessions. We receive no news from San Luis Potosí.

June 12

The twenty-ninth day in prison.

The court-martial will convene in the theater, and numerous tickets are distributed to the public. They are not satisfied to condemn His Majesty; they want to humiliate him.

This triumph, however, they will not have. Maximilian declares to me his firm resolve not to appear in the theater.

Salm-Salm visits the Emperor.

In the evening the monarch feels sick again, and I have Dr. Riva de Nejra summoned to convince him of the suffering. He confirms the illness.

June 13

Today is already the thirtieth day in prison.

At nine o'clock in the morning an escort picks up Mejía and Miramón and leads them to the theater.

How can they so lose all sense of propriety!

As reported to us, in front of the theater a band is playing. In the interior they have festooned the stage with decorations. Most of the members of the court are mere boys. "God forgive me," says the Emperor, "but I believe they have sought out for the court-martial only those with the best uniforms, so that externally at least everything has a decorous appearance."

We have prevailed upon them to excuse Maximilian's appearing. The doctors' official statement confirming his illness will be read before the court-martial, and this will explain his absence.

His Majesty receives Princess Salm-Salm and Baron Lago.

In the afternoon, I use my freedom for the first time and go outside.

Chapter Nineteen

Here end the consecutive notations in my diary. In the days that followed I was primarily occupied in writing the last of the monarch's dispositions. Also, under pressure of approaching catastrophe, I could not find the peace of mind necessary to continuing my diary.

CHAPTER XX

June 13 to 16—Last Day in the Emperor's Life—June 19—The Body —Negotiations With the Government About its Delivery—The Tegett-hoff Mission.

From the moment court sessions began in the theater in Queré-taro, all our illusions completely disappeared. When Maximilian's trial was referred to a court-martial, and the law of January 25 applied against him, the death sentence was pronounced. We could expect no pardon, and the sole possibility of rescue still lay in flight. Even this offered little prospect of success, but it had to be ventured at all costs.

Princess Salm-Salm had already lured a Mexican colonel into our undertaking for a sum of one hundred thousand dollars. He declared himself ready to risk aiding the escape.

However, he could do nothing alone. He demanded that we convince another colonel, whose name he gave the princess. She was confident the plan would succeed.

In the afternoon she visited the Emperor to inform him of the steps taken. With an eye to our scheme, I procured blanket permission to leave the prison, where I still lived at night.

By nine o'clock in the evening, we were completely ready to travel. According to advance preparations, when I received final word from the princess at ten o'clock, His Majesty was only to leave his bed; in five minutes the escape would be made.

It was just a few minutes before ten o'clock when suddenly Dr. Riva de Nejra, who seemed to be extremely worried, came to check on the Emperor's health.

According to agreement, I was to leave the convent under the pretext of summoning the doctor to the sovereign, who had fallen ill. Now that was thwarted, but I had to speak to Princess Salm-Salm at all costs. I quickly wrote out a prescription and hurried to take care of it at the pharmacy.

Riva de Nejra accompanied me to the front of the convent, where we parted.

A few minutes before ten o'clock I reached the princess's house, where I found both colonels. Princess Salm-Salm led me into an adjoining room and gave me Maximilian's signet ring. This was supposed to be a sign to accomplices of the escape.

She said nothing could be done today, that the next day at ten o'clock in the forenoon, she would visit the monarch with the two colonels. One of the officers, who had entered the room, advised me to calm the Emperor; there were still three days before the sentence of the court-martial could be carried out.

I brought the information to His Majesty with his signet ring. He was encouraged that Colonel . . . had openly discussed the scheme with me. This showed his confidence in our success.

At seven o'clock on the morning of the fourteenth, Maximilian summoned me for various instructions. First, 1 was to bring Baron Lago the order to submit today the codicil for the Emperor's signature and to remind the Italian and Belgian chargés d'affaires (Curtopassi and Hoorricks) to hand over for Maximilian's completion letters they were entrusted to prepare. Then I was to speak with Princess Salm-Salm.

As I left her and reached the street, General Refugio González approached me to ask how things really were with my patient. His scornful tone immediately suggested that this was only the introduction to quite a different disclosure. He did not leave me long in doubt. Shortly, turning to an officer accompanying him, he said: "Take this man to the general." He also meant for Herr Schwesinger, who had come with me from the princess's house, to go along. Schwesinger, a German businessman detained in transit from Mexico City to the north, had served as secretary to Prince Salm-Salm during the siege. Now, the Emperor employed him for small services because he was not a prisoner.

We were taken to Escobedo, who questioned me about my presence in the street. I answered him simply: "I am absolutely free to come and go as I choose." "Good," said the affable general, turning to his adjutant. "Take this man into the Quartel Coahuila."*

I was put in solitary confinement. In vain I tried everything to contact Maximilian. I bribed the guard with the little money in my

*The barracks where the battalion from Coahuila was stationed.

possession to pass along a slip of paper to His Majesty. However, I heard that he was too closely guarded to be contacted.

At ten o'clock on the morning of the fifteenth, Colonel Villanueva and Dr. Riva de Nejra took me from my prison. Immediately I was brought to Escobedo, who gave me permission to go to the sovereign. With a sweet smile he remarked, "We know what you have been doing. I make you responsible for everything that happens with Maximilian; you are the first I will have hanged." "Señor," I answered him, "whatever pleases you."

I found the Emperor in bed. He said to me: "I was afraid you were no longer in Querétaro. They told me the order was given yesterday to transport you to San Luis also." Only then did I learn what had happened the day before. The envoys in Querétaro were captured at almost the same time as I was ordered to leave the city within two hours and Princess Salm-Salm was escorted away. His Majesty told me, "Lago left with the codicil unsigned. I, of course, have already telegraphed him, but you must still write him that the codicil must be validated by the three witnesses who have looked over its contents: you, Lago, and Hoorricks."

I had just completed a letter containing several private instructions, which the monarch signed, when Mejía brought the report that the Empress had died. This news affected Maximilian deeply. Saying farewell to life had always seemed easy to him. In battle he had exposed himself to deadly enemy fire with bold courage, and throughout captivity he had looked death in the face with heroic composure and philosophic equanimity.

One thought had overwhelmed him with pain—the thought of the fate of his poor consort, whom he would leave such a bitter lot. Now even this misfortune was past, and, free from this pressure, he prepared himself cheerfully to take his leave of life. Immediately after hearing Mejía's report, the Emperor dictated a postscript to his letter to Lago. Its introduction read as follows: "I have just learned that my poor wife is released from her sufferings; this news, however deeply it grieves me, is at the present moment an inexpressible solace."

To me he said, "One less tie binding me to life."

On the same afternoon, according to his direct instructions and following his notes, I wrote a second letter to the prefect of Miramar, Von Radonetz, executor of His Majesty's will.

In the evening, on the general's instructions one of Escobedo's adjutants came to ask Maximilian if he had heard the sad news about his consort's death.

The court-martial had ended its sessions, and from hour to hour we expected the publication of sentence. The Emperor waited with great peace of mind and self-control. Familiar with death, he occupied himself only with thoughts of those he was leaving behind, his relatives and friends.

Visits from foreigners had stopped; I was now the only European in his entourage (except for the servants Grill and Tüdös). I performed the sad secretarial duty of writing farewell letters—letters beginning "guiltless, facing an undeserved death."

Around noon arrived Father Soria, the father confessor who had been recommended to the sovereign by defense attorney Vázquez. His Majesty said to me, "I do not confess to every cleric, and I called the padre to see if we can agree on certain preliminary questions."

I slept in his room that night, as I did until the nineteenth. He spent a restful night.

On the morning of the sixteenth, we resumed the gloomy business of the previous day. Around eleven o'clock, Colonel Miguel Palacios appeared. With him was General Refugio González, followed by a troop of soldiers who posted themselves in the corridor.

At the open door, González, the new prosecutor, read the death sentence aloud to Maximilian and then to the generals. The monarch listened with a pale but peacefully smiling expression. Immediately after the prosecutor finished, he turned to me with the greatest composure and said, pointing to his watch: "The hour is set for three o'clock; you still have more than three hours' time and can finish everything with ease."

Secretary Blasio, whom the Emperor had summoned earlier, arrived in the meantime, and His Majesty dictated to him the following letter in Spanish:

señor Don Carlos Rubio!

Stripped of all means even for the most necessary expenses, I turn to you confidently with the request that you lend the sum required in my final stipulations. This will be repaid to you by the relatives in Europe whom I appoint as heirs.

It is my wish that my body be brought to Europe to be by the side of the Empress. I entrust this to my physician, Dr. Basch, to whom you will most graciously provide everything necessary for transport and embalming, putting at his disposal the necessary financial means for him and my servants to travel to Europe. My relatives will undertake to repay this loan, either through European companies agreed upon as intermediaries, or by bills of exchange which will be sent to Mexico. The physician mentioned above will take over the arrangements.

Since I am obliged to you in advance for this renewed favor, I send you my farewell greetings and remain wishing you all happiness.

> Yours with kindest regards,
> Maximilian
> Querétaro, June 16, 1867

At twelve o'clock Padre Soria arrived. The writing desk was taken from the sovereign's room into mine, and I wrote until two o'clock in the afternoon.

After one o'clock a mass was read in Miramón's room, and the three condemned men received Holy Communion.

An hour later, I presented to the Emperor for his signature the letters which had been completed in the meantime. He received me with the words: "I can tell you that dying is much easier than I had imagined. I am now completely ready."

His father confessor and those of both generals remained with the men to accompany them on their last trip.

At a quarter to three, Maximilian took leave of me and the servants, who sobbed as they covered his hands with kisses. He gave me his wedding ring and said: "You will go to Vienna. Speak to my parents and relatives and report to them about the siege and the last days of my life. Especially," he enjoined me, "you will tell my mother that I fulfilled my duty as a soldier and that I died a good Christian."

The officer of the guard, who also commanded the firing squad, tearfully begged His Majesty's forgiveness. "You are a soldier," the ruler answered, "and you must carry out your duty."

It was three o'clock, and no one came for the condemned men. A full hour the Emperor waited in the corridor with both generals for the order calling them to the place of execution.

Unconstrained and cheerful, just as in happier days, Maximilian spent this hour conversing with the priests and the defense attorneys Ortega and Vázquez. He expressed his joy at the beautiful blue sky: "I have always wanted to die in beautiful weather; this wish at least is fulfilled." Several times he turned to me to give instructions and repeat his earlier ones. In a last remembrance of his friends, he charged me with greetings to Prince and Princess Salm-Salm, Pitner, Schaffer, Günner, Gröller, and Bilimek.

Both generals sat, rapt in their prayer books or in conversation with their spiritual counselors.

At four o'clock Colonel Palacios arrived, brandishing a sheet of paper. It was a telegram from the government in San Luis Potosí informing the prisoners that the execution of sentence would be postponed until Saturday the nineteenth.

After Palacios had read the telegram, Maximilian remarked: "That is hard to take; I had already settled accounts with this world."

A glimmer of hope for pardon stirred; all the more, since officers I spoke with were firmly convinced that postponement betokened lifting the sentence. Nor did I want to believe that the sentence would be carried out later. It would be uncivilized brutality to play such a barbarous game with prisoners—allowing them to suffer the torments of death, then returning them to a life with which they had already settled accounts. The Emperor, however, remained indifferent to this hope. "Come what may," he commented, "I no longer belong to this world." All his thoughts and actions from the sixteenth to the nineteenth were in harmony with this exalted resignation.

At that time I had to write new farewell letters and add several new points on the one to Radonetz.

Padre Soria came daily, and the sovereign told me: "I have exchanged roles with the father confessor. I have to comfort him so

216

the poor man does not lose courage."

That day His Majesty addressed the following letter to the generals in prison:

"Querétaro, Prison of the Capuchinas, June 17, 1867.

Generals and leaders imprisoned in this city!

In this solemn moment I write you to express my gratitude for the loyalty with which you have served me, as well as to assure you the most sincere respect.

> Yours with kindest regards,
>
> Maximilian"

June 17 passed on wings of lead. Each minute lasted an eternity, and yet despite our desperate hope we were not rescued.

Evening came without good news or bad—a gloomy, chilly solitude. The Emperor slept well that night; the morning of the eighteenth dawned and still no sign of life from the government in San Luis Potosí.

Vázquez brought an answer from the generals which Maximilian passed on to me. The letter read:

Querétaro, Prison of the Teresitas, June 18, 1867.

Sire!

We received Your Majesty's affectionate and moving letter dated yesterday, in which you expressed in your own hand your noble sentiments for the generals and leaders who have followed you to this horrible crisis.

Since we cannot communicate with the rest of our comrades, we have unfortunately not yet informed them of the contents of Your Majesty's letter, but this will be done as soon as possible.

Sire! We the defeated generals, your admirers and friends, are also on the path to the place of execution, and should implacable fate be unfortunate to us all, then, Sire! in heaven we will unite around Your Majesty as around our noble Empress, who sojourns already among the angels. Sire! We are Your Majesty's

> Inspired servants
>
> M. M. Escobar
> J. L. Casanova
> C. Morett
> V. Herrera y Lozada

Around noon Baron Magnus and Bahnsen, the vice-consul from Hamburg, appeared in the prison. They had come from San Luis Potosí during the night. Magnus, having learned in San Luis of my new imprisonment, had brought a German physician, Dr. Szanger, for the embalming. He did not expect my release so soon.

On the sixteenth the Emperor had given all the relics I later brought to Europe to the lawyer Vázquez with instructions to deliver them to me after his death. On the afternoon of the eighteenth, in the presence of Magnus and Bahnsen, he also handed the letters over to Vázquez with the same instructions. For reasons of security I entrusted all my papers to the same man for storage.

In a special handwritten letter, the sovereign thanked his defense attorneys for their "perseverance and energy," and he sent the following telegram to the government: "I wish that señores Miguel Miramón and Tomás Mejía, who the day before yesterday suffered all the torments and bitterness of death, be pardoned and that, as I stated when captured, I be the only one sacrificed."

To Juárez he addressed the following letter of farewell:*

señor Benito Juárez:

> On the verge of suffering death for having tried new political institutions to end the bloody war which has so long ravaged this unfortunate land, I shall gladly lay down my life if this contributes to the peace and welfare of my adopted country. I am deeply convinced that nothing permanent can be established in a land drenched with blood and stirred by violent agitation. Therefore, I most earnestly entreat you with the sincerity suitable to my current situation that my blood be the last shed. With the same perseverance with which you defend the cause now triumphant—a perseverance I recognized and valued in the midst of my own good fortune—I implore you to dedicate yourself to the most noble goal of firm reconciliation and restoration of peace and calm to this beleaguered land.

At around three o'clock, with Magnus and Colonel Villanueva present, Colonel Palacios came to inform the baron and me that Maximilian would have to address himself personally to General Escobedo.

*This letter bears the date June 19 because, according to His Majesty's instructions, it was dispatched on that day.

Chapter Twenty

The Emperor, who saw us talking with Palacios, asked what the conversation was about. Mastering my emotions, I repeated the colonel's words. "What an insult," he exploded. I dictated a letter to Colonel Villanueva, who knew German and immediately wrote it down in Spanish. This letter stated that His Majesty wished his body to be delivered to Baron Magnus and me. I was to bring it to Europe, and the baron would take care of the necessary transportation arrangements. The sovereign calmly read the letter and signed it at the bottom with strong, sure strokes of the pen.

The negative answer to his telegram requesting clemency for the generals arrived from San Luis around five o'clock.

He went to bed after eight o'clock, and I remained alone with him in the room.

Towards nine, Palacios appeared with an explicit reply from Escobedo, assuring the Emperor he would follow his last dispositions in all details.

Maximilian read an hour in Thomas á Kempis's *Imitation of Christ,* which Padre Soria had brought at his request, extinguishing the candles at around ten o'clock.

At eleven-thirty, he had just fallen asleep when someone stepped into the room. I jumped up, half in joy, half in terror; it was Dr. Riva de Nejra, who told me General Escobedo was there and wished to speak to the condemned man. The noise had awakened Maximilian. He lit the candles, Escobedo entered, and I left the room with the doctor. After several minutes the general came out, and I went back in to the monarch. "Escobedo was here to take leave of me. What a pity! I had just gotten to sleep so well."

Shortly afterwards he put out the lights again, and, after an hour —an eternity for me—I noticed from his calm, regular breathing that he had fallen asleep.

He awoke at three-thirty, and I aroused the servants, sleeping in a room on the corridor. Within half an hour the father confessor appeared. At five o'clock His Majesty heard mass with the generals, and at a quarter to six he breakfasted on coffee, chicken, half a glass of red wine, and bread.

For the second time he gave me his wedding ring, which I had

219

returned to him on the sixteenth. He repeated his instructions and stuck a scapulary the father confessor had given him in the breast pocket of his vest: "You will take this to my mother" was his last request.

At six-thirty, with the arrival of Colonel Palacios, my last spark of hope was extinguished.

The Emperor walked to the middle of the escort, while I accompanied him to the steps. There he reached his hand towards me once more with a slight nod of his head and a friendly smile. I tried to follow, but my strength left me and I could not.

After about half an hour, ringing bells awakened me from my brooding—the catastrophe had occurred.

At around eight o'clock Colonel Palacios returned. I could see he had difficulty suppressing his emotions. He offered me his hand and said in a strained voice: "Era una alma grande." (He was a great soul.)

The colonel informed me I was free forever and had permission to attend the embalming. He took me down to the church where the Emperor's cloth-covered body now lay on a table. His features were not disfigured; the head uninjured; the body shot through by six bullets.

Since I did not witness the execution, I cannot describe it. This I gladly forego, as the memories are painful enough. I shall limit myself to refuting current inaccurate reports about it, expressing my opinion as a physician, according to what I found upon examining the body, as to whether Maximilian died a difficult death.

As I remarked above, the head was free of any wound whatsoever. Of the six bullets in the body, three were located in the abdomen and three almost in a straight line in the chest.

On the Cerro de las Campanas, the firing squad had received an express order from Commanding General Díaz de León to aim at the chest rather than the head. Shots were fired at close range, and all six bullets went through the body; none were found at the autopsy. The three chest wounds were fatal. One penetrated the heart (the right atrium and the left ventricle); the second, the chest membrane, cutting through the large veins; the third bullet, the right lung.

Because of the nature of the wounds, death throes could have been only very brief. The hand motions and words by which gruesome fantasy pictured the Emperor commanding renewed fire could have been nothing but convulsions, which, according to physiological law, accompany any quick death from bleeding.

As for the many speeches attributed to him, I can only refer to the report given by Dr. Reyes, a Mexican physician who was present at the catastrophe. According to him, His Majesty distributed a handful of gold coins among the soldiers and requested them to shoot straight. He then spoke the following words in a clear voice:

"Que mi sangre sea la ultima que se derrame en sacrificio de la patria; y si fuere necesario alguno de sus hijos sea para bien de la nacion y nunca en traicion de ella." (May my blood be the last shed as a sacrifice to the Fatherland; and if another of its sons is required, may it be for the good and never for the betrayal of the nation.)

On the morning of the nineteenth, Doctors Licea and Riva de Nejra began the embalming. It was conducted in the Church of the Capuchinas and required eight days.

Despite General Escobedo's promise to the sovereign the government refused to hand over the body to Magnus and me. On the morning of June 20, Baron Magnus traveled to San Luis Potosí to represent our just demands with the president. Two days later, the secretary of the Austrian embassy, Von Schmidt, came to Querétaro. But he returned to Mexico City after several days since his superior had received a negative answer from the government in the meantime. He took the Emperor's clothes, which I had given him for immediate forwarding to Europe.*

I remained in Querétaro after the embalming since at headquarters they had evaded direct answer and given me hope that this would be forthcoming upon the president's arrival.

Juárez arrived at eleven o'clock on the night of the seventh and traveled on to Mexico City early the following morning without my speaking to him. My mission in Querétaro was accomplished, and I went to the capital to make arrangements with the government about

---

*To this simple fact are reduced the pompous newspaper reports of Herr von Schmidt's dangerous adventures with the clothes of the unlucky monarch.

obtaining the body.

Before I left Querétaro, I viewed the body once more. It was set out in the Church of the Capuchinas and lay in a coffin of rough wood covered with zinc on the inside and velvet on the outside. The coffin had a double lid; the inner was composed of three panes of glass inserted next to each other. The middle one bore a golden "M".

Arriving in the capital, I had an audience July 27 with Minister Lerdo de Tejada and handed him a petition. Two days later I received a definite negative reply like that previously given Magnus and Lago.

I could not start the trip home since I had to await the arrival of the relics entrusted to me by Maximilian for delivery to Europe. On June 20, I had given these to Vice-Consul Bahnsen for him to safeguard and take along to San Luis Potosí. At that time Mexico City and Veracruz were still in the hands of the imperial forces, and both cities were besieged by the republicans. For that reason, because we still entertained the heresy that the government would redeem its pledge, we had chosen the route from Querétaro to San Luis Potosí and Tampico for transporting the body. The corvette *Elizabeth* had already been ordered to that port by Lago, and we would embark there.

I therefore awaited in the capital the convoy's arrival. In the course of time Vice-Admiral von Tegetthoff landed in Veracruz, and delivery of the body now seemed certain. But the government blocked the admiral because he could present no written authorization. They wanted at all costs to make political capital out of the negotiations. The ministers showed the admiral all respect due a man of his rank and character. However, they declared themselves ready to hand over the body only if "it is requested by an official document from the Austrian government or by an express desire from the family." Negotiations finally concluded with an official note from Imperial Chancellor Beust to Lerdo de Tejada. At the same time the admiral's efforts brought about release of all foreign prisoners.

During negotiations the republican government ordered the body brought to the Church of San Andrés in Mexico City. The admiral viewed it there in my presence immediately after its arrival and a second time after it was laid in a new coffin. It was well preserved, mummified; the face, deeply tanned. The new coffin, made of Granadilla wood, was lined on the inside with cedar. The lid, a massive piece of the same wood, bore a tastefully carved cross.

On November 12 the body finally left the capital. Accompanying it were Vice-Admiral von Tegetthoff, Colonel von Tegetthoff, both of the Admiral's adjutants, von Gaal and von Henneberg, and I. The escort comprised one hundred cavalrymen.

On November 25 in Veracruz the coffin and contents were officially accepted by the admiral, and the key to the coffin delivered to him.

The next day, the *Novara* pushed off from the fateful shore with the body of the beloved dead. The ship which had brought the Emperor to that country in the prime of his years now carried his mortal remains home to the crypt of his ancestors.

CHAPTER XXI

The Trial

It is not my duty to render judgment about the legal issues in the trial of Emperor Maximilian. However, I will take the liberty, in view of the manifold assertions on this matter, to throw light on the inner motives upon which it was based. I will be permitted to unmask the lowness with which the republican government veiled the vengeful deed of June 19 with the precepts of a sham law, trumpeting it as an exalted act of justice.

I speak harsh words, but I speak with calm deliberation. Because of the methods by which the trial was instituted and conducted, Maximilian was not condemned by legitimate sentence; he was murdered.

A military court with cynical, wanton disregard and caprice, like those in Europe after 1848, was convened according to the provisions of an exceptional law—a law which in effect was no longer valid. When the Emperor was captured, the "usurpation" was effectively ended, and constitutional stipulations and ordinances derived therefrom negated the law. Before this court of justice—criticized even by republicans courageous enough to express their opinions for being a victory-drunk, incompetent, unruly soldiery—an indictment was drawn up. This awkwardly, defectively organized register of false accusations contradicted itself repeatedly. Every argument dispensed with evidence, and the emptiness and open falseness would have been the most eloquent speech in His Majesty's defense, even in a regular Mexican court.

Like the trial, everything about the indictment was a mere formality to the disciplined officers, who were there on command for the sole purpose of passing sentence. With its thirteen counts, the indictment epitomizes the miserable hypocrisy, blind animosity, and cowardly vindictiveness which dictated the trial and stamped it with infamy.

Using Paschen's German edition of the trial documents as reference for the wide-ranging charge, I refer to the ninth count as characteristic of the whole document. Here it is maintained that the Emperor was captured on the Cerro de las Campanas, offering armed resistance. The president, these ministers, this general-in-chief, and these judges—without blushing at their own baseness—adduced this lie, the curse of José Rincón Gallardo's good deed, as an accusation against Maximilian. The whole army knew full well that we were already Escobedo's prisoners that night and that on the Cerro not a single shot was fired by our side, nor the slightest defense attempted.

The tenor of the indictment is most evident in the last two counts. Count 12: " . . . that His Majesty refuses to recognize the competence of the court-martial summoned according to the law of January 25, 1862, to pass judgment on transgressions" specified in it. Count 13: This accuses "Maximilian of obstinacy and rebellion under the pretext of the alleged incompetence of the court-martial and the Supreme Commander to judge him." This count holds the accused criminally responsible for defense techniques adopted by his attorneys.

I expect to be criticized for subjectivity; I believe on the contrary that I have maintained objectivity enough in demonstrating the procedural irregularity and arbitrariness of this so-called trial.

I will now briefly touch upon essential phases in the history of the trial.

On May 24, preliminary investigation began with interrogation by the prosecutor. The next day, the sovereign had Baron Magnus and both defense attorneys Mariano Riva Palacios and Rafael Martínez de la Torre, summoned by telegraph from Mexico City. The preliminary inquest ended, and the Emperor composed the defense notes reproduced at the end of this book. These served henceforth as subject for discussion at conferences with his attorneys. I include this with a translation so that you will understand the enclosure:

El min[istro] d[e] relac[iones] Conde Rechberg llega el 18. de Setiembre de 1862 á Miramar, donde vivo retirado. Proposiciones, Condiciones mias; voluntad nacional. Llega una deputacion el 3. de Octubre de 1863 á Miramar, con la acta de Notables. Mi contestacion. Otra deputacion á principios de Abril 1864 con todas las actas de adhesion, que se encuentran originales en Londres. Gutierrez y Aguilar prueban con el mapa la grande mayoria. Aceptacion y juramento de indep[endencia] y integridad. Reconocimiento de casí todos los gobiernos del mundo entre ellos Inglaterra y Suizza.— Llegado al pais vista la trahicion de los Franceses todo mi trabajo protejer la independencia y integridad; negocio de la

226

Sonora. En consecuencia inemistad con los franceses.—Los Franceses roban todo el dinero, de los dos prestamos no entran que 19. mill[iones] en las arcas del tesoro y la guerra, que ellos hacen, cuesta mas que 60. mill[iones] sobre todo esto quejas fuertes á Paris documentos.—El gobierno imp[erial] el mas barato del pais, pruevas [pruebas] hechas por Escudero.

Llegada de Langlais, que consta el mismo los robos y el despilfarro.—

En Setiembre 1865 llega la noticia a Mexico que Juarez abandonó el territorio nacional. Impulso de los franceses para medidas fuertes para como dicen terminar pronto y completamente. Se elabora la ley del 3. de Octubre Bazaine dicta personalmente pormenores delante testigos. Los ministros responsables y muy liberales como Escudero, Cortez Esparza etc. etc. discuten la ley con todo el Consejo de Estado. Todos los puntos principales de la ley existieron ya antes bajo Juarez; así lo dijeron los ministros. La ley fué bien ejécutada de los mexicanos, por lo que hicieron los franceses, no po-demos tomar la responsabilidad.—

Los franceses siguieron á robar y rovinar [-arruinar] el pais y el mismo gobierno de ellos québro los solemnes tratados con Mejico. Declaran su salida. Deseo mio de un congreso. Junta en Chapultepec. Jda de Mejico á Orizaba. Anulacion imediata el Decreto del 3. de Oct.[ubre], deseo de salir llamado de los consejos.—

Dictamen y apelacion al deber y al honor, Convite al Congreso*]. Llegada imprevista de Miramon y Marquez.— Los franceses exijen mi salida para areglarse con Ortega y hacer pagar á Mejico, mi permanencia salva el pais de este peligro, tanto mas que yo quebro el tratado de aduanas.— Vuelta á Mejico, entrevista en Puebla con Dano y Castelnau. —Otra junta de los consejos en Mejico, mismo dictamen.— Trabajo assiduo para juntar el congreso, agentes á Juarez y Porfirio Diaz.

El mariscal declaró en nombre del gobierno francés que la corte de cassacion de París determinó que donde se encuentre un ejercito francés todas las cuestiones mixtas deben ser juzgados por leyes franceses; Ejemplo con la firma de Napoleon.—

Hecho de Miramon y de los 109 franceses.
Base revolucionario del plan de Ayutla.
La presidencia de Juarez concluyó el 30. de Noviembre de 1865.

*Envio (-enviada) de Garcia con el hijo de Iglesias cerca de Juarez.

227

Marquez era llamado deste 6 meses como otros diplomaticos pas razones de economia Miramon no fué
llamado.

The Minister of Foreign Affairs Count Rechberg arrives
September 18, 1862, at Miramar, where I live in retirement.
Proposals. My condition—the national will. A deputation
arrives at Miramar on October 3, 1863 with the document
from the notables. My answer. Another deputation at the
beginning of April, 1864, with all documents of loyalty, whose
originals are in London. Gutiérrez and Aguilar prove the
large majority with the map. Acceptance and oath of independence and territorial integrity. Recognition by almost all
the governments of the world, among them England and
Switzerland. Arrival in the country, in view of the treason of
the French; all my work, protecting independence and integrity; the Sonora Affair. As a result of this, enmity of the
French; they stole all the money. Of the two loans, merely
nineteen million flows into the state coffers, and the war they
wage costs more than sixty million. Strong complaints about
this to Paris, documents. The imperial government is the most
inexpensive for the country; attestation by Escudero.

Arrival of Langlais, who himself confirms the plundering
and wastefulness.

In September, 1865, the report reaches Mexico City that
Juárez has left the national territory. Impulse on the part of
the French to strong measures in order, as they say, to finish
up quickly and completely. The Law of October 3 is drafted.
Bazaine personally dictates details in front of witnesses. The
responsible and very liberal ministers like Escudero, Cortez
Esparza, etc. discuss the law with the whole state council. All
the main points previously existed under Juárez; the ministers
told me so. The law was mildly administered by the Mexicans;
for what the French did we can take no responsibility.

The French continued to rob and destroy the country,
and their own government broke solemn agreements with
Mexico. They announce their withdrawal. My wish for a
congress. Junta in Chapultepec. Trip from Mexico City to
Orizaba. The immediate revocation of the October 3 Decree.
I want to leave, calling the councils. Declaration of opinion
and appeal to duty and honor. Invitation to the Congress.*
Unexpected arrival of Miramón and Márquez.

The French require my departure in order to come to
terms with Ortega and to make Mexico pay. My remaining
saves the country from this danger, all the more because I

*[Note in his handwriting] Sending of Garcia with Iglesia's son to Juárez.

break the customs treaty.—Return to Mexico City. Interview in Puebla with Dano and Castelnau.—Another junta of the councils in Mexico City; same opinion.—Constant work to set up the congress. Agents to Juárez and Porfirio Díaz.

The Marshal declares in the name of the French government that the French Bureau of the Budget in Paris has decided that everywhere a French army is located, all joint questions have to be judged according to French laws. Example with Napoleon's signature.

Miramón's deed and the 109 Frenchmen**
Revolutionary basis of the Ayutla Plan***
Juárez presidency ended on November 30, 1865.
Márquez was recalled six months ago for reasons of economy. Miramón was not recalled.

May 28—Escobedo ordered the court-martial to convene. Two days' time was given to the defense.

May 29—Defense attorney Vázquez delivered Escobedo a protest from Maximilian, signed by him, against the competence of the court-martial.

On the same day His Majesty's telegram finally reached Baron Magnus, officially confirming rumors about the capture. Since the seventeenth they had spread in the capital, which was surrounded by Porfirio Díaz. The defense attorneys conferred with Father Fischer and Baron Magnus at the latter's home, where they learned that the cleric had hired the lawyer Ortega. They were pleased that he had agreed to help. Due to the many difficulties hindering departure, Magnus and the attorneys were unable to leave the city until the morning of the thirty-first.

In the republican camp Magnus learned of a telegram from Escobedo ordering General Díaz "that if the people required by Maximilian can reach Querétaro promptly, without obstructing the proceedings of the trial or lengthening the time period established for it by law, no sort of hindrance should block compliance with his wishes."

**The shooting of Miramón's brother and the 109 Frenchmen after the defeat at San Jacinto.

***The Constitution of 1857 resulted from it under the presidency of Commonfort.

The baron telegraphed Minister Lerdo de Tejada, requesting that he persuade the president "to postpone legal proceedings so that the defense attorneys have sufficient time to fulfill their mission." This request from the Prussian envoy was granted only to a limited degree. A telegram from Lerdo de Tejada to Escobedo intended for communication to Baron Magnus and dated the evening of June 3, San Luis Potosí, contained the following, omitting the unessential:

> That this afternoon the time limit established by law for defense of Archduke Maximilian expired; then began that for defense of Don Miguel Miramón. The Ministry of War informed you on May 28 that if, within the legal time limit for defense, Maximilian's defense attorneys have not come, you can comply with his wish and begin the time limit anew so that he can prepare his defense. In agreement with that decision I must tell you on instruction from the president that, since the time limit for Miramón's defense expires tomorrow, from then on the legal period for Maximilian's defense starts anew. In this case, the new deadline should be applied for both the other defendants so that they can use it for their defense. Kindly inform Baron Magnus of this answer to his telegram which I received yesterday evening.

Signed, etc.

On June 5, the attorneys from Mexico City held their first conversation with the Emperor. They began defense efforts by telegraphing the government a request "to be granted a few more days." A response wired from the minister of war that evening granted three days beyond the previous postponement.

With His Majesty's consent the lawyers agreed that Riva Palacios and Martínez de la Torre should go to San Luis to intervene with the government while Vázquez and Ortega conducted the defense before the court-martial.

On the eighth Riva Palacios and de la Torre arrived in San Luis. That first day they petitioned the president and ministers for a new, month-long postponement. The next day they learned that their request would in no way be granted.

Both attorneys—interpreting their task as not so much one of legal advocacy as of personal intercession with men in the government—endeavored to secure cooperation from the most influential people. They immediately turned to General Treviño, who had great influence in the army and had declared himself ready to work for a pardon. Earlier, too, he had expressed his opinion about López's betrayal. On the same day Treviño wrote General Escobedo the most urgent complaints. The defense attorneys hoped the general's example would be imitated by other commanders, their endeavors thus attracting the most powerful support.

At the same time, Riva Palacios and de la Torre in no way neglected avenues open to them as lawyers. On June 10 they also submitted to the president a protest against the competence of the military court. However, the same day the minister of war gave them the government's negative reply.

Overcome by zeal and convinced beyond a doubt that Maximilian was as much as sentenced to death when his trial was assigned to a court-martial, both attorneys proceeded directly to seek a pardon "in case Ferdinand Maximilian von Hapsburg in the trial decreed for him be sentenced to death." On the second day they received the president's answer to their petition through the minister of war. He informed them "that it is not legitimate to decide on a petition for clemency before the defendant is actually sentenced."

Lerdo de Tejada refrained from pointing out to the defense "that they expected the death sentence for Maximilian in the verdict of the court-martial," that they themselves held their client's cause for lost.

On June 13, the day the court in Querétaro began final deliberations, Baron Magnus arrived in San Luis. On the same day he had lengthy conversations with the president, as well as with Minister Lerdo de Tejada, beseeching pardon for the Emperor and promising all possible guarantees on the part of his government. On the fifteenth he repeated his request in writing. In the meantime a telegram arrived from Vázquez and Ortega with word that the court session had begun, so Riva Palacios and de la Torre renewed their plea for clemency.

However, Juárez and the ministers remained unshakeable, and the court-martial in Querétaro pronounced the death sentence on the three defendants.

To depict the proceedings, I borrow the following extract from the newspaper *Sombra de Arteaga** which appeared in Querétaro.

At eight o'clock on the morning of June 13, the court-martial installed itself in the Iturbide Theater. The hall was brightly lit; the dais was set up at the back of the stage. All remaining space was reserved for the public.

On the right was the table for the tribunal. Facing this were benches for the accused and chairs for their attorneys. All around were candelabras with high wax candles. The greatest excitement was written on the faces of the spectators. Deep silence reigned in the whole hall. At nine o'clock Miramón and Mejía were fetched from prison in an open coach, escorted on both sides by a company of Supremos Poderes. At the theater they were turned over to the court guards.

The president of the court-martial opened the session. Members of the tribunal in full uniform and defense attorneys took their places.

Public prosecutor Colonel Manuel Aspiroz read the indictment and a number of documents. [These were published in detail, at length, in the newspaper. The two most crucial ones, however, were the protest against the competence of the court and the attestation of illness.]

After the documents were read aloud, the accused Tomás Mejía appeared. They made him take his place in the prisoner's dock, with an escort of Supremos Poderes at his side.

Mejía's defense attorney, Prospero C. Vega, now presented his case [which the newspaper discusses knowledgably].

After the speech the president of the court asked the accused whether he had any other remarks to make in his defense. Mejía said no. His defense attorney had already said what there was to say. If there was anything else, the attorney would know best how to bring it out.

Mejía was now removed, and Miramón entered.

After pleadings by his defense attorneys, Jauerguí and Moreno, he was also led away. Now would begin the trial of the Archduke. First, the prosecutor himself went to the prisoner—it was around three o'clock in the afternoon—and returned several minutes later. He explained to the tribunal that the accused was in no condition to appear. His trial

*Shadow of Arteaga, a republican from Querétaro whom Méndez had had shot.

would proceed in his absence and continue the next day. The court reconvened at nine o'clock in the forenoon and stayed in session until ten o'clock in the evening. One hour earlier it went into secret session.

I have reported in detail in an earlier chapter pronouncement of sentence; I need only discuss here steps taken to save the Emperor afterwards.

On June 15, after the sessions of the court-martial had ended but before confirmation of the death sentence by Escobedo, Riva Palacios and de la Torre presented a new petition in San Luis, requesting clemency or at least postponement of execution. The president's answer was analagous to those he had previously given: "It is impossible to consider a petition for clemency before the sentence is pronounced, for a formal sentence takes effect only when the verdict of the court-martial has been confirmed by the Supreme Commander."

From all parts of the land, from both men and women, arrived numerous requests for pardon. All were denied.

At noon on the sixteenth the telegram from Querétaro arrived in San Luis with word that Escobedo had confirmed the sentence. The execution was set for six o'clock (it read, erroneously, instead of three o'clock).

Immediately Riva Palacios and de la Torre asked for clemency, receiving a refusal a few hours later.

At one o'clock the government telegraphed Querétaro "that it has refused a pardon. However, to allow the condemned men time to put their affairs in order, it has decided the execution will not take place before the nineteenth."

Baron Magnus had accompanied the attorneys to the Government Palace and there joined his request to theirs. He could no longer remain in San Luis, where with unusual sacrifice he had done everything possible to save the life of the unlucky monarch. When he left Querétaro the Emperor had expressed the wish to see him once more before his death.

On the evening of the sixteenth Riva Palacios and de la Torre received the following telegram from the lawyers in Querétaro:

"The three accused had confessed and received Holy Communion when the order to postpone the execution arrived. Morally speaking, they had already suffered death at that moment when they were supposed to be led forth to execution. It would be frightful to have them die on Wednesday a second time after going through the torments of death today."

On the eighteenth even Baron Magnus addressed a similar telegram to Lerdo de Tejada from Querétaro. In the most moving words he stressed the monstrosity of a second execution. The telegram ended with the words:

"I entreat you in the name of humanity and heaven not to threaten their lives any longer, and I repeat once again that I am certain my sovereign, His Majesty the King of Prussia, and all the monarchs of Europe related by ties of blood to the captured prince— namely, his brother the Emperor of Austria, his cousin the Queen of Great Britain, his father-in-law the King of the Belgians, and his cousin the Queen of Spain—as well as the Kings of Italy and Sweden will easily arrange to guarantee His Excellency señor Benito Juárez that none of the prisoners ever will return or set foot again on Mexican territory."

Once more the defense attorneys requested clemency of the president as well as all the ministers; telegrams with the same message were still arriving; ladies of Querétaro and San Luis repeated their pleas, and the citizenry of the former city offered to ransom the Emperor "with gold." All to no avail! On the evening of the eighteenth, Riva Palacios and de la Torre ended defense efforts with a telegram to Vázquez and Ortega:

"Dear friends! All has been in vain. We regret this from the depths of our souls and beg Baron Magnus to express to our client our feelings of deepest pain."

After I have retraced the course of the trial, the only task left is to look into the defense. As a layman I must limit myself to a short, general characterization, to speaking more about the attorneys than about the defense itself. The four lawyers chosen could not have had better personal qualifications. They were republicans of recognized conviction; they enjoyed the best legal reputation.

Riva Palacios, father of the republican general of that name, had extensive connections in Juárez government circles, a circumstance

234

which offered much hope. Therefore, he and de la Torre chose the seat of government as their theater of operations. From the beginning they assumed the role of supplicants—a legal tactic often successfully employed in Mexico, land of the *compadres*. I do not wish to examine further whether in this case their strategy failed.

In any case the chief attorneys had a stricter conception of their duties. Vázquez and Ortega were two men of qualities seldom united in an endeavor of this kind: one with his eminent knowledge of the law and sharp dialectic; the other with his penetrating intellect and overpowering rhetoric.

I believe that I best do justice to them both by reproducing their closing arguments of June 14, stressing outstanding passages in résumé.*

Of the two defense attorneys, Ortega spoke first. He repeated and sharpened his protest against the court's competence, whereupon Vázquez subjected the preliminary inquest to penetrating criticism.

> Not one single witness has been examined, not one solitary document presented, to show that the crimes charged to the Archduke were actually committed and that he is the author of the alleged behavior. No deposition was taken of our defendant; there was not produced one piece of evidence implicating him. All documents introduced are concerned with naming defense attorneys, lengthening the time limit, and rejection of jurisdiction. Without further ado they proceed to accuse our defendant.

> To support the indictment the prosecutor could do nothing except vaguely refer to public knowledge. . . . And no one alleges that in the summary inquest there is evidence for the accusations leveled at our defendant—namely an implied, substantiated, or conjectural confession based on his refusal to answer interpolations from judicial authorities about his case in the summary inquest as well as in the final hearing. Such objections evoke different responses, all decisive and irrefutable. The first is that, as we shall see later, it cannot be admitted as true that the implied, substantiated, or conjectural confession deduced from his silence has the same effect as an expressed statement made in relationship to an established fact. Keeping silent only implies confession when done out of caprice or without justification, but never when someone refuses to answer for legal and well-founded reasons. In the case before us there can be no more just, legal, and well-

---

*Based upon Paschen's translation, this text has been checked for accuracy against the memorandum of the defense attorneys.

founded explanation of our defendant's refusal to answer than that the tribunal set over him is incompetent and that the law applied against him is unconstitutional.

Vázquez now attacked notoriety as it was used as evidence in the trial. He denied its validity in the present case. This gave the defense attorney the opportunity to show brilliantly his greatest strength, his knowledge of the law. He masterfully drew on Mexican military law for his arguments, closing with the words:

"However, since the prosecutor has taken the liberty of searching for weapons to attack the defendant outside the arsenal of preliminary investigation, we demand the same privilege—in defense of our client."

Now Ortega relieved him and examined each count in the indictment, refuting them one by one.

Usurper of public power, enemy to national independence and security, destroyer of order and public peace, violator of human rights—these are in summary the principal accusations leveled against Archduke Maximilian. But in these sonorous and high-sounding phrases, suitable to embellish a speech in a club or fill out a couple of columns in a newspaper, much is lacking to satisfy a tribunal deciding life or death for a human being. Legal, solid, and strong reasons, not frivolous empty declamations, are all that in such a case can appease the conscience of public officials who must decide a punishment with the irrevocable consequences of the death sentence.

It is certain that the rebellion of a village, a city, a province, of a small minority, against nationally accepted institutions is a heavy offense and deserves punishment. Whether it deserves death we will want to examine later. But there is enormous difference between a rebellion—the uprising of some few against the immense majority of a nation—and a true civil war—the severe cleavage of the community into two parties of equal size, when one group wants to go a new way and the other to stick to well-known paths. Those two social situations are completely different in kind; equally different are the applicable legal rules. If what occurs within a nation, or a society, is severe rebellion, the uprising of an insignificant minority against the majority, the former necessarily and infallibly are defeated. The victors have the right to punish legally unauthorized breaches of the public peace.

Sometimes societies, especially those ruled by popular institutions, find themselves in a completely different situation—the nation is almost divided into two halves; each makes

236

opposing claims. When a proportionately small minority opposes the decisions of the majority, the former must submit. It is the law of societies that the minority must yield to the majority for what does not alter the basis of that society. But when a real and severe division takes place among the members; when the strengths of both sections into which a nation divides itself are well balanced; when both take an extraordinarily keen interest in the points of dispute; when neither will make concessions, then the conflict can be divided only by recourse to arms, as if it had arisen between sovereign and independent nations.

To decide international questions without the destructive and bloody warfare, to eliminate war among nations, philosophical and philanthropic writers have come forward century after century with different systems which so far have been ineffective and fruitless. The present condition in the political sciences makes insoluble the problem of eternal peace among nations, just as insoluble in international science as squaring the circle in mathematics. In constitutional law too, we find a gap like that observed in international law. No people has yet found a constitutional solution for the problem of peacefully settling the social rifts which occasionally divide nations, which are decided always by resort to violence. When civil war rages among a people, it is ended by the same means as international wars: by an agreement—once the parties become tired of destruction and end their fighting—just as two warring nations end hostilities with a treaty.

Once more one party succeeds ultimately in becoming ruler over the other, in defeating and subjugating its opponent. Such were the religious wars which erupted among different nations of Central and Northern Europe as a result of the religious Reformation first preached by Luther in Wittenberg. Of the same kind are the political wars which since the end of the previous century have convulsed, will continue to convulse, Europe and America—wars in which the new ideas of freedom and progress, spread throughout the world by modern philosophy and the advancement of the human spirit, struggle with the obsolete traditions of the Middle Ages. When one of those great cleavages disrupts a nation, and when one of the disputing parties gains mastery over the other and defeats it, the victorious party can misuse its triumph at will. Force can be limited only by opposing force which, in my hypothesis, becomes stifled and subjugated. Between what is done and what should be done, between facts and justice, there is a gap as broad as the sky. The victors, overcome with passion of the moment and impulse to revenge which a long and bloody fight always engenders, can misuse their triumph at will. But history and justice, having no share in passion, see through a prism different from that of participants. They stamp the mark of severe reproach on bloody executions and consider them superfluous and unwarranted.

Ortega discussed at length the trials of Charles I and Louis XVI and continued:

> . . . . In his critical essay on *The Constitutional History of England* by Hallam, Macaulay, the greatest English writer of the present century, addresses himself to the trial and execution of Charles I. Contradicting the Tory interpretation, he shows in detail that from the constitutional point of view Charles I, because he had broken the law, could be judged and beheaded. In reference to Charles I's defeat and capture in a civil war, he agrees completely with Hallam's opinion: "Mr. Hallam unreservedly damns Charles's execution, and, in everything he says about this point, we heartily agree. We concur that a great social division, such as a civil war, cannot be confused with ordinary treason and that the vanquished must be dealt with according to the rules of international law rather than statute. It is therefore no longer in dispute that in the present century the victors do not have the right to take the lives of those vanquished in a civil war." For this reason we must now investigate whether the struggle in which the Archduke Maximilian was defeated has the character of a civil war or a simple rebellion.

The defense attorney now proved that the last decade has seen a real civil war brought about by violent disagreement over the Reform Laws. He addressed himself to the main accusation, that Maximilian was guilty of "usurpation." All other charges were merely "the repetition of the same facts from different viewpoints, or, if usurpation is admitted, the enumeration of some of its results."

Recalling the most recent history of Mexico, he demonstrated what an important role "assemblies of notables repeatedly played. Proclamation of the Empire and choice of Maximilian as Emperor by the assembly of notables in Mexico City (1863) were not unusual procedures in the constitutional history of the country." He told how the accused, after obtaining the advice of European legal experts, who explained that the official document from the municipalities was the expression of national will, had only then accepted the crown offered him.

Ortega enumerated Maximilian's attempts to call a congress loyal to Mexico and described the circumstances which reenforced

238

belief in the legitimacy of his title. Going over recent events, he closed this part of the defense with the words:

> Such doubts might have arisen if after removal of foreign pressure and before their occupation by liberal troops, the villages had voluntarily raised the banner of the republic. Whether from enervation, worry that withdrawal of French troops was only a feint, or certainty that within a very short while national armed forces would secure them from any invasion, Mexican as well as foreign—this much is established: the villages generally behaved passively. This behavior was not suited to destroy our client's delusion that he was the nation's choice.

Similarly, Ortega rejected the accusations leveled against the prince for filibustering and promulgation of the law of October 3 and added:

> . . . yet despite the fact that the law, of January 25, 1862, according to which the present trial is supposedly conducted, had the same object in mind as the decree of October 3; despite the fact that the latter was issued by a ruler unbound by constitutional limitations, we are of the opinion that a comparison of the two would benefit the second and that today's vanquished would be pleased to be measured by the same gauge they intended for their opponents.

After refuting further accusations, he discussed the objectionable nature of the death penalty in general and referred to the principles of the Constitution of 1857, which had abolished capital punishment, specifically for political criminals.

His speech for the defense ended with the following appeal to the tribunal:

> On our continent there is a great people, master of liberal institutions, the Republic of the United States. Its treatment of Jefferson Davis, usurper of public power as president of the South, offers a noble example, worthy of imitation. Jefferson Davis was a subject of the government he sought to overthrow. Maximilian was not born in Mexico; he came here in the belief that the nation had summoned him to rule. The one provoked civil war in a country which since independence had enjoyed proverbial peace. The other came to a land torn by years of civil war with the noble intention of ending the strife and found himself drawn by intractable circumstances into participation in his adopted

country's internal quarrels. The former cruelly and obstinantly persecuted partisans of the American Union. The latter not only tolerated his political opponents, the partisans of republican institutions, but even leaned decisively in their direction. He defended and protected them. The former took pains in the territory under his control to nullify principles adopted by the government he was fighting. The latter, with the sole exception of the principle of monarchy—a stipulation essential to his political existence—watched over, defended, and supported principles based on the constitutional government, while slighting his natural allies. Nevertheless, Jefferson Davis, a prisoner since 1865, has been judged neither by an exceptional tribunal nor a privative, unconstitutional law. He is not robbed of guarantees in the constitution of the country whose peace he disturbed; two years after his defeat, no public accuser has yet come forward to demand his head.

Soldiers of the republic, who have just reaped such glorious fame on the field of battle and have given the Fatherland a day of such inexpressible exultation, do not soil your laurels. Do not besmirch such a pure, general joy by misusing your triumph over a defeated foe and decreeing an execution which is bloody, superfluous, and foreign to the noble-hearted character of the compassionate and kind Mexican people.

CONCLUSION

When I claim historical worth for my memoirs, I do so after careful deliberation. They were conceived with the purpose of providing an authentic source for the last ten months of the Empire and enlightening public opinion misled in so many essential respects. For this very reason they have remained within the limits of objectivity. The endeavors of the unfortunate prince to whose memory they are dedicated call for and allow faithful recital, and I could not better fulfill my task "to stand in for the Emperor" than by affording a full insight into his emotional and intellectual life.

My judgments about people, my opinions about events, are the result of an unprejudiced examination and are based on my own experiences or trustworthy information.

I have let the facts speak for themselves, and they are sufficient to disarm the boundless accusations and reproaches raised by all sides. In the face of facts, what significance can there be if French ordnance officers, on command from their master, become enraged and dare reproach the Emperor Maximilian with what their own consciences tell them is their own sovereign's responsibility.

In the face of fact becomes evident the true value of criticism

241

which merely sees things through rose-colored glasses and finds shadows only where the republican sun does not shine. Bias and prejudice are found in all camps, and judgment without thorough investigation of inner motives is still incorrect if adorned with pompous clichés.

History, I am convinced, will ignore the petty calumny and deliberate misunderstanding. Present and future generations will revere the prince's memory.

The Emperor's life, they will have to admit, was no blind advance along time-honored paths; it was a continuous striving—a conscious struggle between prejudice and freedom. This struggle alone is enough to guarantee his fame.

Circumstances thwarted his every endeavor, and he was not permitted to complete what he undertook with enthusiasm.

The fleet he created he could not lead to victory; the great duty he chose for himself—regeneration of an entire nation—that too proved unsuccessful. . . .

Vienna, May 20, 1868

242

The Translator

Hugh McAden Oechler, a native of New York, holds the A. B. degree from Princeton University's Woodrow Wilson School of Public and International Affairs. A world traveler, he attended the University of Grenoble and has worked in France, Italy, and Argentina. While serving in the United States Army, he underwent intensive language training in Malay. From November, 1969, until his release from the military in 1971, he worked for the Fourth United States Army Language Training Facility at Ft. Hood, Texas. During this interim he aided in writing the French course, taught French, and translated French, Italian, and Indonesian. Mr. Oechler is now doing graduate work at Ohio University in South-East Asian Studies.

Hac.da de Alvarado

C. San Pablo

S. Pablo

Rancho de Jesus Mar

Garita

C. San Gregorio

Garita

C. La Trinidad

C. de la Cruz
del Cerro

S a n

Rio Blanco

Cerro La Campana

Calle

Calle de Hospital

Garita de Ceraja

Hacienda de Juanico

Garita del Pueblo

Casa Blanca

Hacienda de Jacal

El Jacal

1000

1500

2000 meter

G.E.v.Gerst in 2.

QUERETARO.

C a n t e r a

H.Q.Escobedo

Banos de Patche

La Parisima   Fabrica de Hercules

Hac.da de Carreas

Sta Cruz

Garita de Mexico

San Francisquito

Hac.da de Calleja

Cuesta China

El Cimatario

1. Casino,
2. Klooster San Teresila,
3. Klooster de Capuchinas,
4. Theater Iturbide,
5. Brug,
6. Meson San Sebastian,
7. San Sebastian,
8. Santa Crara,
9. Plaza de Toros,
    rood Linie der Keizerlijken,
    geel Linie der Liberalen.

Colegio de la Santa Cruz.

Meson de la Cruz

Plaza de la Cruz

S.Cruz

Gardin de la Cruz   Huerta de la Cruz

Pantheon

500   1000

El min. d. relac. Conde Rechberg llega el 18 de Setiembre de 1862 á Miramar, donde vive retirado. Proposiciones. Condiciones mías; voluntad nacional ~~[tachado]~~ ~~[tachado]~~. Llega una diputación el 3 de Octubre de 1863 á Miramar con la acta de Notables. Mi contestación. Otra diputación á principios de Abril 1864, con todas las actas de adhesión, que se encuentran originales en Londres. Gutiérrez y Aguilar perciben con el mayor la grande mayoría. Aceptación; y juramento di indep. y libertad (SDO.) Reconocimiento de casi todos los gobiernos del mundo, entre ellos Ingla-terra y Suiza. — Llegado el país vista la traición de los Franceses todo mi trabajo protejer la independencia y integridad; negocio de la Sonora. En consecuencia enemistad con los franceses. — Los Franceses roban todo el dinero; de los dos prestamos no entran que 19 mill. en las arcas del tesoro. y la guerra que ellos hacen [sobre todo esto quejas fuertes á Paris, documentos] nuestra experimenta mas de 60 mill. — El gobierno imp. el mas barato del país, pruebas hechas por Escudero. Llegada de Langlais que consta de mismo los robos y el despilfarro. —

En Setiembre 1865 llega la noticia á Mexico que Juarez abandonó el territorio nacional — Impulso de los franceses para medidas fuertes para como dicen terminar pronto y comple-tamente. Se elabora la ley del 3 de Octubre. Bazaine dicta personalmente [por sus ...] delante testigos. Los ministros responsables y muy liberales como Escudero, Cortez Esparza etc. etc. discuten la ley con todo el Consejo de Estado. Todos los [principales] puntos de la ley existieron ya antes bajo Juarez; así lo dijeron los ministros. La ley fué bien ejecutada de los mexicanos, por lo que hicieron los franceses, no po-demos tomar la responsabilidad. —

Los franceses siguieron á robar y saquear el país y el mismo gobierno de ellos quebró los solemnes tratados con Méjico. *declaran su salida. Deseo de un congreso.* *Junta en Chapultepec.* Méjico. Anulación inmediata del decreto del 3 de ... Daría brigada y deseo de salir, llamada de los consejos. Dictamen y apelación al deber y al honor, ~~la patria~~ ~~........~~ *Convite al congreso* ✶ y llegada imprevista de Miramón y Marquez. — Los franceses exigen mi salida para arreglarse con Ortega y hacer pagar á Méjico, mi permanencia salva el país de este peligro, tanto mas que yo quebré el tratado de Aduanas. — Vuelta á Méjico, entrevista en Puebla con Bazaine y Castelnau. — Otra junta de los consejos en Méjico, mismo dictamen. — Trabajo asiduo para juntar el congreso, agentes á Juárez y Porfirio Díaz. —

✶ Envío de García con el hijo de Iglesias cerca de Juárez.

El mariscal declaró en nombre del gobierno francés que la costa de ocupación de París determina que donde se encuentre su ejército francés todas las cuestiones mixtas deben ser juzgadas por leyes francesas. Ejemplo con la firma de Napoleón. —

Hecho de Miramón y de los 109 franceses.
Base revolucionaria del plan de Ajutla.
La presidencia de Juárez concluyó el 30 de Noviembre de 1865
Marquez es llamado desde 6 meses como otros diplomáticos por razones de economía, Miramón no fué llamado.

Index

248

251